Mark Twain's Notebooks

Journals, Letters, Observations, Wit, Wisdom, and Doodles

Edited by

CARLO DEVITO

BLACK DOG
& LEVENTHAL
PUBLISHERS
NEW YORK

Copyright © 2015 Black Dog & Leventhal Publishers

Published by
Black Dog & Leventhal Publishers, Inc.
151 West 19th Street
New York, NY 10011

Distributed by
Workman Publishing Company
225 Varick Street
New York, NY 10014

Manufactured in China

Cover and interior design by Liz Driesbach

Cover image courtesy of The Mark Twain House & Museum

ISBN-13: 978-1-57912-997-2

h g f e d c b a

Library of Congress Cataloging-in-Publication Data on file.

CONTENTS

~

Introduction

Mark Twain in 1895.

Samuel Langhorne Clemens, also known as Mark Twain, is a cultural and literary icon. Although he is best known as a writer and humorist, his interests included journalism, travel, inventions, boating, smoking, billiards, and much more. He was also a constant note taker and scrapbooker. This volume is a tour of Twain's notes, letters, licenses, stock certificates, communications, newspaper articles, magazine articles, books, cartoons, caricatures, photographs, and other documents from throughout his life, brought together to create a colorful glimpse at one of America's greatest and most celebrated authors.

Notebooks

Clemens was born in Florida, Missouri on November 30, 1835, during the passing of Halley's Comet. He became an avid note taker when, at twenty-one, he first endeavored to become a cub pilot to the well-regarded steam boatman Horace Bixby. The twists and turns of the Mississippi were copious and dangerous. Young Sam Clemens could not remember them all.

"His hunger for the life aboard the steamers became a passion. To be even the humblest employee of one of those floating enchantments would be enough; to be an officer would be to enter heaven; to be a pilot was to be a god," wrote biographer Albert Bigelow Paine.

"You can hardly imagine what it meant," Twain reflected once, "to a boy in those days, shut in as we were, to see those steamboats pass up and down, and never to take a trip on them.

"I entered upon the small enterprise of learning 12 or 13 hundred miles of the great Mississippi River with the easy confidence of my time of life. If I had really known what I was about to require of my faculties I should not have had the courage to begin. I supposed that all a pilot had to do was to keep his boat in the river and I did not consider that that could be much of a trick, since it was so wide."

"A day or two later the easy confidence was all gone. Bixby, asking him [Clemens] to repeat some of the instruction we had furnished him, found that he could remember none of it. His head was a mere jumble of 'points' and 'bends' and 'bars' and 'crossings,' " wrote Paine in In *The Boy's Life of Mark Twain*.

"'My boy,' said Mr. Bixby, 'you must get a little memorandum-book and every time I tell you a thing, put it down, right away. There's only one way to be a pilot and that is to get this entire river by heart. You have to know it just like A B C.'"

Contrary to many falsely reported pieces of information, Mark Twain was never a ship captain. He was a pilot, which is quite a different thing. Still, it was his youth's ambition, and he achieved it. Here is a drawing from *Life on the Mississippi*. Also pictured in the inset is Mr. Bixby in later years.

"He probably bought the little memorandum-book at the next landing-place where such things were to be had—at Cairo, most likely, for there his first entry appears to have been made," wrote biographer Albert Bigelow Paine. "He began with great diligence and enthusiasm. The first three or four pages are crowded with confused entries, microscopic lead-pencil abbreviations, today all but illegible. Later his enthusiasm waned, or he recognized the futility of such a confusion. He systematized his entries under blue pencil headings, and wrote more legibly . . ."

This experience became an enduring practice. He kept notebooks for the rest of his life, especially when traveling, and filled them with notes, ideas, quips, questions and story lines. At one point in his life, he ordered custom-made notebooks for himself of his own design—narrow with a notch that jutted out at the top to the right.

In 1935, Albert Bigelow Paine published the selected writings from Mark Twain's notebooks. Later, in 1975, a complete and definitive edition of all his surviving notebooks was published by the University of California Press. Twain had not written the notebooks with an eye toward publishing them. That was the act of scholars and fans. Like any personal notebook, they were scribbled in by hand, and some were illegible.

"At certain periods it becomes the dearest ambition of a man to keep a faithful record of his performances in a book; and he dashes at this work with an enthusiasm that imposes on him the notion that keeping a journal is the veriest pastime in the world, and the pleasantest," Twain wrote humorously in *The Innocents Abroad*. "But if he only lives twenty-one days, he will find out that only those rare natures that are made up of pluck, endurance, devotion to duty for duty's sake, and invincible determination, may hope to venture upon so tremendous an enterprise as the keeping of a journal and not sustain a shameful defeat." Later in the book he opined, "If you wish to inflict a heartless and malignant punishment upon a young person, pledge him to keep a journal a year."

According to Albert Bigelow Paine, "In one of the final chapters of *The Innocents Abroad* Mark Twain tells of a diary he once began with the new year: 'When I was a boy and a confiding and a willing prey to those impossible schemes of reform which well-meaning old maids and grandmothers set for the feet of unwary youths at that season of the year. . . . Please accept an extract:

'Monday—Got up, washed, went to bed.
'Tuesday—Got up, washed, went to bed.'"

The diary continued this line through the week or at least until Friday, then skipped to the next Friday, and finally to the Friday of the following month. It seems to have been abandoned then. Discouraged, he said, "Startling events appeared to be too rare, in my career, to render a diary necessary. I still reflect with pride, however, that even at that early age I washed when I got up. That journal finished me. I never had the nerve to keep one since."

"That final statement is true so far as any formal and regular diary is concerned," Bigelow continued. "Mark Twain never kept a consistent, orderly journal. He was not as prosaic as that. But he was always making notes, capturing the moment—the occurrence, the theme, the purpose, the fancy that flitted through his mind: whatever came and went, if he could get hold of a notebook and pencil quickly enough, he fixed it to his page; when he couldn't he forgot, and was profane. It is a long record, for it covers, intermittently, about forty years. The only thing uniform about it is the form—the books he kept it in."

There are between thirty and forty of them, filled with his neat, beautiful writing, smooth and graceful in the beginning, becoming angular and uncertain with age. Except for the two little black-bound river logs all are nearly of the same size and style—books to fit the pocket—buffalo-leather-covered during the early years—limp morocco later, evidently made to order, with a projecting ear or flange on each leaf, to be torn off when used, so that he might always, and quickly, find his place. This was his own idea, and my recollection is that it was patented—he was always patenting things. Sometimes he lost a notebook, but for the most part he preserved them. One wonders how he managed it—he had a gift for mislaying his belongings."

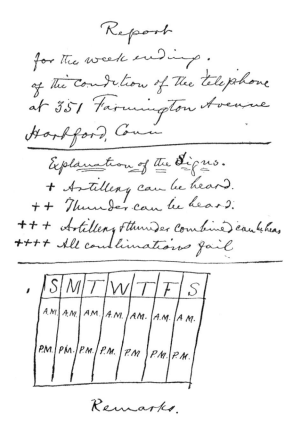

Twain had a love-hate relationship with the telephone. He was among the first to have a one in Hartford, Connecticut, though he continued to lampoon the invention in his writings:

Report for the week ending.

Of the condition of the telephone at 351 Farmington Avenue, Hartford, Conn.

Explanation of the signs:

+ Artillery can be heard.

++Thunder can be heard.

+++ Artillery & thunder combined can be heard.

++++All combinations fail.

Remarks.

Scrapbooking

Twain's notebooks are entertaining in their own right, but it is important to note that some notes later went on to become books, stories, articles, or other printed material. Much of what he wrote in them was revisited by Bigelow later in life, when Paine edited Twain's autobiography. Some of these notes were incorporated into that work. Many were not. While the notebooks are fascinating because they show when and where the germination of some published writings began, these are not the only sources of text for this book. It is also important to note the other passion of Twain—he was an avid scrapbooker.

Mark Twain's "preoccupation with what others were saying about his various performances led him to spend a lot of time with scrapbooks," wrote University of Virginia Library's Kevin Mac Donnell for an exhibition of the Barrett collection. "That was how he came to discover a way to improve the scrapbook by making it self-pasting. In 1872 he patented the idea and marketed it as 'Mark Twain's Patent Scrapbook.' In 1881 he said in a letter to Charles Webster that 'the scrapbook gravels me because while [the company producing it has] been paying me about 1800 or 2000 a year, I judge it ought to have been 3 times as much.' In any case, this one Mark Twain book with no words in it was probably his most lucrative: according to an item in the *St. Louis Post-Dispatch* (8 June 1885), he had made $200,000 from all his other books, and $50,000 from the scrapbook alone."

Here's a collection of Twain's scrapbook covers from this very successful series. Some were plain while others were highly stylized. His most popular were those with self-adhesive pages.

According to Mac Donnell, "contrary to a popular myth, it was a success." There were US and English editions, which listed the dozens of formats and bindings available to the public. "Twain's scrapbook came in various leather bindings, a variety of cloth bindings, and even in pocket size manilla covers."

Rebecca Greenfield wrote in the *Atlantic* magazine in 2010, "As an avid scrapbooker, Twain tired of hand gluing his life into books and figured his fellow scrapbookers felt the same way. After acquiring the patent, Twain successfully marketed and sold the invention…

This invention made scrapbooking more accessible to the less crafty. While Twain likely pasted his accolades into those pages, less prominent folk probably co-opted the invention, using it to store all manner of unconventional documents and personal archives."

In addition to these two sources, there was way too much source material in his published works (books, articles, lectures, and speeches) as well as in his personal correspondence to ignore. By taking something of each of these streams, a more complete and complex version of Mr. Twain may be drawn.

Journalism and Lectures

From his youth, Mark Twain had been trained in the art of casting type, which served him well. It made for great entry into the trade, and he worked for many newspapers such as the *Territorial Enterprise* in Virginia City, Nevada. Sam Clemens's typesetting skills opened up many opportunities for him as the burgeoning young writer, Mark Twain. By the time he'd gotten to the *Enterprise* he was being paid $25 per week as a local reporter. According to Paine, "The *Territorial Enterprise* was one of the most remarkable frontier papers ever published. Its editor-in-chief, Joseph Goodman, was a man with rare appreciation, wide human understanding, and a comprehensive newspaper policy. Being a young man, he had no policy, in fact, beyond the general purpose that his paper should be a forum for absolutely free speech, provided any serious statement it contained was based upon knowledge."

Shown here is a metal movable type case, part of the typesetter's trade, in the office of the *Territorial Enterprise.*

The office of the *Territorial Enterprise*.

While Twain plied his trade as a newspaperman, he never gave up being a celebrity on the stage. His lectures were popularly sold out. His letters and lectures about his trip to the Sandwich Islands, now known as Hawaii, made him a celebrity. As a lecture circuit guest, Twain made a small fortune but the job brought on a mixed bag of feelings. He liked the money and adulation but hated the grueling schedules and missed his wife and family.

Twain was popular on the lecture circuit and spoke in halls all around the country. Here's an advertisement for his lecture at the Cooper Institute in New York City, 1867.

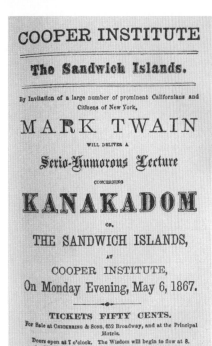

COOPER INSTITUTE

The Sandwich Islands.

By Invitation of a large number of prominent Californians and Citizens of New York,

MARK TWAIN

WILL DELIVER A

Serio-Humorous Lecture

CONCERNING

KANAKADOM

OR,

THE SANDWICH ISLANDS,

AT

COOPER INSTITUTE,

On Monday Evening, May 6, 1867.

TICKETS FIFTY CENTS.

For Sale at CHICKERING & Sons, 652 Broadway, and at the Principal Hotels.

Doors open at 7 o'clock. The Wisdom will begin to flow at 8.

Twain was great on stage and became one of the most popular speakers on what was known as the lyceum circuit. From November to April, the public halls of large cities and small towns played host to a number of famed lecturers, who would come and entertain as well as inform. Twain was very much in demand. Committees oversaw the selections of speakers, and speaking was by invitation only. In some towns, the circuit was so popular that the committee members became as well known as their guest lecturers.

Harper's Weekly November 15, 1873, "The Lyceum Committeeman's Dream— Some Popular Lecturers in Character."

Even with his success as a lecturer, Twain was determined to ply his journalism vocation. Eventually his newspaper career brought him to Buffalo, New York, where he was co-editor of the *Buffalo Express* from 1869–1871.

On August 18th, 1869, he famously wrote to the newspapers readers:

Being a stranger, it would be immodest for me to suddenly and violently assume the associate editorship of the *Buffalo Express* without a single word of comfort or encouragement to the unoffending patrons of the paper, who are about to be exposed to constant attacks of my wisdom and learning. But the word shall be as brief as possible. I only want to assure parties having a friendly interest in the prosperity of the journal that I am not going to hurt the paper deliberately and intentionally at any time. I am not going to introduce any startling reforms, nor in any way attempt to make trouble. . . . I shall not make use of slang and vulgarity upon any occasion or under any circumstances, and shall never use profanity except when discussing house rent and taxes. Indeed, upon a second thought, I shall not use it even then, for it is unchristian, inelegant, and degrading; though, to speak truly, I do not see how house rent and taxes are going to be discussed worth a cent without it. I shall not often meddle with politics, because we have a political Editor who is already excellent and only needs to serve a term or two in the penitentiary to be perfect. I shall not write any poetry unless I conceive a spite against the subscribers.

Such is my platform. I do not see any use in it, but custom is law and must be obeyed.

Twain always enjoyed toiling for the newspapers long after he became a celebrated writer and lecture-circuit star. He was constantly scribbling articles and editorials, sometimes under a nom de plume, but often in his own name.

Mark Twain lived in this sumptuous house with his young bride, Olivia Langdon Clemens, who he doted on, and called "Livy." She returned his affection, and for many years called him simply, "Youth." He was in his mid-thirties when he became co-editor of the *Buffalo Express*, where he owned a stake in the business.

In the *Miraposa Gazette*, on December 18, 1868, he wrote an article entitled "Horace Greeley: A Humorous Description of Him by Mark Twain."
In it, Twain lambasted Greeley, the formidable and famous editor of the *New York Tribune*. After describing Greeley's exaggerated morning rituals, Twain wrote:

He then goes out into his model garden and applies his vast store of agricultural knowledge to the amelioration of his cabbages; after which he writes an able agricultural article for the instruction of American farmers, his soul cheered the while with the reflection that if cabbages were worth $11 apiece his model farm would pay." Twain continued, "After breakfast he writes a short editorial, and puts a large dash at the beginning of it, thus (——), which is the same as if he put H. G. after it, and takes a savage pleasure in reflecting that none of us understrappers can use that dash, except in profane conversation . . . He writes this editorial in his own handwriting. He does it because he is so vain of his penmanship. He always did take an inordinate pride in his penmanship. He hired it out once, in his young days, as a writing master, but the enterprise failed. The pupils could not translate his remarks with any certainty. His first copy was, "Virtue is its own reward," and they got it, "Washing with soap is wholly absurd,"

The article drew an immediate response from Greeley.

MARK,—You are mistaken as to my criticisms on your farming. I never publicly made any, while you have undertaken to tell the exact cost per pint of my potatoes and cabbages, truly enough the inspiration of genius. If you will really betake yourself to farming, or even to telling what you know about it, rather than what you don't know about mine, I will not only refrain from disparaging criticism, but will give you my blessing.

Yours, HORACE GREELEY.

Albert Bigelow Paine remarked of the exchange, "The letter is in Mr. Greeley's characteristic scrawl, and no doubt furnished inspiration for the turnip story in *Roughing It*, also the model for the pretended facsimile of Greeley's writing."

Letter from Horace Greeley to Mark Twain, 1871. Transcription is above.

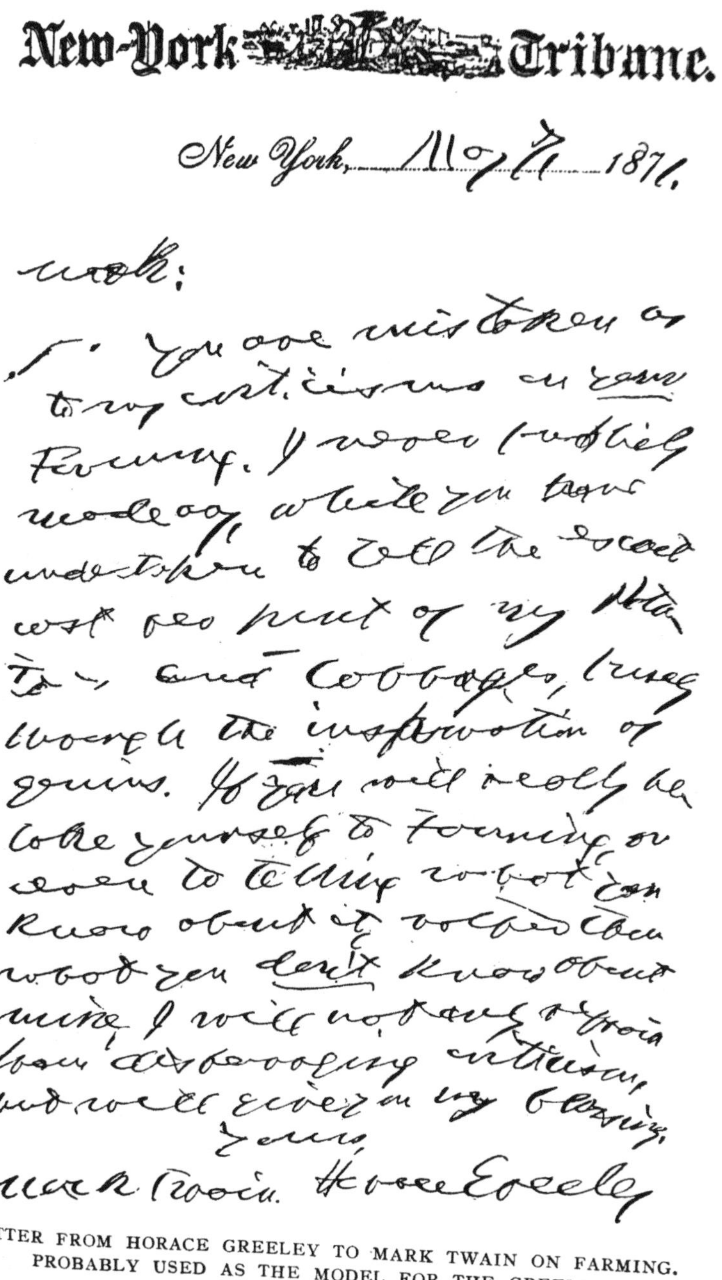
New-York Tribune.
New York, Nov 7 1871.
Horace Greeley

LETTER FROM HORACE GREELEY TO MARK TWAIN ON FARMING. PROBABLY USED AS THE MODEL FOR THE GREELEY FACSIMILE IN "ROUGHING IT"

Books

The 1870s found Twain and his family firmly ensconced in Hartford, Connecticut, where their famous home still stands today. It was during these years that he and Livy raised their three daughters and summered in Elmira, New York, near Livy's family home. It was there—high up in the New York hills of Quarry Farm, while looking out over the Chemung River from a small octagonal study set off from the house—that Twain wrote often and best.

"He worked steadily there . . ." Paine wrote of Twain. "He would go up mornings, after breakfast, remaining until nearly dinner-time, say until five o'clock or after, for it was not his habit to eat luncheon. Other members of the family did not venture near the place, and if he was urgently wanted they blew a horn. Each evening he brought down his day's performance to read to the assembled family. He felt the need of audience and approval. Usually he earned the latter . . ."

Original manuscript pages of famous authors are always fun to examine. And Twain's are no exception. In 1876, Twain published *Tom Sawyer*. It remains a seminal work of American fiction. The final manuscript was written largely at his study on Quarry Farm, but it was originally started sometime around 1872 as a play. In this first draft, Act 1, Scene 1, Tom's relation is "Aunt Winny" who later became "Aunt Polly."

Tom Sawyer actually started out as a play. Here is the first page of that manuscript.

Twain became so wealthy and prosperous—and so sure of himself—that he decided to try his hand as a publisher. His first book was his greatest success: Ulysses S. Grant's memoirs. Grant had been facing financial ruin after his presidency, and Twain offered him an outrageous sum to publish the work, sure that it would be a hit. Grant wrote the book with a death sentence hanging over his head, suffering from terminal cancer.

Twain wrote of Grant, "I then believed he would live several months. He was still adding little perfecting details to his book, and preface, among other things. He was entirely through a few days later. Since then the lack of any strong interest to employ his mind has enabled the tedious weariness to kill him. I think his book kept him alive several months. He was a very great man and superlatively good." Grant died days after finishing his memoir, which was a huge success, restoring his family's fortunes and making Twain even richer. However, few books Twain subsequently published did anywhere near as well.

These were among Grant's last written words, referring to his memoirs, "There is much more that I could do if I was a well man. I do not rite quite as clearly as I could if well. If I could read it over myself many little matters of anecdote and incident would suggest themselves to me."

Still, it always came back to writing for Twain, who continued copious correspondences as well as writing articles and other things. As his career drew to a close, he spent much time looking back over his achievements and failures: numerous books, plays, articles, and editorials.

In 1869, his book *The Prince and the Pauper* was turned into a stage adaptation for the first time. "Abby Sage Richardson had dramatized *The Prince and the Pauper*, and Daniel Frohman had secured Elsie Leslie (Lyde) to take the double role of the Prince and Tom Canty. The rehearsals were going on, and the Clemens children were naturally a good deal excited over the outcome," wrote Paine. "Pretty Elsie Leslie became a favorite of the Clemens household. She was very young, and when she visited Hartford Jean and she were companions and romped together in the hay-loft. She was also a favorite of William Gillette. One day when Clemens and Gillette were together they decided to give the little girl a surprise—a unique one. They agreed to embroider a pair of slippers for her—to do the work themselves." Twain wrote to her about to Elsie about the slippers:

Either one of us could have thought of a single slipper, but it took both of us to think of two slippers. In fact, one of us did think of one slipper, and then, quick as a flash, the other of the other one. It shows how wonderful the human mind is. . . .

Gillette embroidered his slipper with astonishing facility and splendor, but I have been a long time pulling through with mine. You see, it was my very first attempt at art, and I couldn't rightly get the hang of it along at first. And then I was so busy that I couldn't get a chance to work at it at home, and they wouldn't let me embroider on the cars; they said it made the other passengers afraid. They didn't like the light that flared into my eye when I had an inspiration. And even the most fair-minded people doubted me when I explained what it was I was making—especially brakemen. Brakemen always swore at it and carried on, the way ignorant people do about art. They wouldn't take my word that it was a slipper; they said they believed it was a snow-shoe that had some kind of disease.

Take the slippers and wear them next your heart, Elsie dear; for every stitch in them is a testimony of the affection which two of your loyalest friends bear you. Every single stitch cost us blood. I've got twice as many pores in me now as I used to have; and you would never believe how many places you can stick a needle in yourself until you go into the embroidery line and devote yourself to art.

Do not wear these slippers in public, dear; it would only excite envy; and, as like as not, somebody would try to shoot you.

Merely use them to assist you in remembering that among the many, many people who think all the world of you is your friend,

MARK TWAIN.

Twain wrote:
Dear Elsie: I forgot the presentation speech I made, and I find that the letter I have written in place of it to put in here, won't go in—wouldn't go in a canal boat, let alone a slipper, examine it yourself, and you will see. Will you please explain that I embroidered this slipper without any instruction in Art, and all for love of you?
Mark Twain

October 5, 1889

The embroidery was not Twain's.

The play of *The Prince and the Pauper*, dramatized by Mrs. Richardson and arranged for the stage by David Belasco, was produced at the Park Theater, Philadelphia, on Christmas Eve of 1889, approximately seven years after the book had been published.

Twain published his last completed novel, *The Personal Recollections of Joan of Arc, by the Sieur Louis de Conte* in 1896. He was sixty-one years old. He scribbled this into his notebook about his book Joan of Arc:

November 30, 1908

I like the Joan of Arc best of all my books: and it *is* the best, I know it perfectly well. And besides, it furnished me seven times the pleasure afforded me by any of the others: 12 years of preparation and 2 years of writing, the others needed no preparation, and got none.

Mark Twain

Mark Twain, the celebrated writer, died on April 21, 1910. He had remarked in the previous year, "I came in with Halley's Comet in 1835. It is coming again next year, and I expect to go out with it. It will be the greatest disappointment of my life if I don't go out with Halley's Comet. The Almighty has said, no doubt: 'Now here are these two unaccountable freaks; they came in together, they must go out together.'" He died of a heart attack at his home Stormfield in Redding, Connecticut, as Halley's Comet was passing earth.

This is just a smattering of what awaits inside, to celebrate a life filled with incredible accomplishment, foolish mistakes, great joys, and bottomless sorrows. It is impossible to encapsulate an entire being's experience into one small volume, especially such a towering personality as Mark Twain. He was a typesetter, a journalist, a miner, a steamboatman, a publisher, a scrapbooker, a billiards-player, a cat-lover, a husband, and a father. It is hoped that the selections chosen for this book will give you a glimpse into the rich and complex life of one of the most important figures of American literature.

Twain wrote this notebook entry regarding The Personal Recollections of Joan of Arc when he was seventy-three years old, fifteen months before his death.

"A successful book is not made of
what is in it, but of what is left out of it."
—Letter to Henry H. Rogers,
April 26–28, 1897

"… great books are weighed and measured
by their style and matter and not by the
trimmings and shadings of their grammar."
—*Mark Twain, a Biography*

I. Writers and Writing

Writing

Criticism

Criticism is a queer thing. If I print "She was stark naked"—& then proceeded to describe her person in detail, what critic would not howl?—who would venture to leave the book on a parlor table.—but the artist does this & all ages gather around & look & talk & point. I can't say, "They cut his head off, or stabbed him, &c" describe the blood & the agony in his face.

—*Notebook #18, February–September 1879*

The young lady is Miss Olivia L. Langdon — (for you would naturally like to know her name.)

Remember me to the boys — & recollect Jim The whenever you or Dick have chance to stumble into Buffalo we shall always have a knife & fork for you, & an honest welcome.

Truly Your Friend
Saml. L. Clemens.

P. S. California plums are good Jim — particularly when they are stew Do they continue to name all the young Injuns after me — whe you pay them for the compliment

Elmira, N.Y., Jan. 26/70.

Dear Jim —

I remember that all right just as well! And somewhere among my relics I have your remembrancer stored away. It makes my heart ache yet to call to mind some of those days. — Still, it shouldn't — for right in the depths of their poverty & their pocket-hunting vagabondage lay the germ of my coming good-fortune. You remember the one gleam of jollity that shot across our dismal sojourn in the rain & mud of Angel's Camp — I mean that day we sat around the tavern stove & heard that chap tell about the frog & how they

Letter to pocket miner Jim Gillis recalling the trip they made five years prior that inspired the story "The Celebrated Jumping Frog of Calaveras County," written from Elmira, New York, January 26, 1870. The complete text of the letter is on the next page.

Elmira, N. Y., Jan. 26/70.

Dear Jim—

I remember that old night just as well! And somewhere among my relics I have
your remembrancer stored away. It makes my heart ache yet to call to mind
some of those days. Still, it shouldn't—for right in the depths of their poverty
& their pocket-hunting vagabondage lay the germ of my coming good-fortune.
You remember the one gleam of jollity that shot across our dismal sojourn in
the rain & mud of Angel's Camp—I mean that day we sat around the tavern
stove & heard that chap tell about the frog & how they filled him with shot. And
you remember how we quoted from the yarn & laughed over it, out there on the
hillside while you & dear old Stoker panned & washed. I jotted the story down
in my note-book that day, & would have been glad to get ten or fifteen dollars
for it—I was just that blind. But then we were so hard up. I published that story,
& it became widely known in America, India, China, England,—& the reputation it made for me has paid me thousands & thousands of dollars since. Four
or five months ago I bought into that Express (have ordered it sent to you as
long as you live—& if the bookkeeper bill sends you any bills, you let me hear of
it) & went heavily in debt—never could have dared to do that, Jim, if we hadn't
heard the Jumping Frog story that day.

And wouldn't I love to take old Stoker by the hand, & wouldn't I love to see
him in his great specialty, his wonderful rendition of "Rinaldo" in the "Burning
Shame!" Where *is* Dick, & what is he doing? Give him my fervent love & warm
old remembrances.

A week from to-day I shall be married—to a girl even better than Mahala, & love-
lier than the peerless "Chapparal Quails." You can't come so far, Jim, but still I cordially invite you to come, anyhow—& I invite Dick, too. And if you two boys were
to land here on that pleasant occasion, we would make you right royally welcome.

The young lady is Miss Olivia L. Langdon—(for you would naturally like to
know her name.)

Remember me to the boys—& recollect, Jim, that whenever you or Dick shall
chance to stumble into Buffalo, we shall always have a knife & fork for you, &
an honest welcome.

Truly Your Friend

Samuel L. Clemens.

P. S. California plums *are* good, Jim—particularly when they are stewed. Do they continue to name all the young Injuns after me—when you pay them for the compliment?

~

When Artemus Ward passed through California on a lecturing tour, in 1865 or '66, I told him the "Jumping Frog" story, in San Francisco, and he asked me to write it out and send it to his publisher, Carleton, in New York, to be used in padding out a small book which Artemus had prepared for the press and which needed some more stuffing to make it big enough for the price which was to be charged for it.

It reached Carleton in time, but he didn't think much of it, and was not willing to go to the typesetting expense of adding it to the book. He did not put it in the waste-basket, but made Henry Clapp a present of it, and Clapp used it to help out the funeral of his dying literary journal, *The Saturday Press*. "The Jumping Frog" appeared in the last number of that paper, was the most joyous feature of the obsequies, and was at once copied in the newspapers of America and England. It certainly had a wide celebrity, and it still had it at the time that I am speaking of—but I was aware that it was only the frog that was celebrated.

— Mark Twain's Autobiography

The first appearance of "The Celebrated Jumping Frog of Calaveras County" published by Henry Clapp in *The Saturday Press*.

Sketches New and Old

Elmira, NY May 7, 1874

A.R. Spofford Esq.

Dear Sir:

I enclose of a Pamphlet Cover, upon which I desire a copyright.

Also, the Title-Page of the Pamphlet—upon the contents of which I likewise desire copyright.

Fess $1.oo enclosed.

Very truly yours

Samuel L. Clemens

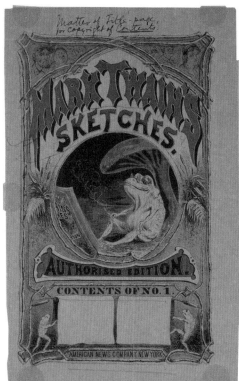

Twain's submission for copyright for a pamphlet of his group of stories called *Sketches New and Old*.

On Publishers

In Mark Twain's letter to author Thomas Bailey Aldrich he references his publisher, Elisha Bliss Jr., at the American Publishing Company.

3/24/74.

My Dear Aldrich:

All right, my boy, send along the proofs.

Never mind Bliss. I don't feel around him. When you've a book ready, I'll only say, "I've the MS here, of a book by Aldrich. Can you pay him 10 per cent royalty, or shall I carry it over the way, to Worthington, Dustin & Co?" The same with a book by Howells. Precious little tortuous diplomacy required when one names his price with a stiff upper lip & mentions the hated rival over the way. I'll attend to the business details, & the framing of the contract, if you'll let me.

Bliss had contracted to pay me 10 p.c. on my next book (contract made 18 months ago) so I made him pay that on *Roughing Gilded Age*. He paid 7½ p.c. on *Roughing It* & 5 p.c. on *Innocents Abroad*. I only made him pay 7½ p.c. on Joaquin Miller's *Modoc* book, because I don't think Miller much of a card in America.

There's an unknown cuss in N. Y. who wants to write a book on a purely commercial subject & make a reputation—but I reckon the lack of a publisher was rather a stumbling block in his way. So I have commissioned him to write the book for me & am to pay him $2,000 when he hands me the MS for said book—500 pages caret—that is 1800 pages of note paper MS. He is to put his own name to it, & read the proofs. I'll make $10,000 out of that books, but not by publishing it as you & Howells publish.

Grief.

There is one discomfort which I fear a man must put up with when he publishes by subscription, & that is wretched paper & vile engravings. I fancy the publisher don't make a very large pile when he pays his author 10 p.c. You notice that the *Gilded Age* is rather a rubbishy looking book; well, the sale has now reached about 50,000 copies—so the royalty now due the authorship is-$-is about $18,000—yet the Company have declared only one ten [per-cent] dividend since the book was issued; they would have declared at least 30-25 per cent in dividends on 50,000 copies of a 7½ p.c. book.

Now I think seriously of printing my own next book & publishing it thro' this same subscription house. It will thus be a mighty starchy book, but I reckon I won't get so much money out of it.

Mrs. C. gets along very, very slowly. But a week hence, if she can travel, we'll leave for Elmira. I must get her away from household & *building* cares. She don't sleep worth a cent.

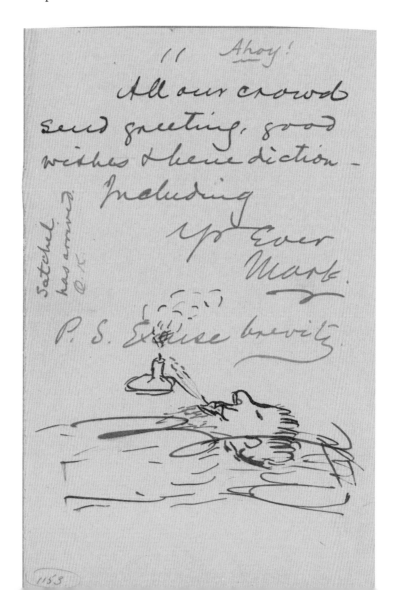

We are also sorry about the "frustration" (as you call it—frustratification is the correct word) of our Cambridge plans. But then the best laid gangs of mice & men are often frustratified, in the providence of

Hope & Gratulation.

God. But never mind—next fall we'll come—or rather you'll come here, for then you'll be no longer at Elmwood & you'd be too high-toned to receive country folk in the city, wouldn't you? We did all most royally enjoy the visit of You Trinity here, & are exceeding glad that you folks enjoyed it, too. Old Joe Twichell, that born prince of men, was in last night, & he is still gloating over the joys of that time. He says that next to being great one's self, is the luxury of meeting the great, face to face. You people made a rare sensation in this neighborhood.

General Observations.

Had a note from the Spectre last night, jolly, splendid old soul. It speaks well for your good heart that you call him Skeleton & so please him with the harmless notion that there is something substantial about his ethereal get-up.

I'm to run back to Hartford in the course of a few weeks, & then I'll try to come up & discuss those plans of yours over a jorum of lager (jorum's good.)

And still no tidings from poor unnecessary but still delightful Keeler! I am getting well discouraged in that direction.

The Little Violinist's prayer struck water in my lower level, as the silver miner says when he is affected. Pretty sketch—good sketch.

Ahoy!

All our crowd send greeting, good wishes & benediction—

Including

Ys Ever

Mark.

Satchel has arrived. O. K

P. S. Excuse brevity.

Left: The last page of Twain's letter to Aldrich.

On The Adventures of Tom Sawyer

My mother had a good deal of trouble with me, but I think she enjoyed it. She had none at all with my brother Henry, who was two years younger than I, and I think that the unbroken monotony of his goodness and truthfulness and obedience would have been a burden to her but for the relief and variety which I furnished in the other direction. I was a tonic. I was valuable to her. I never thought of it before, but now I see it. I never knew Henry to do a vicious thing

From the first edition of *The Adventures of Tom Sawyer*.

toward me, or toward any one else—but he frequently did righteous ones that cost me as heavily. It was his duty to report me, when I needed reporting and neglected to do it myself, and he was very faithful in discharging that duty. He is "Sid" in *Tom Sawyer*. But Sid was not Henry. Henry was a very much finer and better boy than ever Sid was.

It was Henry who called my mother's attention to the fact that the thread with which she had sewed my collar together to keep me from going in swimming, had changed color. My mother would not have discovered it but for that, and she was manifestly piqued when she recognized that that prominent bit of circumstantial evidence had escaped her sharp eye. That detail probably added a detail to my punishment. It is human. We generally visit our shortcomings on somebody else when there is a possible excuse for it—but no matter, I took it out of Henry. There is always compensation for such as are unjustly used. I often took it out of him—sometimes as an advance payment for something which I hadn't yet done. These were occasions when the opportunity was too strong a temptation, and I had to draw on the future. I did not need to copy this idea from my mother, and probably didn't. Still she wrought upon that principle upon occasion.

If the incident of the broken sugar-bowl is in "Tom Sawyer"—I don't remember whether it is or not—that is an example of it. Henry never stole sugar. He took it openly from the bowl. His mother knew he wouldn't take sugar when she wasn't looking, but she had her doubts about me. Not exactly doubts, either. She knew very well I would. One day when she was not present, Henry took sugar from her prized and precious old English sugar-bowl, which was an heirloom in the family—and he managed to break the bowl. It was the first time I had ever had a chance to tell anything on him, and I was inexpressibly glad. I told him I was going to tell on him, but he was not disturbed. When my mother came in and saw the bowl lying on the floor in fragments, she was speechless for a minute. I allowed that silence to work; I judged it would increase the effect. I was waiting for her to ask "Who did that?"—so that I could fetch out my news. But it was an error of calculation. When she got through with her silence she didn't ask anything about it—she merely gave me a crack on the skull with her thimble that I felt all the way down to my heels. Then I broke out with my injured innocence, expecting to make her very sorry that she had punished the wrong one. I expected her to do something remorseful and pathetic. I told her that I was not the one—it was Henry. But there was no upheaval. She said, without emotion, "It's all right. It isn't any matter. You deserve it for something you've done that I didn't know about; and if you haven't done it, why then you deserve it for something that you are going to do, that I sha'n't hear about.

—*Mark Twain's Autobiography*

The house pointed out as Huck Finn's home.

On The Adventures of Huckleberry Finn

Tom Blankenship was the inspiration for Huckleberry Finn. He was the son of a saw-laborer and drunkard who lived in Hannibal, Missouri, where Mark Twain grew up.

In *Huckleberry Finn* I have drawn Tom Blankenship exactly as he was. He was ignorant, unwashed, insufficiently fed; but he had as good a heart as ever any boy had. His liberties were totally unrestricted. He was the only really independent person—boy or man—in the community, and by consequence he was tranquilly and continuously happy and envied by the rest of us. And as his society was forbidden us by our parents the prohibition trebled and quadrupled its value, and therefore we sought and got more of his society than any other boy's.

—*Mark Twain's Autobiography*

The double-barreled novel lies torpid. I found I could not go on with it. The chapters I had written were still too new and familiar to me. I may take it up next winter, but cannot tell yet; I waited and waited to see if my interest in it would not revive, but gave it up a month ago and began another boys' book— more to be at work than anything else. I have written 400 pages on it— therefore it is very nearly half done. It is *Huck Finn's Autobiography*. I like it only tolerably well, as far as I have got, and may possibly pigeonhole or burn the MS when it is done.

—Letter to William Dean Howells on August 9, 1876

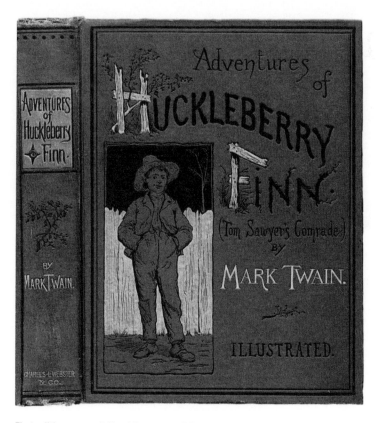

First edition cover of *The Adventures of Huckleberry Finn.*

On Typewriters

BJUYT KIOP M LKJHGFOSA;QWERTYUIOP: _-98V86432QW RT
                                            HA
                        HARTFORD, DEC. 9.
DEAR BROTHER:
I AM TRYING T TO GET THE HANG OF THIS NEW F
FANGLED WRITING MACHINE, BUT AM NOT MAKING
A SHINING SUCCESS OF IT. HOWEVER THIS IS THE
FIRST ATTEMPT I EVER HAVE MADE, & YET I PER-
CEIVETHAT I SHALL SOON & EASILY ACQUIRE A FINE
FACILITY IN ITS USE. I SAW THE THING IN BOS-
TON THE OTHER DAY & WAS GREATLY TAKEN WI:TH
IT. SUSIE HAS STRUCK THE KEYS ONCE OR TWICE,
& NO DOUBT HAS PRINTED SOME LETTERS WHICH DO
NOT BELONG WHERE SHE PUT THEM.
THE HAVING BEEN A COMPOSITOR IS LIKELY TO BE
A GREAT HELP TO ME, SINCE O NE CHIEFLY NEEDS
SWIFTNESS IN BANGING THE KEYS. THE MACHINE COSTS
125 DOLLARS. THE MACHINE HAS SEVERAL VIRTUES
I BELIEVE IT WILL PRINT FASTER THAN I CAN WRITE.
ONE MAY LEAN BACK IN HIS CHAIR & WORK IT. IT
PILES AN AWFUL STACK OF WORDS ON ONE PAGE.
IT DONT MUSS THINGS OR SCATTER INK BLOTS AROUND.
OF COURSE IT SAVES PAPER.
                        SUSIE IS GONE,
NOW, & I FANCY I SHALL MAKE BETTER PROGRESS.
WORKING THIS TYPE-WRITER REMINDS ME OF OLD
ROBERT BUCHANAN, WHO, YOU REMEMBER, USED TO
SET UP ARTICLES AT THE CASE WITHOUT PREVIOUS-
LY PUTTING THEM IN THE FORM OF MANUSCRIPT. I
WAS LOST IN ADMIRATION OF SUOH MARVELOUS
INTELLECTUAL CAPACITY.
                        LOVE TO MOLLIE.
                YOUR BROTHER,
                        SAM.

Twain typed this letter to his brother Orion in around 1879.

~

Twain invested $300,000 ($5,905,833 today) in a typesetting machine called the Paige Compositor, *invented by James W. Paige around 1872–1888. The machine was a failure and never turned a profit. Twain reportedly invested much of his book profits and a large portion of his wife's inheritance into the* Paige Compositor *and it helped to cause his family's financial decline. Twain filed for bankruptcy at the age of 59 in 1893 and his family was forced to leave his Hartford home.*

The Paige Compositor.

~

Twain believed that Life on the Mississippi, *(1882), was the first work of literature to be written on a typewriter.*

...I will now claim—until dispossessed—that I was the first person in the world to apply the typewriter to literature...The early machine was full of caprices, full of defects—devilish ones. It had as many immoralities as the machine of today has virtues. After a year or two I found that it was degrading my character, so I thought I would give it to Howells...He took it home to Boston, and my morals began to improve, but his have never recovered.

— *The First Writing Machines*

On Censorship

The following story was printed in the New York Times, *March 27, 1906.*

NEVER TOO ILL FOR A STORY.

"Mark Twain's" Only Comment on Brooklyn's Edict Against His Works.

There is a letter over in Brooklyn signed by Samuel L. Clemens, a sad man living at 21 Fifth Avenue. Mr. Clemens, better known as Mark Twain, has been ill for a week with a cold which threatened him with pneumonia. Yesterday he was said to be better, but he did not feel well enough to receive interviewers and explain to them how it had happened that the Brooklyn Public Libraries, through Librarian Frank P. Hill, had put on the "restricted list" both "Huckleberry Finn" and "Tom Sawyer," and what he had said to them in the letter he wrote on the subject.

Mr. Clemens's secretary told the reporters that the humorist had thrown away Dante's "Inferno," which he had been reading, when he learned of the ban on his books in Brooklyn. Then he proceeded to tell a story he knew of an Englishman who "bettered a story." Here is the story as the secretary told it:

There was once a wicked man who stayed late at his club. His wife had a cuckoo clock. As he entered the door he heard it sound twice, and on his own account added more "cuckoos." When he awoke in the morning he was happy in the belief that his wife had been deceived into thinking he had got home by 12 o'clock.

Now this story was told by an American to an Englishman, who, lacking a sense of humor, insisted on telling the sequel. It was to the effect that the too lively gentleman learned from his spouse when he complained about not being wakened in time that she had been out on an errand. During the night she had heard the clock "co-co" and decided that it had the hiccoughs, so she had taken it to the clockmaker.

The doctor who was summoned after this story said that his patient was doing very well, indeed. The fact that Mr. Hill had refused to give out the letter in regard to the edict against "Huckleberry Finn" and "Tom Sawyer" made it impossible for Mr. Clemmens's [sic] secretary to make it public, the communication being personal.

Signed copy of the *Adventures of Huckleberry Finn* to Edward and Charles Sisson of San Francisco on March 12, 1885. To the left of Twain's signature are two "sparring" figures Twain drew and what appears to be the words "guess it."

~

Some people can smoke to excess. Let them beware. There are others [who] can't smoke to excess because there isn't time enough in the day which contains only 24 hours. But never mind about that: The matter which touches me much nearer is the question who got this book from poor Edward & Charles?

Truly Yours,

Mark Twain

Montreal, ☀ day. 27, 1881

(The blank means that there is no-vem-
ber there.)

Livy

, A [squirrel] kept me awake

[sock] night till 3 or 4 o' [clock] — so

[eye] [am] lying a— [bed] this morning

I would [give] [give]

[bottles] 2 [birds flying] oct 14

Yonder in the [snow storm scene]

although it is only snow.

There. — thats for the children
— was not sure that they could read
writing, especially Jean, who is strangely
ignorant in some things.

A Rebus Letter

Clemens, away on copyright business in Montreal in November 1881, wrote home to his wife, Livy, and his three young daughters, Susy, Clara, and Jean, in the form of a "rebus letter," in which pictographs were substituted for words or syllables. For those who may find his doodles difficult to decode, here is a translation:

Livy dear, a mouse kept me awake last night till 3 or 4 o'clock—so I am lying abed this morning. I would not [a log with a "knot"] give sixpence [the nibs of six pens] to be out yonder in the storm, although it is only snow.

There—that's for the children—was not sure that they could read writing, especially Jean, who is strangely ignorant in some things.

On Weather

The text on the next page was originally intended to be part of Pudd'nhead Wilson *which Twain finished drafting on December 12, 1892. In a subsequent revision of his draft, he sent the below to the printer, offering various symbols be inserted in facsimile at the heads of chapters. The idea was discarded before the book was published on November 28, 1894.*

According to the Morgan Library curators, "Twain wrote Pudd'nhead Wilson *in a blaze of creativity, spurred by his imminent bankruptcy. The finances of Twain's publishing firm, Webster and Company, were failing, and his continued investment in the Paige typesetting machine was becoming overwhelming. He needed to write a commercially successful novel quickly and completed 60,000 words between November 12 and December 14, 1892. Making light of his haste, Twain used seven symbols to denote weather conditions and instructed the printer to insert them at the head of each chapter. They do not appear in the printed edition.*

The rebus letter excerpted above.

Key to Signs used in this book.

To save the space usually

devoted to, explanations of the state

of the weather, in books of this

kind, the author, ~~will~~ begs leave to substitutes

a simple system of weather-signs.

The hieroglyph at the head of each chapter

~~which~~ will instantly convey to

the reader's mind a perfect com-

prehension of the ~~condi~~

kind of weather which is going to

prevail below.

The signs & their meanings here

follow:

Sunny.

Pitch Dark

Starlight.

Rainy.

Moonlight.

SNOW.

Fog.

When two or more signs occur together, the ensuing weather is

going to be more, or more yet, or still more

~~mixed~~ according to number of signs employed.

variable,

When Twain finished the novel in July 1893, he told Fred Hall that 'there ain't any weather in it, & there ain't any scenery—the story is stripped for flight!' "

To printer: Please make facsimiles of these signs and use them at chapter tops—sometimes two—it is not necessary that they fit the weather of that chapter always.

Key to signs used in this book.

To save the space usually devoted to explanations of the state of the weather in books of this kind, the author begs leave to substitute a simple system of weather signs. Their hieroglyph at the head of each chapter will instantly convey to the reader's mind a perfect comprehension of the kind of weather which is going to prevail below.

The signs and their meanings here follows:

When two or more signs occur together the ensuing weather is going to be more, or none yet, or still more variable, according to number of signs employed.

~~

Twain was appalled by weather in books, and played with the idea of eliminating it altogether in yet another work:

No weather will be found in this book. This is an attempt to pull a book through without weather. It being the first attempt of the kind in fictitious literature, it may prove a failure, but it seemed worth the while of some dare-devil person to try it, and the author was in just the mood.

Many a reader who wanted to read a tale through was not able to do it because of delays on account of the weather. Nothing breaks up an author's progress like having to stop every few pages to fuss-up the weather. Thus it is plain that persistent intrusions of weather are bad for both reader and author.

Instructions to Mark Twain's printer regarding the weather indicators he drew at the start of each chapter, "to save the space usually devoted to explanations of the state of the weather in books of this kind."

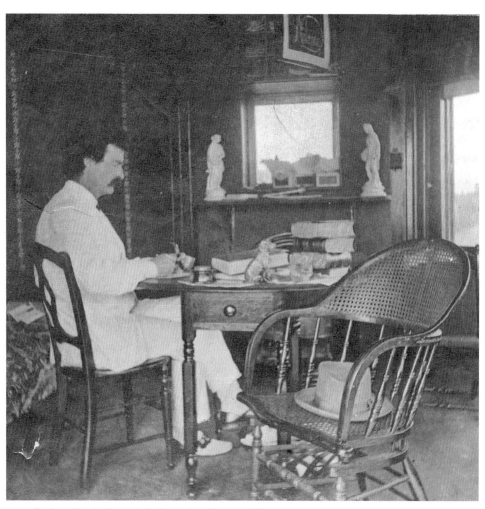

Twain writing in his study in Elmira, New York, in 1874.

Of course weather is necessary to a narrative of human experience. That is conceded. But it ought to be put where it will not be in the way; where it will not interrupt the flow of the narrative. And it ought to be the ablest weather that can be had, not ignorant, poor-quality, amateur weather. Weather is a literary specialty, and no untrained hand can turn out a good article of it. The present author can do only a few trifling ordinary kinds of weather, and he cannot do those very good. So it has seemed wisest to borrow such weather as is necessary for the book from qualified and recognized experts-giving credit, of course. This weather will be found over in the back part of the book, out of the way. See Appendix. The reader is requested to turn over and help himself from time to time as he goes along.

—*The American Claimant*

Autobiography

This autobiography of mine is a mirror, and I am looking at myself in it all the time. Incidentally I notice the people that pass along at my back—I get glimpses of them in the mirror—and whenever they say or do anything that can help advertise me and flatter me and raise me in my own estimation, I set these things down in my autobiography. I rejoice when a king or a duke comes my way and makes himself useful to this autobiography, but they are rare customers, with wide intervals between. I can use them with good effect as lighthouses and monuments along my way, but for real business I depend upon the common herd....

An autobiography that leaves out the little things and enumerates only the big ones is no proper picture of the man's life at all; his life consists of his feelings and his interests, with here and there an incident apparently big or little to hang the feelings on.

—*Mark Twain's Autobiography*

An autobiography is the truest of all books; for while it inevitably consists mainly of extinctions of the truth, shirkings of the truth, partial revealments of the truth, with hardly an instance of plain straight truth, the remorseless truth is there, between the lines, where the author-cat is raking dust upon it which hides from the disinterested spectator neither it nor its smell (though I didn't use that figure)—the result being that the reader knows the author in spite of his wily diligences.

—Letter to William D. Howells, March 14, 1904

∿

I will construct a text:

What a wee little part of a person's life are his acts and his words! His real life is led in his head, and is known to none but himself. All day long, and every day, the mill of his brain is grinding, and his thoughts, not those other things, are his history. His acts and his words are merely the visible, thin crust of his world, with its scattered snow summits and its vacant wastes of water—and they are so trifling a part of his bulk! a mere skin enveloping it. The mass of him is hidden—it and its volcanic fires that toss and boil, and never rest, night nor day. These are his life, and they are not written, and cannot be written.

Every day would make a whole book of eighty thousand words—three hundred and sixty-five books a year. Biographies are but the clothes and buttons of the man—the biography of the man himself cannot be written.

M. T.

—*Mark Twain's Autobiography*

Twain often wrote in bed, 1905.

A DOUBLE-BARRELLED DETECTIVE STORY.

IN TWO PARTS. PART FIRST.

I

We ought never to do wrong when people are looking.

in the country, in Virginia;
The first scene is ~~in a Southern State~~;
the time, 1880. There has been a wedding,
between a *handsome* young man of slender means,
& a rich young girl — a romantic
case of love at first sight & a precipitate marriage; a marriage
bitterly opposed by the girl's widowed, *father.*
Jacob Fuller, the bridegroom, is 26 years old. OVER

bride is 19 & beautiful.
She is intense, romantic, *high-strung,*
measurelessly proud of her Cavalier blood, & 'passionate in her love for her young
husband. For its sake she braved
her father's displeasure, endured his
reproaches, listened with loyalty
unshaken to his warning predictions, & went from his house
without his blessing, proud & happy
~~in what she~~
in the proofs she was thus giving of the
quality of the affection which had made
its home in her heart.

A Double-Barreled Detective Story

First Page of A Double Barreled Detective Story, *first published in 1902.*

PART I

"We ought never to do wrong when people are looking."

The first scene is in the country, in Virginia; the time, 1880. There has been a wedding, between a handsome young man of slender means and a rich young girl—a case of love at first sight and a precipitate marriage; a marriage bitterly opposed by the girl's widowed father.

Jacob Fuller, the bridegroom, is twenty-six years old, is of an old but unconsidered family which had by compulsion emigrated from Sedgemoor, and for King James's purse's profit, so everybody said—some maliciously the rest merely because they believed it. The bride is nineteen and beautiful. She is intense, high-strung, romantic, immeasurably proud of her Cavalier blood, and passionate in her love for her young husband. For its sake she braved her father's displeasure, endured his reproaches, listened with loyalty unshaken to his warning predictions, and went from his house without his blessing, proud and happy in the proofs she was thus giving of the quality of the affection which had made its home in her heart.

James Fenimore's Literary Offenses

Mark Twain on writing.

1. A tale shall accomplish something and arrive somewhere.

2. The episodes of a tale shall be necessary parts of the tale, and shall help develop it.

3. The personages in a tale shall be alive, except in the case of corpses, and that always the reader shall be able to tell the corpses from the others.

4. The personages in a tale, both dead and alive, shall exhibit a sufficient excuse for being there.

5. When the personages of a tale deal in conversation, the talk shall sound like human talk, and be talk such as human beings would be likely to talk in the

given circumstances, and have a discoverable meaning, also a discoverable purpose, and a show of relevancy, and remain in the neighborhood of the subject in hand, and be interesting to the reader, and help out the tale, and stop when the people cannot think of anything more to say.

6. When the author describes the character of a personage in his tale, the conduct and conversation of that personage shall justify said description.

7. When a personage talks like an illustrated, gilt-edged, tree-calf, hand-tooled, seven-dollar Friendship's Offering in the beginning of a paragraph, he shall not talk like a Negro minstrel at the end of it.

8. Crass stupidities shall not be played upon the reader by either the author or the people in the tale.

9. The personages of a tale shall confine themselves to possibilities and let miracles alone; or, if they venture a miracle, the author must so plausibly set it forth as to make it look possible and reasonable.

10. The author shall make the reader feel a deep interest in the personages of his tale and their fate; and that he shall make the reader love the good people in the tale and hate the bad ones.

11. The characters in tale shall be so clearly defined that the reader can tell beforehand what each will do in a given emergency.

An author should:

12. *Say* what he is proposing to say, not merely come near it.

13. Use the right word, not its second cousin.

14. Eschew surplusage.

15. Not omit necessary details.

16. Avoid slovenliness of form.

17. Use good grammar.

18. Employ a simple, straightforward style.

—*The Literary Offenses of James Fenimore Cooper*

From *Roughing It*, Mark Twain's semi-autobiographical (travel literature) book first published in 1872.

A True Story

Mark Twain's article published in *The Atlantic* called "A True Story: Repeated Word for Word as I Heard It." Transcription follows.

This is the first page of Mark Twain's manuscript, "A True Story: Repeated Word for Word as I Heard It," which was the first piece of his to be published in the Atlantic Monthly *by William Dean Howells. It was the first story he had written for publication with absolutely no humor in it whatsoever.*

The article told the story of a former slave, while in chains, who had been brutally separated from her husband and her children, only to be reunited with her youngest sons many years later as she was feeding a group of Union soldiers.

A True Story, repeated word for word as I heard it.

It was summer time, and twilight. We were sitting on the porch of the farm-house on the summit of the hill and "Aunt Rachel" was sitting respectfully below our level on the steps—for she was our servant and colored. She was a of mighty frame and stature; she was sixty…

~⁊

This is the letter to Howells that accompanied the story:

Elmira, Sept. 12.

My Dear Howells:

Your telegram just rec'd. Shall await your letter.

But I made a mistake in writing you. It would take too long to explain. Suffice it that I was charging about 33 per cent more than I meant to.

This disgusts me. But I send the "Fable for Old Boys & Girls" anyway. Since its price is lowered I don't know but what you might really come to like it. But hurl it back with obloquy if you don't. I can dodge.

I enclose also a "True Story" which has no humor in it. You can pay as lightly as you choose for that, if you want it, for it is rather out of my line. I have not altered the old colored woman's story except to begin it at the beginning, instead of the middle, as she did—& worked both ways.

I told this yarn to Hay & some company & they liked it. So I thought I'd write it.

Ys Ever

Mark.

—Letter to Dean Howells, Septemver 2, 1874.

Language

On Adjectives

Mark Twain had several things to say about adjectives. He succinctly wrote in his 1894 novel Pudd'nhead Wilson, *"As to the Adjective: When in doubt, strike it out."*

But his true feelings he made clear in a letter on March 20, 1880 to D. W. Bowser, when he wrote, "I notice that you use plain, simple language, short words and brief sentences. That is the way to write English—it is the modern way and the best way. Stick to it; don't let fluff and flowers and verbosity creep in. When you catch an adjective, kill it. No, I don't mean utterly, but kill most of them—then the rest will be valuable. They weaken when they are close together. They give strength when they are wide apart. An adjective habit, or a wordy, diffuse, flowery habit, once fastened upon a person, is as hard to get rid of as any other vice.

On Adverbs

I am dead to adverbs; they cannot excite me. To misplace an adverb is a thing which I am able to do with frozen indifference; it can never give me a pang…. There are subtleties which I cannot master at all,—the confuse me, they mean absolutely nothing to me,—and this adverb plague is one of them….Yes, there are things which we cannot learn, and there is no use in fretting about it. I cannot learn adverbs; and what is more I won't," *Twain wrote in "Reply to a Boston Girl,"* Atlantic Monthly, *June 1880.* He also advised at a different time, "Substitute 'damn' every time you're inclined to write "very;" your editor will delete it and the writing will be just as it should be.

On Spelling

I have had an aversion to good spelling for sixty years and more, merely for the reason that when I was a boy there was not a thing I could do creditably except spell according to the book. It was a poor and mean distinction, and I early learned to disenjoy it. I suppose that this is because the ability to spell correctly is a talent, not an acquirement. There is some dignity about an acquirement, because it is a product of your own labor. It is wages earned, whereas to be able to do a thing merely by the grace of God, and not by your own effort, transfers the distinction to our heavenly home—where possibly it is a matter of pride and satisfaction, but it leaves you naked and bankrupt.

—Mark Twain's Autobiography

Writers

On Charles Dickens

Twain saw Charles Dickens read during Dickens' second tour of America. Twain filed the following report on February 5, 1868, in the Alta California *newspaper (San Francisco):*

I only heard him read once. It was in New York, last week. I had a seat about the middle of Steinway Hall, and that was rather further away from the speaker than was pleasant or profitable.

Promptly at 8 P.M., unannounced, and without waiting for any stamping or clapping of hands to call him out, a tall, "spry," (if I may say it,) thin-legged old gentleman, gotten up regardless of expense, especially as to shirt-front and dia-monds, with a bright red flower in his button-hole, gray beard and moustache, bald head, and with side hair brushed fiercely and tempestuously forward, as if its owner were sweeping down before a gale of wind, the very Dickens came! He did not emerge upon the stage—that is rather too deliberate a word—he strode. He strode—in the most English way and exhibiting the most English general style and appearance—straight across the broad stage, heedless of everything, unconscious of everybody, turning neither to the right nor the left—but striding eagerly straight ahead, as if he had seen a girl he knew turn the next corner. He brought up handsomely in the centre and faced the opera glasses. His pictures are hardly handsome, and he, like everybody else, is less handsome than his pictures. That fashion he has of brushing

Wood engraving from a sketch by Charles A. Barry of Charles Dickens from *Harper's Weekly*, December 1867.

his hair and goatee so resolutely forward gives him a comical Scotch-terrier look about the face, which is rather heightened than otherwise by his portentous dignity and gravity. But that queer old head took on a sort of beauty, bye and bye, and a fascinating interest, as I thought of the wonderful mechanism within it, the complex but exquisitely adjusted machinery that could create men and women, and put the breath of life into them and alter all their ways and actions, elevate them, degrade them, murder them, marry them, conduct them through good and evil, through joy and sorrow, on their long march from the cradle to the grave, and never lose its godship over them, never make a mistake! I almost imagined I could see the wheels and pulleys work. This was Dickens—Dickens. There was no question about that, and yet it was not right easy to realize it. Somehow this puissant god seemed to be only a man, after all. How the great do tumble from their high pedestals when we see them in common human flesh, and know that they eat pork and cabbage and act like other men.

Mr. Dickens had a table to put his book on, and on it he had also a tumbler, a fancy decanter and a small bouquet. Behind him he had a huge red screen—a bulkhead—a sounding-board, I took it to be—and overhead in front was suspended a long board with reflecting lights attached to it, which threw down a glory upon the gentleman, after the fashion in use in the picture-galleries for bringing out the best effects of great paintings. Style!—There is style about Dickens, and style about all his surroundings.

He read *David Copperfield*. He is a bad reader, in one sense—because he does not enunciate his words sharply and distinctly—he does not cut the syllables cleanly, and therefore many and many of them fell dead before they reached our part of the house. [I say "our" because I am proud to observe that there was a beautiful young lady with me—a highly respectable young white woman.] I was a good deal disappointed in Mr. Dickens' reading—I will go further and say, a great deal disappointed. The *Herald* and *Tribune* critics must have been carried away by their imaginations when they wrote their extravagant praises of it. Mr. Dickens' reading is rather monotonous, as a general thing; his voice is husky; his pathos is only the beautiful pathos of his language—there is no heart, no feeling in it—it is glittering frostwork; his rich humor cannot fail to tickle an audience into ecstasies save when he reads to himself. And what a bright, intelligent audience he had! He ought to have made them laugh, or cry, or shout, at his own good will or pleasure—but he did not. They were very much tamer than they should have been.

He pronounced Steerforth "St'yaw-futh." This will suggest to you that he is a little Englishy in his speech. One does not notice it much, however. I took two or three notes on a card; by reference to them I find that Pegotty's anger when he learned the circumstance of Little Emly's disappearance, was "excellent acting—full of spirit;" also, that Pegotty's account of his search for Emly was "bad;" and that Mrs. Micawber's inspired suggestions as to the negotiation of her husband's bills, was "good;" (I mean, of course, that the reading was;) and that Dora the child-wife, and the storm at Yarmouth, where Steerforth perished, were not as good as they might have been. Every passage Mr. D. read, with the exception of those I have noted, was rendered with a degree of ability far below what his reading reputation led us to expect. I have given "first impressions." Possibly if I could hear Mr. Dickens read a few more times I might find a different style of impressions taking possession of me. But not knowing anything about that, I cannot testify.

~◡

Twain later recalled in October 10, 1907:

What is called a "reading," as a public platform entertainment, was first essayed by Charles Dickens, I think. He brought the idea with him from England in 1867. He had made it very popular at home and he made it so acceptable and so popular in America that his houses were crowded everywhere, and in a single season he earned two hundred thousand dollars. I heard him once during that season; it was in Steinway Hall, in December, and it made the fortune of my life—not in dollars, I am not thinking of dollars; it made the real fortune of my life in that it made the happiness of my life; on that day I called at the St. Nicholas Hotel to see my Quaker City Excursion shipmate, Charley Langdon, and was introduced to a sweet and timid and lovely young girl, his sister. The family went to the Dickens reading, and I accompanied them. It was forty years ago; from that day to this the sister has never been out of my mind nor heart.

Mr. Dickens read scenes from his printed books. From my distance he was a small and slender figure, rather fancifully dressed, and striking and picturesque in appearance. He wore a black velvet coat with a large and glaring red flower in the button-hole. He stood under a red upholstered shed behind whose slant was a row of strong lights—just such an arrangement as artists use to concentrate a strong light upon a great picture. Dickens's audience sat in a pleasant twilight, while he performed in the powerful light cast upon him from the concealed lamps. He read with great force and animation, in the lively passages, and with stirring effect. It will be understood that he did not merely read but also acted. His reading of the storm scene in which Steerforth lost his life was so vivid, and so full of energetic action, that his house was carried off its feet, so to speak.

Dickens had set a fashion which others tried to follow, but I do not remember that anyone was any more than temporarily successful in it. The public reading was discarded after a time and was not resumed until something more than twenty years after Dickens had introduced it; then it rose and struggled along for a while in that curious and artless industry called Authors' Readings. When Providence had had enough of that kind of crime the Authors' Readings ceased from troubling and left the world at peace.

On Walt Whitman

Mark Twain called Walt Whitman the "the father of free verse." He sent this letter to the author on Whitman's 70th Birthday.

Hartford, May 24/89

To Walt Whitman:

You have lived just the seventy years which are greatest in the world's history & richest in benefit & advancement to its peoples. These seventy years have done much more to widen the interval between man & the other animals than was accomplished by any five centuries which preceded them.

What great births you have witnessed! The steam press, the steamship, the steel ship, the railroad, the perfected cotton-gin, the telegraph, the telephone, the phonograph, the photograph, photo-gravure, the electrotype, the gaslight, the electric light, the sewing machine, & the amazing, infinitely varied & innumerable products of coal tar, those latest & strangest marvels of a marvelous age. And you have seen even greater births than these; for you have seen the application of anesthesia to surgery-practice, whereby the ancient dominion of pain, which began with the first created life, came to an end in this earth forever; you have seen the slave set free, you have seen the monarchy banished from France, & reduced in England to a machine which makes an imposing show of diligence & attention to business, but isn't connected with the works. Yes, you have indeed seen much—but tarry yet a while, for the greatest is yet to come. Wait thirty years, & then look out over the earth! You shall see marvels upon marvels added to these whose nativity you have witnessed; & conspicuous above them you shall see their formidable Result—Man at almost his full stature at

Twain's letter to Walt Whitman. Transcript on previous page.

last!—& still growing, visibly growing while you look. In that day, who that hath a throne, or a gilded privilege not attainable by his neighbor, let him procure his slippers & get ready to dance, for there is going to be music. Abide, & see these things! Thirty of us who honor & love you, offer the opportunity. We have among us 600 years, good & sound, left in the bank of life. Take 30 of them—the richest birth-day gift ever offered to poet in this world—& sit down & wait. Wait till you see that great figure appear, & catch the far glint of the sun upon his banner; then you may depart satisfied, as knowing you have seen him for whom the earth was made, & that he will proclaim that human wheat is worth more than human tares, & proceed to organize human values on that basis.

Mark Twain

On Colonel William L. Brown

THE ANNUAL NEW YORK PRESS CLUB DINNER,
NOVEMBER 13, 1900

Colonel William L. Brown, the former editor of the Daily News, as president of the club, introduced Mr. Clemens as the principal ornament of American literature. Twain then said:

I must say that I have already begun to regret that I left my gun at home. I've said so many times when a chairman has distressed me with just such compliments that the next time such a thing occurs I will certainly use a gun on that chairman. It is my privilege to compliment him in return. You behold before you a very, very old man. A cursory glance at him would deceive the most penetrating. His features seem to reveal a person dead to all honorable instincts—they seem to bear the traces of all the known crimes, instead of the marks of a life spent for the most part, and now altogether, in the Sunday-school of a life that may well stand as an example to all generations that have risen or will rise—I mean to say, will rise. His private character is altogether suggestive of virtues which to all appearances he has not. If you examine his past history you will find it as deceptive as his features, because it is marked all over with waywardness and misdemeanor—mere effects of a great spirit upon a weak body—mere accidents of a great career. In his heart he cherishes every virtue on the list of virtues, and he practices them all—secretly—always secretly. You all know him so well that there is no need for him to be introduced here. Gentlemen, Colonel Brown.

On Bret Harte

Francis Bret Harte (August 25, 1836–May 5, 1902) was a contemporary of Mark Twain. Harte was an American author and poet, best remembered for his accounts of pioneering life in California.

According to Albert Bigelow Paine, Twain's biographer, Twain wrote in a letter that both Bret Harte and himself quit the "Californian" expecting to write for Eastern papers in the future. He added:

Though I am generally placed at the head of my breed of scribblers in this part of the country, the place properly belongs to Bret Harte, I think, though he denies it, along with the rest. He wants me to club a lot of old sketches together with a lot of his, and publish a book. I wouldn't do it, only he agrees to take all the trouble. But I want to know whether we are going to make anything out of it, first. However, he has written to a New York publisher, and if we are offered a bargain that will pay for a month's labor we will go to work and prepare the volume for the press.

∿

Mark Twain's first little volume, "The Celebrated Jumping Frog," appeared in the Californian in 1865. To Bret Harte he wrote about the publication of the book:

The book is out and it is handsome. It is full of damnable errors of grammar and deadly inconsistencies of spelling in the Frog sketch, because I was away and did not read proofs; but be a friend and say nothing about these things. When my hurry is over, I will send you a copy to poison the children with.

∿

Twain and Harte became estranged after their co-written play, "Oh, Sin!" was a failure. Twain wrote about Harte to his friend, William Dean Howells, in June of 1878, "Harte is a liar, a thief, a swindler, a snob, a sot, a sponge, a coward, a Jeremey Diddler, he is brim full of treachery... How do I know? By best of evidence, personal observation."

My Dear Howells:

I have mailed one set of the slips to London, & told Bentley you would print Sept. 15 ~~for~~ in October *Atlantic*, & he must not print earlier in *Temple Bar.* Have I got the dates & things right?

I am powerful glad to see that No. 1 reads a nation sight better in print than it did in MS. I told Bentley we'd send him the slips each time 6 weeks before day of publication. We can do that, can't we? Two months ahead would be still better I suppose, but I don't know.

"Ah Sin" went a-booming at the Fifth Avenue. The reception of Col. Sellers was calm compared to it. If Bret Harte had suppressed his name (it didn't occur to me to suggest it) the play would have received as great applause in the papers as it did in the Theatre. x The criticisms were just; the criticisms of the great New York ~~press~~ dailies are always just, intelligent, & square & honest—notwithstand-ing ~~by~~ by a blunder which nobody was seriously to blame for I was made to say exactly the opposite of this in a Baltimore paper some time ago. Never said it at all, & moreover I never thought it. I could not publicly correct it before the play appeared in New York, because that would look as if I had really said that thing & then was moved by fears for my pocket & my reputation to take it back. But I can correct it now, & shall do it; for now my motives cannot be impugned. When I began this it had not occurred to me to use you in this connection, but it occurs to me now. Your opinion & mine, uttered a year ago, & repeated more than once since, that the candor & ability of the New York critics were beyond question, is a matter which makes it proper that I should speak through you at this time. Therefore if you will print this somewhere, it may remove the impression that I say unjust things which I do not think, merely for the pleasure of talking.

There, now. Can't you say—

"In a letter to Mr. Howells of the Atlantic Monthly, *Mark Twain describes the reception of the new comedy "Ah Sin," & then goes on to say:" &c*

~~Beg~~

Beginning at the x with The words, "The criticisms were just."

Will you cut that paragraph out of this letter & precede it with the remarks suggested (or with better ones,) & send it to the *Globe* or some other paper? You can't do me a bigger favor; & yet if it is in the least disagreeable, you mustn't think of it. But let me know, right away, for I want to correct this thing before it grows stale again. I explained myself to only one critic (the *World*)— the consequence was a noble notice of the play. This one called on me, else I shouldn't have explained myself to him. [in margin: Mrs. Clemens says, "*Don't* ask that of Mr. Howells—it will be disagreeable to him." I hadn't thought it, but I will bet two to one on the correctness of her instinct. We shall see.]

I have been putting in a deal of hard work on that play in New York, & have left hardly a foot-print of Harte in it anywhere. But it is full of incurable defects: to-wit, Harte's deliberate thefts & plagiarisms, & my own unconscious ones. I don't believe Harte ever had an idea that he came by honestly. He is the most abandoned thief that defiles the earth.

My old Plunkett family seemed wonderfully coarse & vulgar on the stage, but it was because they were played in such an outrageously & inexcusably coarse way. The Chinaman is killingly funny. I don't know when I have enjoyed anything as much as I did him. The people say there isn't enough of him in the piece. That's a triumph—there'll never be any more of him in it.

John Brougham said, "Read the list of things which the critics have condemned in the piece, & you have unassailable proof that the play contains all the requirements of success & a long life."

That is true. Nearly every time the audience roared I knew it was over some-thing that would be condemned in the morning (justly, too) but must be left in—for low comedies are written for the drawing-room, the kitchen & the stable, & if you cut out the kitchen & the stable the drawing-room can't support the play by itself.

There was as much money in the house the first 2 nights as in the first 10 of Sellers. Haven't heard from the third—I came away.

Yrs Ever

Mark.

4 - Ah Sin Enters - goes to table & looks at cards — looks at Broderick's hand) Two littlee tenee — two littlee ~~drews~~ trrose — velly good han (looks at Plunketts hand) Two littlee fivee — (disgusted) Some mellican man no can deal - don't know how. (goes up stage & shuff cards — watching off R occasionally — picks ou 4 Kings & gives them to Broderick & then gives 4 Aces to Plunkett.) Him all littlee now. (looks about jabbering in chinese - tries to put fist in his waist - but not having time puts its in the barrel and exits quickly L.U.E. talking Chinese)

Ah Sin. Broderick he likee hand, velly good hand — Chinaman deal to ———.

without looking at hands. R. 3. E.

Brod.

Whats that?

Plunk.

There's a man for breakfast!

Exeunt both R.3.E.

(Music) Enter Ah Sin. ✗ —

He puts revolver in barrell con=
ceals himself — Re-enter Plunkett
and Brod.

Brod. (resuming former position) Didn't you think you heard a
shot! (looks at hand and shows furtive
signs of delight which he instantly
suppresses.)

Plunk.

I know I heard it, and it wasn't
20 steps from where we're — (aside)
My soul, what a hand: (Looks at his
hand and shows signs of delight which
he tries to suppress.)

Brod. (aside)

Oh, but I'll sweat him this time, if I
can only draw him on to bet.

Ah Sin.

Chinaman deal alle same like poker sharp.

Brod. (Dissimulating)

Consorn it, I don't seem to have
any luck, Give me 4 cards (Discarding)
Never mind, no use to try to improve
such a hand as this. (aside exultingly)
There aint much lie about that (takes
back his discard)

Ah Sin.

Him old smarty from Mud Springs.

Plunk. (pretending disgust)

On Jane Austen

Whenever I take up *Pride and Prejudice* or *Sense and Sensibility*, I feel like a barkeeper entering the Kingdom of Heaven. I mean, I feel as he would probably feel, would almost certainly feel. I am quite sure I know what his sensations would be—and his private comments. He would be certain to curl his lip, as those ultra-good Presbyterians went filing self-complacently along. ...

She makes me detest all her people, without reserve. Is that her intention? It is not believable. Then is it her purpose to make the reader detest her people up to the middle of the book and like them in the rest of the chapters? That could be. That would be high art. It would be worth while, too. Some day I will examine the other end of her books and see.

—"Jane Austen," by Mark Twain, collected in Who Is Mark Twain?

I haven't any right to criticize books, and I don't do it except when I hate them. I often want to criticise Jane Austen, but her books madden me so that I can't conceal my frenzy from the reader; and therefore I have to stop every time I begin. Every time I read *Pride and Prejudice* I want to dig her up and beat her over the skull with her own shin-bone.

—Letter to Joseph Twichell, September 13, 1898

Twain's Hand

The sane man readeth but the ass signeth without looking.

—Twain inscription of *Innocents Abroad* to Judge John N. Nickerson

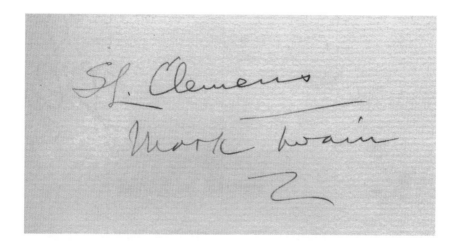

Self-Caricature

The copperplate on the next page was one of the souvenirs presented to each of the guests at the dinner honoring Twain on his sixty-seventh birthday, November 28, 1902, at the Metropolitan Club in New York. The engraved note reads:

Done by / Truly Yours / Mark Twain

"N.B. I cannot make a good / mouth, therefore I leave it out. / There is enough without it anyway. / Done with the best ink. M.T."

According to the Morgan Library, it is housed in a brown leather case and lettered "Mr. J. Pierpont Morgan in gilt." To further personalize these facsimile engravings, a slip of paper was inset below the image, with a characteristically ironic hand-written note to the recipient from Twain: Twain gave it to J. Pierpont Morgan with the note: "For financial advice apply without diffidence to Mark Twain."

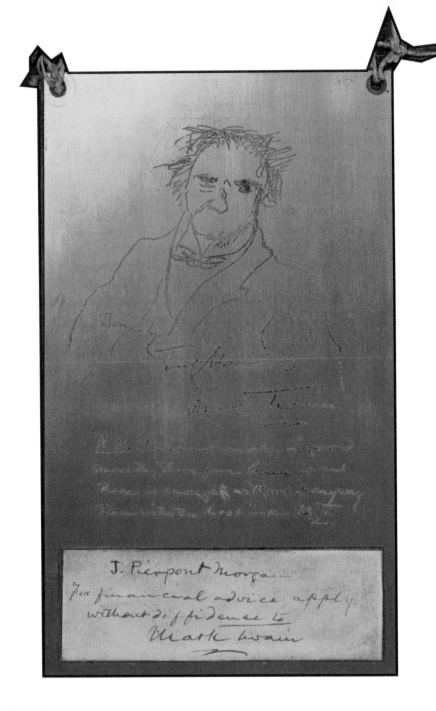

Speeches, Readings, and Dinners

The Lotos Club is one of the oldest literary clubs in the United States. Twain be-
came a life member in 1895. The club held several dinners in his honor including
this one in 1908 that was covered by the New York Times.

The *New York Times,* January 12, 1908

MARK TWAIN NOW AFTER COMPLIMENTS

Says at Lotos Club Dinner He's Collecting Them as some Others Do Stamps.

Author Took a Nap Between Courses Because He Was Going to be Up So Late.

Through Innocent Oysters Abroad, Roughing It Soup, Fish Huckleberry Finn,
and Joan of Arc Filet of Beef, which the menu of the Lotos Club's dinner to
Mark Twain told the guests they were eating last night, the guest of honor in
his white suit, sat in an armchair at the speaker's table. But when Jumping Frog
Terrapin had been reached, the author, the names of whose works had been
perpetuated in the dishes, thought he would be out of bed pretty late for him,
and consequently he would like to take a nap.

While the guests cheered him and he waved his hand to them, he was escorted
to the upper floor. Those left in the dining room continued with Punch, Brothers, Punch; Gilded Age duck, Hadleyburg salad, Life on the Mississippi salad,
Prince and the Pauper cakes, Puddin'head [sic] cheese, and White Elephant
coffee. Toward the end of the menu, Mark Twain reappeared.

When his turn to speak came he announced that he had discovered a new
idea. People collected postage stamps, cats, dogs, and autographs, but he was
collecting compliments, he declared. He had a number of specimens and he
would read them. He did. And then he added his appreciation of their authors'
sincerity. The paying of compliments was an art by itself, he said.

At the speakers' table with Mark Twain were Frank R. Lawrence, President of
the club; Col. Robert P. Porter, Andrew Carnegie, Dr. Robert S. MacArthur,
Hamilton W. Mabie, James M. Beck, Col. George M. Harvey, Col. William C.
Church, Gen. Steward L. Woodford, H. H. Rogers, Chester S. Lord, Dr. Alex-
ander C. Humphreys, and William H. McElroy. Near the close of the dinner
Gov. Fort of New Jersey entered.

Menu for Twain's 1908 Lotos Club dinner.

After Mark had taken his armchair again and the other guests had sipped their White Elephant coffee, President Lawrence as a prelude to the introduction of the guest of honor pointed out one significant feature of the occasion.

The first club dinner in he present clubhouse, at 558 Fifth Avenue, held fourteen years ago, had been in honor of Mark Twain. Seven years later, "on his return from diverse and irregular wanderings," he was the guest at another dinner.

At that time it had been jokingly proposed that at regular intervals of seven years dinners should be held for the author. Last night was the night. It was possible, Mr. Lawrence said, that this dinner might be the last given in the old house. (The new house, 110 West Fifty-seventy Street, may be ready on Jan. 15.)

Mr. Lawrence then called upon Col. Robert P. Porter, who had accompanied Mr. Clemens to Oxford on the occasion of the conferring upon him of the degree of Doctor of Literature, to tell something of the author as he appeared then.

Dr. Porter said among other things that he had been impressed abroad at the number and kind of persons who knew Mr. Clemens. The people on the street —even the London policemen who had been sent down to the university town to help their comrades of Oxford with the pageant knew him.

Then after a toast had been drunk to him, Mr. Clemens began in his drawling gentle way:

"I wish to begin at the beginning, lest I forget it altogether," he said. "I wish to thank you for your welcome now and for that of seven years ago, which I forgot to thank you for at the time, also for that of fourteen years ago which I also forgot to thank you for. I know how it is; when you have been in a parlor and are going away, common decency ought to make you say the decent thing, what a good time you have had. Everybody does it except myself.

"I hope that you will continue that excellent custom of giving me dinners every seven years. I had had it on my mind to join the hosts of another world—I do not know which world - but I have enjoyed your custom so much that I am willing to postpone it for another seven years.

"The guest is in an embarrassing position, because compliments have been paid to him. I don't care whether you deserve it or not, but it is hard to talk up to it.

"The other night at the Engineers' Club dinner they were paying Mr. Carnegie here discomforting compliments. They were all compliments and they were not deserved, and I tried to help him out with criticisms and references to things nobody understood.

"They say that one cannot live on bread alone, but I could live on compliments. I can digest them. They do not trouble me. I have missed much in life that I did not make a collection of compliments, and keep them where I could take them out and look at them once in a while. I am beginning now. Other people collect autographs, dogs, and cats, and I collect compliments. I have brought them along.

"I have written them down to preserve them, and think that they're mighty good and exceedingly just."

Then Mr. Clemens read a few. The first, by Hamilton W. Mabie, said that La Salle might have been the first man to make a voyage of the Mississippi, but that Mark Twain was the first man to chart light and humor for the human race.

"If that had been published at the time that I issued that book (*Life on the Mississippi*) it would have been money in my pocket," he said. "I tell you it is a talent by itself to pay compliments gracefully and have them ring true. It's an art by itself.

"Now, here's one by my biographer. [Loud laughter.] Well, he ought to know me if anybody does. He's been at my elbow for two years and a half. This is Albert Bigelow Paine:

"'Mark Twain is not merely the great writer, the great philosopher, but he is the supreme expression of the human being with its strengths and weaknesses.'"

Mark Twain looked up from he paper which the compliments were written.

"What a talent for compression!" he exclaimed.

W. D. Howells, Mark Twain said, spoke of him as first of Hartford and ultimately of the solar system, not to say of the universe.

"You know how modest Howells is," he commented. "If it can be proved that my fame reaches to Neptune and Saturn, that will satisfy even me. You know how modest and retiring Howells is, but deep down he is as vain as I am."

Mark Twain said Mr. Howells had been granted a degree at Oxford, whose gown was red. He had been invited to an exercise at Columbia, and upon inquiry had been told that it was usual to wear the black gown. Later he had found that three other men wore bright gowns and he had lamented that he had been one of the black mass, and not a red torch.

Edison wrote: "The average American loves his family. If he has any love left over for some other person he generally selects Mark Twain."

"Now here's the compliment of a little Montana girl, " continued Mark Twain, "which came to me indirectly. She was in a room in which there was a large photograph of me. After gazing at it steadily for a time, she said:

"'We've got a John the Baptist like that.'"

When the diners' laughter allowed him, Mr. Clemens added:

"She also said: 'Only ours has more trimmings.'"

"I suppose she meant the halo. Now here is a gold miner's compliment. It is forty-two years old. It was my introduction to an audience to which I lectured in a log schoolhouse. There were no ladies there. I wasn't famous then. They didn't know me. Only the miners were there with their breeches tucked into their boot tops and with clay all over them. They wanted some one to introduce me, and then selected a miner, who protested that he didn't want to do on the ground that he had never appeared in public. This is what he said:

"I don't know anything about this man. Anyhow, I only know two things about him. One is he has never been in jail and the other is I don't know why.

"There's one thing I want to say about the English trip. I knew his Majesty, the King of England, long years ago, and I didn't meet him for the first time then. One thing that I regret was that some newspapers said I talked with the Queen of England with my hat on. I don't do that with any woman. I did not put it on until she asked me to. Then she told me to put it on, and it's a command there. I thought I had carried my American democracy far enough. So I put it on. I have no use for a hat, and never did have.

"Who was it who said that the police of London knew me? Why, the police knew me everywhere. There never was a day over there when a policeman did not salute me, and then put up his hand and stop the traffic of the world. They treated me as though I were a Duchess."

Andrew Carnegie, who followed Mr. Clemens, said that the English public had made much of the author's literary attainments but there was another Mark Twain—Mark Twain the man. He eulogized Mark Twain at length, and referred to his action in paying every cent of the debts of the publishing firm with which he had once been connected.

Other speakers were Dr. Robert S. MacArthur, Hamilton W. Mabie, James M. Beck, Col. George M. Harvey, Col. William C. Church, and Gen. Stewart L. Woodford.

The menu card was a large sheet rolled as a diploma or degree with its central feature a picture of Mark Twain in his Oxford doctor's robes. The margins contained small pictures of scenes and characters from the author's books.

There were also shown the old homes and the new of the Lotos club. A woman below the Mark Twain portrait held in one a scroll with Mr. Clemens's various degrees, and in the other a mask whose features were those of Mark Twain. Near the bottom in the centre was the menu with its book and character names and titles.

HERE IS WHAT THE DINERS ATE:

Innocent Oysters Abroad.

Roughing It Soup.

Huckleberry Finn Fish.

Joan of Arc Filet of Beef.

Jumping Frog Terrapin.

Punch Brothers Punch.

Gilded Duck.

Hadleyburg Salad.

Life on the Mississippi Ice Cream.

Prince and the Pauper Cake.

Pudd'nhead Cheese.

White Elephant Coffee.

Chateau Yuem Royals.

Pommery Brut.

Henkow Cognac.

After it was all over President Lawrence told the company that while this might be the final gathering in the old quarters, the Lotos spirit must be made to burn brightly in the new quarters.

～

The famous white suit

The New York Times: *December 8, 1906*

MARK TWAIN IN WHITE AMUSES CONGRESSMEN

Advocates New Copyright Law and Dress Reform.

WEARS LIGHT FLANNEL SUIT

Says at 71 Dark Colors Depress Him—Talks Seriously of Author's Right to Profit

Special to the *New York Times*

An Advocate of Dress Reform.

While waiting to appear before the committee Mr. Clemens talked to the reporters.

"Why don't you ask why I am wearing such apparently unseasonable clothes? I'll tell you. I have found that when a man reaches the advanced age of 71 years as I have, the continual sight of dark clothing is likely to have a depressing effect upon him. Light-colored clothing is more pleasing to the eye and enlivens the spirit. Now, of course, I cannot compel every one to wear such clothing just for my especial benefit, so I do the next best thing and wear it myself.

"Of course, before a man reaches my years, the fear of criticism might prevent him from indulging his fancy. I am not afraid of that. I am decidedly for pleasing color combinations in dress. I like to see the women's clothes, say, at the opera. What can be more depressing than the sombre black which custom requires men to wear upon state occasions. A group of men in evening clothes looks like a flock of crows, and is just about as inspiring.

"After all, what is the purpose of clothing? Are not clothes intended primarily to preserve dignity and also to afford comfort to the wearer? Now I know of nothing more uncomfortable than the present day clothes of men. The finest clothing made is a person's own skin, but, of course, society demands something more than this.

"The best-dressed man I have ever seen, however, was a native of the Sandwich Islands, who attracted my attention thirty years ago. Now, when that man wanted to don especial dress to honor a public occasion or a holiday, why he occasionally put on a pair of spectacles. Otherwise the clothing with which God had provided him sufficed.

"Of course, I have ideas of dress reform. For one thing, why not adopt some of the women's styles? Goodness knows, they adopt enough of ours. Take the peek-a-boo waist, for instance. It has the obvious advantages of being cool and comfortable, and in addition it is almost always made up in pleasing colors, which cheer and do not depress.

It is true that I dressed the Connecticut Yankee at King Arthur's Court in a plug hat, but let's see, that was twenty-five years ago. Then no man was considered fully dressed until he donned a plug hat. Nowadays I think that no man is dressed until he leaves it home. Why, when I left home yesterday they trotted out a plug hat for me to wear.

"'You must wear it,' they told me; 'why, just think of going to Washington without a plug hat!' But I said no; I would wear a derby or nothing. Why, I believe I could walk along the streets of New York—I never do—but still I think I could —and I should never see a well dressed man wearing a plug hat. If I did I should suspect him of something. I don't know just what, but I would suspect him.

"Why, when I got up on the second story of the Pennsylvania ferryboat coming down here yesterday, I saw Howells coming along. He was the only man on the boat with a plug hat, and I tell you he felt ashamed of himself. he said he had been persuaded to wear it against his better sense, but just think of a man nearly 70 years old who has not a mind of his own on such matters!"

Author Readings

Letter to Richard R. Bowker, editor of Publishers Weekly *and* Harper's Magazine, *and founder of the R.R. Bowker Company, on October 9, 1889. Printed in the* Philadelphia Inquirer, *December 8, 1889, p. 4, which reprinted the letter from the* New York Sun.

I have worked for copyright in all the different ways that its friends have suggested ever since 1872, seventeen or eighteen years, and I am cordially willing to continue to work for it all the rest of my life in all those ways but one—but I want to draw the line there—the platform.

We can point to an aggregate of about twelve authors' readings now, since the first attempt, but we can't point to a single one of them and say it was rationally conducted. Conducting a show is a trade. To do it well must be done by a

"MARK TWAIN,"
AMERICA'S BEST HUMORIST.

master, not novices or apprentices. There is no master with grit enough for the place. You can't find him. He hasn't been born yet. Consider what is required of him. He must say to the small fry: 'You are allowed ten minutes of platform time; if you overpass it two minutes I shall bring down the gavel and shut you off.' To the very greatest poet he must say: 'For your own sake you are allowed but fifteen minutes; you must test your piece at home, and time it by a friend's watch, and allow for the difference between platform time and parlor time, which is three minutes. If it overpasses twelve minutes at home you must cut it down to twelve. If you try to ring in an extra piece you'll hear the gavel.' He must say to the audience: 'The performance will close at 10 o'clock whether the programme is finished or not,' and then keep his word. He must find obscurities who are willing to take the tailpieces on the plain condition that they may possibly never be called up, or notorieties who will promise that they will not answer to their names after 10 o'clock, and will honorably keep that promise.

There is no such man alive, unless it might be General Sherman, author of the brisk and delightful personal memoirs. And even then you would have to appoint me to police him and whisper from time to time, 'General, your time's up;' for possibly you have noticed it, in no instance in history has the chairman of an authors' reading failed to add an hour to the already intolerably long bill.

No: an authors reading, conducted in the customary way, turns what ought to be the pleasantest of all entertainments into an experience to be forever remembered with bitterness by the audience. Remember Washington. There are now living but four persons who paid to get into that house; it is also a fact, howsoever privately it has been kept, that twenty-two died on the premises and eight-one on their way home. I am miserable when I think of my share in that wanton, that unprovoked massacre.

Tell me any other way that I can help the cause and I will do my level best.

Book Tour

Selection from a speech on Morals, July 15, 1895, Cleveland, Ohio

I was solicited to go around the world on a lecture tour by a man in Australia. I asked him what they wanted to be lectured on. He wrote back that those people were very course, and serious, and that they would like something solid, something gigantic; and he proposed that I prepare about three or four lectures at any rate, on just morals, any kind of morals, but just morals, and I liked that idea. I liked it very much, and was perfectly willing to engage in that kind of work, and I should like to teach morals. I have a great enthusiasm in doing that, and I shall like to teach morals to those people. I do not like to have them taught to me, and I do not know of any duller entertainment than that, but I know I can produce a quality of goods that will satisfy those people.

If you teach principles, why, you had better let your illustrations come first, illustrations which shall carry home to every person. I planned my first lecture on morals. I must not stand here and talk all night; get out a watch; I am talking the first time now, and I do not know anything about the length of it.

I would start with two or three rules of moral principles which I want to impress upon those people. I will just make the lecture gradual, by and by. The illustrations are the most important, so that when that lecture is by and by written and completed, it will just be a waveless ocean with this archipelago of smiling green islands of illustrations in the midst of it.

"I thought I would state a principle which I was going to teach. I have this theory for doing a great deal of good out there, everywhere in fact, that you should prize as a priceless thing every transgression, every crime that you commit—the lesson of it, I mean.

"Make it permanent; impress it so that you may never commit that same crime again as long as you live; then you will see yourself what the logical result of that will be—that you get interested in committing crimes. You will lay up in that way, course by course, the edifice of a personally perfect oral character. You cannot afford to waste any crime; they are not give to you to be thrown away, but for a great purpose. There are 462 crimes possible, and you cannot add anything to this; you cannot originate anything. These have been all thought out, all experimented on, and have been thought out by most capable men in the penitentiary. When you commit a transgression lay it up in your memory, and without stopping, it will all lead toward moral perfection. When you have committed your 462 you are released of every other possibility and have ascended the staircase of faultless creation, and you finally stand with your 462 complete with absolute moral perfection, and I am more than two-thirds up there. It is immense inspiration to find yourself climbing that way, and have not much further to go. I shall have, then, that moral perfection, and shall then see my edifice of moral character standing fair before the world all complete. I know that this would produce it. Why, the first time that I ever stole a watermelon—I think it was the first, but this is no matter, it was right along there somewhere—I carried that watermelon to a secluded bower. You may call it a bower, and I suppose you may not. I carried that watermelon to a secluded bower in the lumber yard, and broke it open and it was green.

"Now then, I began to reflect; there is the virtual—that is the beginning of reformation, when you reflect. When you do not reflect, that transgression is wasted on you. I began to reflect, and I said to myself, I have done wrong; it was wrong in me to steal that watermelon—that kind of watermelon. And I said to myself: Now what would a right-minded and right-intentioned boy do, who found that he had done wrong—stolen a watermelon like this. What would he do, what must he do? Do right; restitution; make restitution. He must restore that property to its owner; and I resolved to do that, and the moment I made that good resolution I felt that electrical moral uplift which becomes a victory over wrongdoing. I was spiritually strengthened and refreshed, and carried that watermelon back to that wagon and gave it to the farmer—restored it to him, and I told him he ought to be ashamed of himself going around working off green watermelons in that way on people who had confidence in him, and I told him in my perfectly frank manner it was wrong. I said that if he did not stop he could not have my custom and he was ashamed. He was ashamed; he said he would never do it again, and I believe that I did that man a good turn, as well as one for myself. He did reform; I was severe with him a little, but that was all. I restored the watermelon and made him give me a ripe one. I morally helped him, and I have no doubt that I helped myself the same time, for that was a lesson which remained with me for my perfection. Ever since that day to this I never stole another one—like that.

Then I have another theory, and that is to teach that when you do a thing do it with all your might; do it with all your heart. I remember a man in California, Jim. What-is-his-name, Baker. He was a hearty man of most gentlemanly spirit, and had many fine qualities. He lived a good many years in California among the woods and mountains; he had no companionship but that of the wild creatures of the forest. To me he was an observant man. He watched the ways of the different creatures so that he got so that he could understand what the creatures said to each other and translate it accurately. He was the only man I ever knew who could do this. I know he could, because he told me so himself, and he says that some of he animals have very slight education and small vocabulary. These creatures are very fond of talking. They like to show off and he placed the bluejay at the head of that list. He said: "Now, there is more to the bluejay than any other animal. He has got more different kinds of feeling. Whatever a bluejay feels he can put into language, and not mere commonplace language, but straight out-and-out book talk. And there is such a command of language. You never saw a bluejay get stuck for a word. He is a vocabularized geyser. Now, you must call a jay, a bird, and so he is in a measure, because he wears feathers, and don't belong to any church, but otherwise he is just as human nature made him. A bluejay hasn't any more principle than an ex-Congressman, and he will steal, deceive, and betray four times out of five; and as for the sacredness of an obligation you cannot scare him in the detail of principle. He talks the best grammar of all the animals. You may say a cat talks good grammar. Well, a cat does; but you let a cat get excited, you let a cat get a pulling fur with another cat on a shed nights, and you will hear grammar. A bluejay is human; he has got all a man's faculties and a man's weakness. He likes especially scandal; he knows when he is an ass as well as you do."

From "Mark Twain's First Appearance" speech, 1906.

I recall the occasion of my first appearance...I got to the theatre forty-five minutes before the hour set for the lecture. My knees were shaking so that I didn't know whether I could stand up. If there is an awful, horrible malady in the world, it is stage fright—and seasickness. They are a pair. I had stage fright then for the first and last time. I was only sea-sick once, too. It was on a little ship on which there were two hundred other passengers. I—was—sick. I was so sick there wasn't any left for the other passengers.

I had got a number of friends of mine, stalwart men, to sprinkle themselves through the audience armed with big clubs. Every time I said anything they could possibly guess I intended to be funny they were to pound those clubs on the floor. Then there was a kind lady in a box up there, also a good friend of mine, the wife of the Governor. She was to watch me intently, and whenever I glanced towards her she was going to deliver a gubernatorial laugh that would lead the whole audience into applause.

Well, after the first agonizing five minutes, my stage fright left me, never to return. I know if I'm going to be hanged I could get up and make a good show-ing, and I intend to.

Twain's lecture notes for an unknown event.

"Good friends, good books and a
sleepy conscience: this is the ideal life."
—Notebook, 1898

"Let us endeavor so to live
that when we come to die even the
undertaker will be sorry."
—*The Tragedy of Pudd'nhead Wilson and
the Comedy of the Extraordinary Twins*

2. Life

Samuel Clemens at age fifteen holding holding a printer's
composing stick with the letters SAM.

Youth

Being told I would be expected to talk here, I inquired what sort of talk I ought
to make. They said it should be something suitable to youth—something didac-
tic, instructive, or something in the nature of good advice. Very well. I have

a few things in my mind which I have often longed to say for the instruction of the young; for it is in one's tender early years that such things will best take root and be most enduring and most valuable. First, then. I will say to you my young friends—and I say it beseechingly, urgently—

Always obey your parents, when they are present. This is the best policy in the long run, because if you don't, they will make you. Most parents think they know better than you do, and you can generally make more by humoring that superstition than you can by acting on your own better judgment.

Be respectful to your superiors, if you have any, also to strangers, and sometimes to others. If a person offends you, and you are in doubt as to whether it was intentional or not, do not resort to extreme measures; simply watch your chance and hit him with a brick. That will be sufficient. If you shall find that he had not intended any offense, come out frankly and confess yourself in the wrong when you struck him; acknowledge it like a man and say you didn't mean to. Yes, always avoid violence; in this age of charity and kindliness, the time has gone by for such things. Leave dynamite to the low and unrefined.

Go to bed early, get up early—this is wise. Some authorities say get up with the sun; some say get up with one thing, others with another. But a lark is really the best thing to get up with. It gives you a splendid reputation with everybody to know that you get up with the lark; and if you get the right kind of lark, and work at him right, you can easily train him to get up at half past nine, every time—it's no trick at all.

Now as to the matter of lying. You want to be very careful about lying; otherwise you are nearly sure to get caught. Once caught, you can never again be in the eyes to the good and the pure, what you were before. Many a young person has injured himself permanently through a single clumsy and ill-finished lie, the result of carelessness born of incomplete training. Some authorities hold that the young out not to lie at all. That of course, is putting it rather stronger than necessary; still while I cannot go quite so far as that, I do maintain, and I believe I am right, that the young ought to be temperate in the use of this great art until practice and experience shall give them that confidence, elegance, and precision which alone can make the accomplishment graceful and profitable. Patience, diligence, painstaking attention to detail—these are requirements; these in time, will make the student perfect; upon these only, may he rely as the sure foundation for future eminence. Think what tedious years of study, thought, practice, experience, went to the equipment of that peerless old master who was able to impose upon the whole world the lofty and sounding maxim that "truth is mighty and will prevail"—the most majestic compound fracture of fact which any of woman born has yet achieved. For the history of our race, and each individual's experience, are sewn thick with evidences that a truth is not hard to kill, and that a lie well told is immortal. There is in Boston a monument of the man who discovered anesthesia; many people are aware, in these latter days, that that man didn't discover it at all, but stole the discovery from another man. Is this truth mighty, and will it prevail? Ah no, my hearers, the monument is made of hardy material, but the lie it tells will outlast it a million years. An awkward, feeble, leaky lie is a thing which you ought to make it your unceasing study to avoid; such a lie as that has no more real permanence than an average truth. Why, you might as well tell the truth at once and be done with it. A feeble, stupid, preposterous lie will not live two years—except it be a slander upon somebody. It is indestructible, then of course, but that is no merit of yours. A final word: begin your practice of this gracious and beautiful art early—begin now. If I had begun earlier, I could have learned how.

Never handle firearms carelessly. The sorrow and suffering that have been caused through the innocent but heedless handling of firearms by the young! Only four days ago, right in the next farm house to the one where I am spending the summer, a grandmother, old and gray and sweet, one of the loveliest spirits in the land, was sitting at her work, when her young grandson crept in and got down an old, battered, rusty gun which had not been touched for many years and was supposed not to be loaded, and pointed it at her, laughing and threatening to shoot. In her fright she ran screaming and pleading toward the door on the other side of the room; but as she passed him he placed the gun almost against her very breast and pulled the trigger! He had supposed it was not loaded. And he was right—it wasn't. So there wasn't any harm done. It is the only case of that kind I ever heard of. Therefore, just the same, don't you meddle with old unloaded firearms; they are the most deadly and unerring things that have ever been created by man. You don't have to take any pains at all with them; you don't have to have a rest, you don't have to have any sights on the gun, you don't have to take aim, even. No, you just pick out a relative and bang away, and you are sure to get him. A youth who can't hit a cathedral at thirty yards with a Gatling gun in three quarters of an hour, can take up an old empty musket and bag his grandmother every time, at a hundred. Think what Waterloo would have been if one of the armies had been boys armed with old muskets supposed not to be loaded, and the other army had been composed of their female relations. The very thought of it makes one shudder.

There are many sorts of books; but good ones are the sort for the young to read. Remember that. They are a great, an inestimable, and unspeakable means of improvement. Therefore be careful in your selection, my young friends; be very careful; confine yourselves exclusively to Robertson's *Sermons*, Baxter's *Saints' Rest*, *The Innocents Abroad*, and works of that kind.

But I have said enough. I hope you will treasure up the instructions which I have given you, and make them a guide to your feet and a light to your understanding. Build your character thoughtfully and painstakingly upon these precepts, and by and by, when you have got it built, you will be surprised and gratified to see how nicely and sharply it resembles everybody else's.

— "Advice to Youth," 1882 speech

Houses and Homes

Hannibal, Missouri

HANNIBAL—BY A NATIVE HISTORIAN

Hannibal has had a hard time of it ever since I can recollect, and I was "raised" there. First, it had me for a citizen, but I was too young then to really hurt the place. Next, Jimmy Finn, the town drunkard, reformed, and that broke up the only saloon in the village. But the temperance people liked it; they were willing enough to sacrifice public prosperity to public morality. And 80 they made much of Jimmy Finn—dressed him up in new clothes, and had him out to breakfast and to dinner, and so forth, and showed him off as a great living curiosity—a shining example of the power of temperance doctrines when earnestly and eloquently set forth. Which was all very well, you know, and sounded well, and looked well in print, but Jimmy Finn couldn't stand it. He got remorseful about the loss of his liberty; and then he got melancholy from thinking about it so much; and after that, he got drunk. He got awfully drunk in the chief citizen's house, and the next morning that house was as if the swine had tarried

Mark Twain never tired of writing about his youth, especially his time spent in Hannibal, Missouri. Here is an introduction to *The Adventures of Huckleberry Finn* dedicating the book to the boys and girls of Hannibal, Missouri, that was never used.

To the Once Boys & Girls

who comraded with me in the morning of ~~time~~ time & the youth of antiquity, in the village of

Hannibal, Missouri,

this book is inscribed, with affection for themselves, respect for their virtues, & reverence for their honorable gray hairs.

The Author.

(Never used Chas L Webster)

Twain's boyhood home in Hannibal, Missouri.

in it. That outraged the temperance people and delighted the opposite faction. The former rallied and reformed Jim once more, but in an evil hour temptation came upon him, and he sold his body to a doctor for a quart of whiskey, and that ended all his earthly troubles. He drank it all at one sitting, and his soul went to its long account and his body went to Dr. Grant. This was another blow to Hannibal. Jimmy Finn had always kept the town in a sweat about something or other, and now it nearly died from utter inanition.

After this, Joe Dudding, a reckless speculator, started a weekly stage to the town of Florida, thirty miles away, where a couple of families were living, and Hannibal revived very perceptibly under this wild new sensation.

But then the scarlet fever came, and the hives, and between them they came near hiving all the children in the camp. And so Hannibal took another back-set. But pretty soon a weekly newspaper was started, which bred a fierce spirit of enterprise in the neighboring farmers, because when they had any small potatoes left over that they couldn't sell, they didn't throw them away as they used to do, but they took them to the editor and traded them off for subscriptions to his paper. But finally the potato-rot got him, and Hannibal was floored again.

However, somebody started a pork-house, and the little village showed signs of life once more. And then came the measles and blighted it. It stayed blighted a good while, too.

After a while they got to talking about building a plank road to New London, ten miles away, and after another while, they built it. This made business. Then they got excited and built a gravel road to Paris, 30 or 40 miles. More business. They got into a perfect frenzy and talked of a railroad—an actual rail road—a railroad 200 miles long—a railroad from Hannibal to St. Joseph! And behold, in the fullness of time—in ten or fifteen years—they built it.

A sure enough prosperity burst upon the community, now. Property went up. It was noted as a significant fact that instead of selling town-lots by the acre people began to sell them by the front foot. Hannibal grew fast—doubled its population in two years, started a daily paper or two, and came to be called a city—sent for a fire engine and had her out, bedecked with ribbons, on Fourth of July, but the engine-house burned down one night and destroyed her, which cast a gloom over the whole community. And they started militia companies, and Sons of Temperance and Cadets of Temperance. Hannibal always had a weakness for the Temperance cause. I joined the Cadets myself, although they didn't allow a boy to smoke, or drink or swear, but I thought I never could be truly happy till I wore one of those stunning red scarfs and walked in procession when a distinguished citizen died. I stood it four months, but never an infernal distinguished citizen died during the whole time; and when they finally pronounced old Dr. Norton convalescent (a man I had been depending on for seven or eight weeks,) I just drew out. I drew out in disgust, and pretty much all the distinguished citizens in the camp died within the next three weeks.

Well, Hannibal's prosperity seemed to be of a permanent nature, but St. Louis built the North Missouri Railroad and hurt her, and Quincy tapped the Hannibal and St. Joe in one or two places, which hurt her still worse, and then the war came, and the closing years of it almost finished her.

Now they are trying to build a branch railroad to some place in the interior they call Moberly, at a cost of half a million, and if that fails some of the citizens will move. They only talk Moberly now. The church members still talk about religion, but they mix up a good deal of Moberly in it. The young ladies talk fashion and Moberly, and the old ones talk of charity and temperance, piety, the grave, and Moberly. Hannibal will get Moberly, and it will save her. It will bring back the old prosperity. But won't they have to build another road to protect the Moberly? and another and another to protect each enterprise of the kind? A railroad is like a lie—you have to keep building to it to make it stand. A railroad is a ravenous destroyer of towns, unless those towns are put at the end of it and a sea beyond, so that you can't go further and find another terminus. And it is shaky trusting them, even then, for there is no telling what may be done with trestle-work.

—An article published in the *San Francisco Alta California*, May 26, 1867 (written New York, April 16, 1867)

∽

Tom Nash was a boy of my own age—the postmaster's son. The Mississippi was frozen across, and he and I went skating one night, probably without permission. I cannot see why we should go skating in the night unless without permission, for there could be no considerable amusement to be gotten out of skating at midnight if nobody was going to object to it. About midnight, when we were more than half a mile out toward the Illinois shore, we heard some ominous rumbling and grinding and crashing going on between us and the home side of the river, and we knew what it meant—the river was breaking up. We started for home, pretty badly scared. We flew along at full speed whenever the moonlight sifting down between the clouds enabled us to tell which was ice and which was water. In the pauses we waited, started again whenever there was a good bridge of ice, paused again when we came to naked water, and waited in distress until a floating vast cake should bridge that place. It took us an hour to make the trip—a trip which we made in a misery of apprehension all the time. But at last we arrived within a very brief distance of the shore. We waited again. There was another place that needed bridging. All about us the ice was plunging and grinding along and piling itself up in mountains on the shore, and the dangers were increasing, not diminishing. We grew very impatient to get to solid ground, so we started too early and went springing from cake to cake. Tom made a miscalculation and fell short. He got a bitter bath, but he was so close to shore that he only had to swim a stroke or two—then his feet struck hard bottom and he crawled out. I arrived a little later, without accident.

We had been in a drenching perspiration and Tom's bath was a disaster for him. He took to his bed, sick, and had a procession of diseases. The closing one was scarlet fever, and he came out of it stone deaf. Within a year or two speech departed, of course. But some years later he was taught to talk, after a fashion— one couldn't always make out what it was he was trying to say. Of course he could not modulate his voice, since he couldn't hear himself talk. When he supposed he was talking low and confidentially, you could hear him in Illinois.

Four years ago (1902) I was invited by the University of Missouri to come out there and receive the honorary degree of LL.D. I took that opportunity to spend a week in Hannibal—a city now, a village in my day. It had been fifty-five years since Tom Nash and I had had that adventure. When I was at the railway station ready to leave Hannibal, there was a great crowd of citizens there. I saw Tom Nash approaching me across a vacant space, and I walked toward him, for I recognized him at once. He was old and white-headed, but the boy of fifteen was still visible in him. He came up to me, made a trumpet of his hands at my ear, nodded his head toward the citizens, and said, confidentially—in a yell like a fog horn—"Same damned fools, Sam."

—Mark Twain's Autobiography

∿

Twain visited Hannibal later in his life, when he was writing Life on the Mississippi:

The romance of boating is gone, now. In Hannibal the steamboatman is no longer a god. The youth don't talk river slang any more."

∿

Twain wrote in his notebook:

Alas! Everything was changed in Hannibal – but when I reached third or fourth streets the tears burst forth, for I recognized the mud. It, at least, was the same—the same old mud – the same mud that Annie McDonald got stuck in."

∿

He wrote in a letter to Jenny Boardman, in March 25, 1887:

[I returned] like some banished Adam who is revisiting his half-forgotten Paradise and wondering how the arid outside world could ever have seemed green and fair to him.

The Mark Twain House on Farmington Avenue in Hartford, Connecticut.

Hartford

To us our house was not unsentient matter—it had a heart & a soul & eyes to see us with, & approvals & solicitudes & deep sympathies; it was of us, & we were in its confidence, & lived in its grace & in the peace of its benediction. We never came home from an absence that its face did not light up & speak out its eloquent welcome—& we could not enter it unmoved.

—Letter to Joseph Twichell, quoted in *Mark Twain: A Biography*

∽

The house itself was considered by the Clemens's as one of their own. Before the family left for Europe in 1888, they made a sad walk around the house. As Clara recalled forty years later, "We had to leave so much treasured beauty behind. We had showered love on the home itself—the library; the conservatory sweet with the perfume of flowers; the bright bedrooms; and, outside, the trees, the tender eyebrights, the river reflecting clouds and sky." *Clara recalled snowstorms and crackling fires, Shakespeare's plays performed in the schoolroom, concerts on the baby upright piano, and popcorn and roasted chestnuts.* "We passed from room to room with leaden hearts, looked back and lingered—lingered. An inner voice whispered we should never return, and we never did."

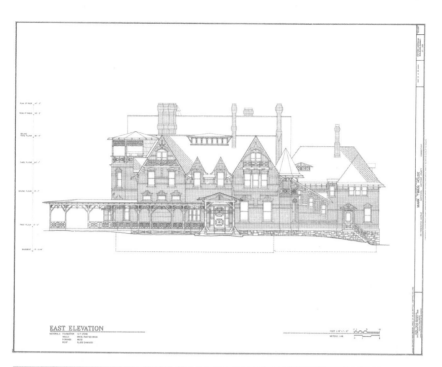

EAST ELEVATION

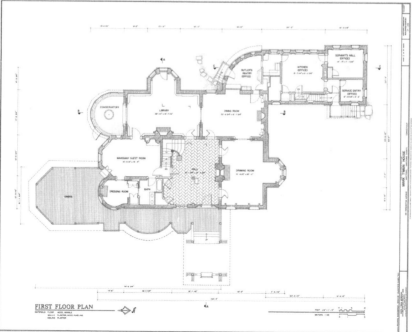

FIRST FLOOR PLAN

Architectural plans for the Hartford house.

Twain returned to the house in March of 1895 while quickly passing through Hartford. He wrote his wife Livy, "As soon as I entered the front door I was seized with a furious desire to have us all in this house again and right away, and never go outside the grounds any more forever....& right away, & never go outside the grounds any more forever..." *Twain wrote of the* "perfect taste of this ground floor, with its delicious dream of harmonious color, and its all-pervading spirit of peace and serenity and deep contentment...It is the loveliest home that ever was. It seemed as if I had burst awake out of a hellish dream, and had never been away, and that you would come drifting down out of those dainty upper regions with the little children tagging after you."

Burglars

On September 8, 1908, two burglars entered Twain's home in Redding, Connecticut while he was sleeping upstairs. The burglars took a sideboard into the garden, breaking it open to steal the silverware. They were eventually caught by the police. The next day, with the help of an aspiring young artist named Dorothy Sturgis, Twain produced the following note. From that day on, it was permanently attached to his front door.

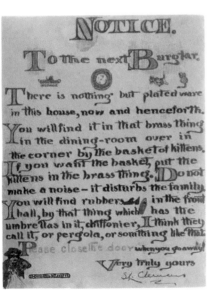

NOTICE.

To the next Burglar.

There is only plated ware in this house now and henceforth.

You will find it in that brass thing in the dining room over in the corner by the basket of kittens. If you want the basket, put the kittens in the brass thing.

Do not make a noise—it disturbs the family. You will find rubbers in the front hall by that thing which has the umbrellas in it, chiffonier, I think they call it, or pergola, or something like that. Please close the door when you go away !

Very truly yours,

S. L. Clemens.

Library

Along one side of the library, in the Hartford home, the bookshelves joined the mantelpiece—in fact, there were shelves on both sides of the mantelpiece. On these shelves, and on the mantelpiece, stood various ornaments. At one end of the procession was a framed oil-painting of a cat's head; at the other end was a head of a beautiful young girl, life size, called Emmeline, an impressionist water-color. Between the one picture and the other there were twelve or fifteen of the bric-à-brac things already mentioned, also an oil-painting by Elihu Vedder, "The Young Medusa." Every now and then the children required me to construct a romance—always impromptu—not a moment's preparation permitted—and into that romance I had to get all that bric-à-brac and the three pictures. I had to start always with the cat and finish with Ernmeline. I was never allowed the refreshment of a change, end for end. It was not permissible to introduce a bric-à-brac ornament into the story out of its place in the procession. These bric-à-bracs were never allowed a peaceful day, a reposeful day, a restful Sabbath. In their lives there was no Sabbath. In their lives there was no peace. They knew no existence but a monotonous career of violence and bloodshed. In the course of time the bric-à-brac and the pictures showed wear. It was because they had had so many and such violent adventures in their romantic careers.

—"Chapters from My Autobiography, " 1906–1907

Twain's library at his home on Hartford, Connecticut.

The Brave Sir Mark

A Yankee Writer at King Arthur's Court

This Louis Rhead illustration of Clemens appeared in *Life Magazine*, 1903.

Advice

On Admiration

It is human nature to take delight in exciting admiration. It is what prompts children to say "smart" things, and do absurd ones, and in other ways "show off" when company is present. It is what makes gossips turn out in rain and storm to be the first to tell a startling bit of news.

—The Innocents Abroad

On Affection

I have received since I have been here, in this one week, hundreds of letters from all conditions of people in England—men, women, and children—and there is in them compliment, praise, and, above all and better than all, there is in them a note of affection. Praise is well, compliment is well, but affection—that is the last and final and most precious reward that any man can win, whether by character or achievement, and I am very grateful to have that reward.

—Address at Pilgrim's Club Luncheon given in honor of Mr. Clemens at the Savoy Hotel, June 25, 1907

On Bravery

To believe yourself brave is to be brave; it is the one only essential thing.

—Personal Recollections of Joan of Arc, 1896

The Need for Swearing

May 5.

My Dear Bro—

It was my private secretary's carelessness—but I enclose them.

I have a very bad cold in the head, therefore cannot enter into particulars; the time is needed for swearing.

Yr Bro Sam.

May 5.

My Dear Bro —
It was my private
Secretary's carelessness —
but I enclose them.
I have a very bad
cold in the head, Therefore
cannot enter into partic-
ulars; the time is needed
for swearing.
Yr Bro
Sam.

Letter to Mark Twain's brother, Orion Clemens, 1877. (U Cal)

Be good + you will be lonesome.

Mark Twain

Morality

Be good + you will be lonesome.

—Mark Twain

There is a Moral Sense, and there is an Immoral Sense. The Moral Sense teaches us what morality is and how to avoid it; the Immoral Sense teaches us what immorality is and how to enjoy it.

Truly Yours

Mark Twain

Wien 5 October, 1897

A dedication to the magazine *Wiener Bilder*, 1897. The quote is also in *Following the Equator, Pudd'nhead Wilson's New Calendar*, 1894.

There is a moral sense and there is an immoral sense. The moral sense teaches us what morality is and how to avoid it; the immoral sense teaches us what immorality is and how to enjoy it.

Truly Yours

Mark Twain

Date 5 October Wein 1897

~

Always do right. This will gratify some people and astonish the rest.

Truly Yours

Mark Twain

New York, Feb. 16, 1901

— Note to the Young People's Society, Greenpoint Presbyterian Church, Brooklyn, 1901

Fault

Always acknowledge a fault. This will hrow those in authority off their guard & give you opportunity to commit more.

Yours Truly

Samuel L. Clemens

Mark Twain

July, '77

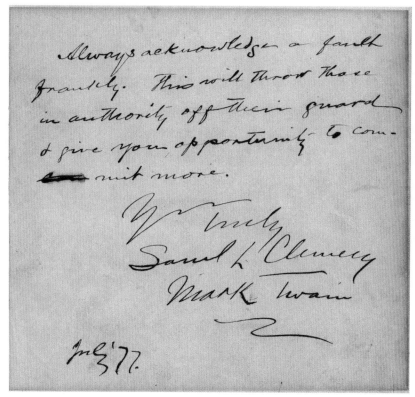

Note signed by Twain using both his names, 1877. The recipient is unknown.

Manners

22 October, 1877, Hartford, Conn.

Monday, P.M.

Dear Charley: My wife has plunged me into an abyss of genuine remorse, by saying, "What! didn't you go to the station with Mr. Stoddard?" I said, "You know I only go when there are ladies, or when the gentlemen do not know the way." "She said, "But this is such a dismal day. It is so forlorn to send anybody away alone." I realized it in an instant & I have felt like a brute ever since—but I do assure you my conduct was innocent & only heedless—but it was hellish, nevertheless. Now you promise me to come again & give me one more chance. Will you?

Yrs Ever

Mark.

We all thoroughly enjoyed your visit, my boy—all the tribe of us.

A note to Twain's friend, author and editor Charles Warren Stoddard.

Death

In time, the Deity perceived that death was a mistake; a mistake, in that it was insufficient; insufficient, for the reason that while it was an admirable agent for the inflicting of misery upon the survivor, it allowed the dead person himself to escape from all further persecution in the blessed refuge of the grave. This was not satisfactory. A way must be conceived to pursue the dead beyond the tomb.

—*Letters from the Earth*

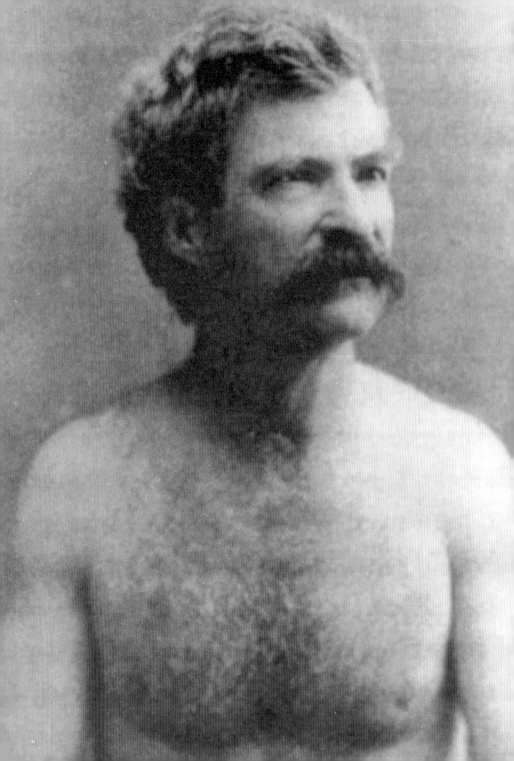

Sex

During your entire life you shall be under inflexible limits and restrictions, sexually…man is only briefly competent; and only then in the moderate measure applicable to the word in his sex's case. He is competent from the age of sixteen or seventeen thence-forward for thirty-five years. After fifty his performance is of poor quality, the intervals between are wide, and its satisfactions of no great value to either party…his candle is increasingly softened and weakened by the weather of age, as the years go by, until at last it can no longer stand, and is mournfully laid to rest in the hope of a blessed resurrection which is never to come.

—*Letters From the Earth*

Women

The Washington Star

January 13, 1868

Mark Twain's Eulogy of the Fair Sex.

The Washington Correspondents' Club held its anniversary on Saturday night. Mr. Clemens, better known as Mark Twain, responded to the toast "Woman, the pride of the professions and the jewel of ours." He said:

Mr. President: I do not know why I should have been singled out to receive the greatest distinction of the evening—for so the office of replying to the toast to woman has been regarded in every age. [Applause.] I do not know why I have received this distinction, unless it be that I am a trifle less homely than the other members of the Club. But, be this as I may, Mr. President, I am proud of the position, and you could not have chosen anyone who would have accepted it more gladly, or labored with a heartier good will to do the subject justice, than I. Because, sir, I love the sex. [Laughter.] I love all the women, sir, irrespective of age or color. [Laughter.]

Mark Twain in 1883. It's not clear why he is shirtless.

Twain's wife, Olivia Langdon Clemens, in 1869.

Human intelligence cannot estimate what we owe to woman, sir. She sews our buttons [laughter], she mends our clothes [laughter], she ropes us in at the church fairs—she confides in us; she tells us whatever she can find out about the little private affairs of the neighbors—she gives us good advice, and plenty of it—she gives us a piece of her mind, sometimes—and sometimes all of it—she soothes our aching brows—she bears our children. In all the relations of life, sir, it is but just, and a graceful tribute to woman to say of her that she is a brick. [Great laughter.]

Wheresoever you place woman, sir—in whatever position or estate—she is an ornament to that place she occupies, and a treasure to the world. [Here Mr. Twain paused, looked inquiringly at his hearers and remarked that the applause should come in at this point. It came in. Mr. Twain resumed his eulogy.] Look at the noble names of history! Look at Cleopatra! Look at Desdemona! Look at Florence Nightengale! look at Joan of Arc! Look at Lucretia Borgia! [Disapprobriation expressed. "Well," said Mr. Twain, scratching his head doubtfully, "suppose we let Lucretia slide."] Look at Joyce Heth! look at Mother Eve! I repeat, sir, look at the illustrious names of history! Look at the Widow Machree! Look at Lucy Stone! Look at Elizabeth Cady Stanton! Look at George

Francis Train! [Great laughter.] And, sir, I say with bowed head and deepest veneration, look at the mother of Washington! She raised a boy that could not lie—could not lie. [Applause.] But he never had any chance. It might have been different with him if he had belonged to a newspaper correspondent's club. [Laughter, groans, hisses, cries of "put him out." Mark looked around placidly upon his excited audience and resumed.]

I repeat, sir, that in whatever position you place a woman she is an ornament to society and a treasure to the world. As a sweetheart she has few equals and no superiors—[laughter;]—as a cousin she is convenient; as a wealthy grandmother with an incurable distemper, she is precious; as a wet nurse she has no equal among men! [Laughter.]

What, sir, would the people of this earth be, without woman? They would be scarce, sir. Then let us cherish her—let us protect her—let us give her our support, our encouragement, our sympathies—ourselves, if we get the chance. [Laughter.]

But, jesting aside, Mr. President, woman is lovable, gracious, kind of heart, beautiful—worthy of all respect, of all esteem, of all deference. Not any here will refuse to drink her health right cordially, for each and every one of us has personally known, and loved, and honored, the very best one of them all—his own mother! [Applause.]

Privacy

In this Autobiography I shall keep in mind the fact that I am speaking from the grave. I am literally speaking from the grave, because I shall be dead when the book issues from the press.

I speak from the grave rather than with my living tongue, for a good reason: I can speak thence freely. When a man is writing a book dealing with the privacies of his life—a book which is to be read while he is still alive—he shrinks from speaking his whole frank mind; all his attempts to do it fail, he recognizes that he is trying to do a thing which is wholly impossible to a human being. The frankest and freest and privatest product of the human mind and heart is a

Preface for all
editions of the book.| To precede the
Florentine dictation.   48
13

PREFACE.

As from the Grave.

I.

In this Autobiography I shall
keep in mind the fact that I am
speaking from the grave. I am
literally speaking from the grave, because
I shall be dead when the book issues
from the press.

I speak from the grave rather
than with my living tongue, for a
good reason: I can speak thence freely.
When a man is writing a book
dealing with the privacies of his life — a book
which is to be read while he is
still alive — he shrinks from speaking
his whole frank mind; all his attempts to
do it fail, he recognizes that he
is trying to do a thing which is wholly
impossible to a human being.
The frankest & freest & privatest product of the
human mind & heart is a love letter;

Handwritten preface for Twain's Autobiography.

love letter; the writer gets his limitless freedom of statement and expression from his sense that no stranger is going to see what he is writing. Sometimes there is a breach-of-promise case by and by; and when he sees his letter in print it makes him cruelly uncomfortable and he perceives that he never would have unbosomed himself to that large and honest degree if he had known that he was writing for the public. He cannot find anything in the letter that was not true, honest, and respect-worthy; but no matter, he would have been very much more reserved if he had known he was writing for print.

It has seemed to me that I could be as frank and free and unembarrassed as a love letter if I knew that what I was writing would be exposed to no eye until I was dead, and unaware, and indifferent.

Sleep

In this Harper's Magazine *article, biographer Albert Bigelow Paine recounts Twain's travels with American novelist George Washington Cable and a visit with cartoonist Thomas Nast, who created an illustration of the incident.*

On Thanksgiving Eve the readers were in Morristown, New Jersey, where they were entertained by Thomas Nast. The cartoonist prepared a quiet supper for them and they remained overnight in the Nast home. They were to leave next morning by an early train, and Mrs. Nast had agreed to see that they were up in due season. When she woke next morning there seemed a strange silence in the house and she grew suspicious. Going to the servants' room, she found them sleeping soundly. The alarm-clock in the back hall had stopped at about the hour the guests retired. The studio clock was also found stopped; in fact, every timepiece on the premises had retired from business. Clemens had found that the clocks interfered with his getting to sleep, and he had quieted them regardless of early trains and reading engagements. On being accused of duplicity he said:

"Well, those clocks were all overworked, anyway. They will feel much better for a night's rest."

THOMAS NAST'S CARTOON OF MARK TWAIN COLLECTING THE OFFENDING CLOCKS

Telephone

One of the very most useful of all inventions, but rendered almost worthless & a cold & deliberate theft & swindle by the black scoundrelism & selfishness of the companies of chartered robbers who conduct it.

—*Mark Twain's Notebooks & Journals*, volume 3, notebook 30, August 1890–June 1891

TWAIN AND THE TELEPHONE

He Hears the Telharmonium and Incidentally Tells a Story.

"The trouble with these beautiful, novel things is that they interfere so with one's arrangements. Every time I see or hear a new wonder like this I have to postpone my death right off. I couldn't possibly leave the world until I have heard this again and again."

Mark Twain said this as he lounged on the keyboard dais in the telharmonium music room in upper Broadway, swinging his legs, yesterday afternoon. The instrument has just played the "Lohengrin Wedding March" for him.

"You see, I read about this in the *New York Times* last Sunday, and I wanted to hear it. If a great Princess marries, what is to hinder all the lamps along the streets on her wedding night playing that march together? Or, if a great man should die—I, for example—they could all be tuned up for a dirge."

Twain's office and pool room in Hartford. He kept his telephone in this room.

"Of course, I know that it is intended to deliver music all over the town through the telephone, but that hardly appeals as much as it might to a man who for years, because of his addiction to strong language, has tried to conceal his telephone number, just like a chauffeur running away after an accident.

"When I lived up in Hartford, I was the very first man, in that part of New England at least, to put in a telephone—but it was constantly getting me into trouble because of the things I said carelessly. And the family were all so thoughtless. One day when I was in the garden, fifty feet from the house, somebody on the long distance wire who was publishing a story of mine, wanted to get the title.

"Well, the title was the first sentence, "Tell him to go to hell." Before my daughter got it through the wire and through him there was a perfect eruption of profanity in that region. All New England seemed to be listening in, and each time my daughter repeated it she did so with rising emphasis. It was awful. I broke into a cold perspiration, and while the neighborhood rang with it, rushed in and implored her to desist. But she would have the last word, and it was "hell," sure enough, every time.

"Soon after I moved to New York; perhaps that had something to do with my moving. When I got there and asked for a fire-proof telephone, the company sent up a man to me. I opened up all my troubles to him, but he laughed and said it was all right in New York. There was a clause in their contract, he said, allowing every subscriber to talk in his native tongue, and of course they would not make an exception against me. That clause has been a godsend to me."

It is my heart-warm and world-embracing Christmas hope and aspiration that all of us, the high, the low, the rich, the poor, the admired, the despised, the loved, the hated, the civilized, the savage (every man and brother of us all throughout the whole earth), may eventually be gathered together in a heaven of everlasting rest and peace and bliss, except the inventor of the telephone.

—A version of this quote was published in "Christmas Greetings,"
Boston Daily Globe, December 25, 1890

Letter from Mark Twain to Gardiner Hubbard, father-in-law of Alexander Graham Bell.

Hartford, Dec.27/90

Dear Sir:

I doubt if it can be arranged.

You see - 1. If it had not been for Professor Bell, there would not be any telephone; 2. & consequently no Hartford telephone; 3 - which makes him primarily & therefore personally responsible for the Hartford telephone. The Hartford telephone is the very worst on the very face of the whole earth. No man can dictate a 20-word message intelligible through it at any hour of the day without devoting a week's time to it, & there is no night-service whatsoever since electric-lighting was introduced. Though mind you they charge for night-service, in their cold calm way, just the same as if they furnished it. And if you try to curse through the telephone, they shut you off. It is this ostentatious holiness that grovels me. Every day I go there to practice & always get shut off. And so what it amounts to is that I don't get any practice that can really be considered practice. Well, as you see, yourself, the inventor is responsible for all this. For your sake I wish I could think of some way to save him, but there doesn't appear to be any. Now, then, reconcilement to his fate will be the next best thing. Let him come up & work the Hartford telephone till he pines for the solace & refuge of his long lost home.

Meantime, good wishes & a Merry Christmas to you, sir!

Mark Twain

Games

Billiards

The game of billiards has destroyed my naturally sweet disposition.

—Speech, April 24, 1906

~ಿ

I wonder why a man should prefer a good billiard-table to a poor one; and why he should prefer straight cues to crooked ones; and why he should prefer round balls to chipped ones; and why he should prefer a level table to one that slants; and why he should prefer responsive cushions to the dull and unresponsive kind. I wonder at these things, because when we examine the matter we find that the essentials involved in billiards are as competently and exhaustively furnished by a bad billiard outfit as they are by the best one. One of the essentials is amusement. Very well, if there is any more amusement to be gotten out of the one outfit than out of the other, the facts are in favor of the bad outfit. The bad outfit will always furnish thirty per cent. More fun for the players and for the spectators than will the good outfit. Another essential of the game is that the outfit shall give the players full opportunity to exercise their best skill, and display it in a way to compel the admiration of the spectators. Very well, the bad outfit is nothing behind the good one in this regard. It is a difficult matter to estimate correctly the eccentricities of chipped balls and a slanting table, and make the right allowance for them and secure a count; the finest kind of skill is required to accomplish the satisfactory result. Another essential of the game is that it shall add to the interest of the game by furnishing opportunities to bet. Very well, in this regard no good outfit can claim any advantage over a bad one. I know, by experience, that a bad outfit is as valuable as the best one; that an outfit that couldn't be sold at auction for seven dollars is just as valuable for all the essentials of the game as an outfit that is worth a thousand…Last winter, here in New York, I saw Hoppe and Schaefer and Sutton and the three or four other billiard champions of world-wide fame contend against each other, and certainly the art and science displayed were a wonder to see; yet I saw nothing there in the way of science and art that was more wonderful than shots which I had seen Texas Tom make on the wavy surface of that poor old wreck in the perishing saloon at Jackass Gulch forty years before.

—Mark Twain's Autobiography, Chapters from the
North American Review, November 1907

The billiard table is better than the doctors. It is driving out the heartburn in a most promising way. I have a billiardist on the premises, & I walk not less than ten miles every day with the cue in my hand. . . . The games begin right after luncheon, daily & continue until midnight, with 2 hours intermission for dinner & music. And so it is 9 hours' exercise per day, & 10 or 12 for Sunday.

—Letter to Emilie Rogers, wife of close friend Henry H. Rogers, November 1906. The Rogers gave Twain a billiard table as a gift and it was installed in his home of Fifth Avenue in New York City.

Mark Twain at a beloved billiard table, circa 1908.

Automobiles

I do not own a motor-car but I recommend them to all my friends and advise them to buy a car—so that they will come around and take me out in it. Somehow or other, riding over a rough road in a motor-wagon jolts certain parts of my torso that need to be jolted, but seldom ever do get jolted, same as when I run up stairs. It's splendid exercise and limbers up and promotes springiness—of the stair boards.

—quoted in "Mark Twain as a Motorist," *Motor*, May 1906

Everyday throughout America, the Overspeeder runs over somebody and "escapes." That is the way it reads. At present the 'mobile numbers are so small that ordinary eyes cannot read them, upon a swiftly receding machine, at a distance of a hundred feet—a distance which the machine has covered before the spectator can adjust his focus. I think I would amend the law. I would enlarge the numbers, and make them readable at a hundred yards. For overspeeding—first offence—I would enlarge the figures again, and make them readable at three hundred yards—this in place of a fine, and as a warning to pedestrians to climb a tree.

— "Overspeeding" *Harper's Weekly*, November 5, 1905

Mark Twain in the back seat in a 1906 Oldsmobile. The driver was reported to be noted race-car driver Ernest Keeler.

Mark Twain and guests at his 70th birthday celebration at Delmonicos, New York City.

Celebrations

Birthdays

The *New York Times*, December 6, 1905
CELEBRATE MARK TWAIN'S SEVENTIETH BIRTHDAY
Fellow-Workers in Fiction Dine with Him at Delmonico's.
HEAR WHY HE LIVED SO LONG
And How They, if They Resemble Him, May Reach Seventy, Too

Speech by Mark Twain:
"I remember that first birthday well," he began. "Whenever I think of it, it is with indignation. Everything was so crude, so unaesthetic. Nothing was really ready. I was born, you know, with a high and delicate aesthetic taste. And then think of—I had no hair, no teeth, no clothes. And I had to go to my first banquet like that.

The menu for Twain's 70th birthday celebration.

Menu

Oysters

Consomme Souveraine
Green Turtle

Timbales Perigerdine

Filets of Kingfish Meunière
Cucumbers
Persillade Potatoes

Saddle of Lamb Colbert
Stuffed Tomatoes

Baltimore Terrapin
Mushrooms on Toast with Cream
Sherbet with Kirsch

Quail
Red Head Duck
Fried Hominy and Currant Jelly

Salad : Celery Mayonnaise

Fancy Ice Cream
Assorted Cakes   Bonbons
Coffee

SHERRY
SAUTERNE
CHAMPAGNE
MINERAL WATERS
LIQUEURS

PRINTER

JOURNALIST

PILOT

TRAVELER

MINER

LECTURER

"BE GOOD AND
YOU WILL BE
LONESOME."

"And everybody came swarming in. It was the merest little hamlet in the back-woods of Missouri, where never anything happened at all. All interest centered on me that day. They came with that peculiar provincial curiosity to look me over and to see if I had brought anything fresh in my particular line. Why, I was the only thing that had happened in the last three months—and I came very near being the only thing that happened there in two whole years.

"They gave their opinions. No one had asked them, but they gave them, and they were all just green with prejudice. I stood it as long as—well, you know, I was born courteous. I stood it for about an hour. Then the worm turned. I was the worm. It was my turn to turn, and I did turn. I knew the strength of my position. I knew that I was the only spotlessly pure person in that camp, and I just came out and told them so.

"It was so true that they could make no answer at all. They merely blushed and went away. Well, that was my cradle song, and now I am singing my swan song. It is a far stretch from that first birthday to this, the seventieth. Just think of it!

Twain's Recipe for Long Life.

"The seventieth birthday! It is the time of life when you arrive at a new and awful dignity; when you may throw aside the decent reserves which have oppressed you for a generation, and stand unafraid and unabashed upon your seven-terraced summit and look down and teach—unrebuked. You can tell the world how you got there. It is what they all do. I have been anxious to explain my own system this long time, and now at last I have the right.

"I have achieved my seventy years in the usual way: by sticking strictly to a scheme of life which would kill anybody else. It sounds like an exaggeration, but that is really the common rule for attaining old age. When we examine the programme of any of these garrulous old people we always find that the habits which have preserved them would have decayed us. I will offer here, as a sound maxim this: that we can't reach old age by another man's road.

"I will now teach, offering my way of life to whomsoever desires to commit suicide by scheme which has enabled me to beat the doctor and the hangman for seventy years. Some of the details may sound untrue, but they are not. I am not here to deceive. I am here to teach.

He Goes to Bed Sometimes.

"We have no permanent habits until we are 40. Then they begin to harden, presently they petrify, then business begins. Since 40 I have been regular about going to bed and getting up—and that is one of the main things. I have made it a rule to go to bed when there wasn't anybody left to sit up with; and I have made it a rule to get up when I had to. This has resulted in an unswerving regularity of irregularity.

"In the matter of diet—which is another main thing—I have been persistently strict in sticking to the things which didn't agree with me until one or the other got the best of it myself. But last Spring I stopped frolicking with mince pie after midnight; up to then I had always believed it wasn't loaded. For thirty years I have taken coffee and bread at 8 in the morning, and no bite nor sup till 7:30 in the evening. Eleven hours. That is all right for me. Headachy people would not reach 70 comfortably by that road. And I wish to urge upon you this—which I think is wisdom—that if you find you can't make 70 by any but an uncomfortable road, don't you go. When they take off the Pullman and retire you to the rancid smoker, put on your things, count your checks, and get out at the first way station where there's a cemetery.

And Smokes in Bed.

"I have made it a rule never to smoke more than one cigar at a time. I have no other restriction as regards smoking. I do not know just when I began to smoke, I only know that it was in my father's lifetime, and that I was discreet. He passed from this life early in 1847, when I was a shade past 11; ever since then I have smoked publicly. As an example to others, and not that I care for moderation myself, it has always been my rule never to smoke when asleep and never to refrain when awake.

"I smoke in bed until I have to go to sleep; I wake up in the night, sometimes once, sometimes twice, sometimes three times, and I never waste any of these opportunities to smoke. This habit is so old and dear and precious to me that if I should break it I should feel as you, Sir, would feel if you should lose the only moral you've got. Meaning the Chairman. If you've got one; I am making no charge. I will grant, here, that I have stopped smoking, now and then, for a few months at a time, but it was not on principle—it was only to show off; it was to pulverize those critics who said I was a slave to my habits and couldn't break my bonds.

"Today it is all of sixty years since I began to smoke the limit. I have never bought cigars with life belts around them. I early found that those were too expensive for me. I have always bought cheap cigars—reasonably cheap, at any rate. Sixty years ago they cost me $4 a barrel, but my taste has improved lately, and I pay $7 now. Six or seven. Seven, I think. Yes; it's seven. But that includes the barrel. I often have smoking parties at my house, but the people that come have always just taken the pledge. I wonder why that is?

Raised on 9 Barrels of Cod Liver Oil.

"As for drinking, I have not rule about that. When the others drink I like to help; otherwise I remain dry, by habit and preference. This dryness does not hurt me, but it could easily hurt you, because you are different. You let it alone.

"Since I was 7 years old I have seldom taken a dose of medicine, and have still seldomer needed one. But up to 7 I have lived exclusively on allopathic medicines. Not that I needed them, for I don't think I did; it was for economy. My father took a drug store for a debt, and it made cod liver oil cheaper than other breakfast foods. We had nine barrels of it, and it lasted me seven years. Then

I was weaned. The rest of the family had to get along with rhubarb and ipecac and such things, because I was the pet. I was the first Standard Oil Trust. I had it all. By the time the drug store was exhausted my health was established, and there has never been much the matter with me since.

Never Exercised.

"I have never taken any exercise, except sleeping and resting, and I never intend to take any. Exercise is loathsome. And it cannot be any benefit when you are tired; I was always tired.

"I desire now to repeat and emphasize that maxim: We can't reach old age by another man's road. My habits protect my life, but they would assassinate you.

"I have lived a severely moral life. But it would be a mistake for other people to try that, or for me to recommend it. Very few would succeed: you have to have a perfectly colossal stock of morals; and you can't get them on a margin. Morals are an acquirement—like music, like a foreign language, like piety, poker, paralysis—no man is born with them. I wasn't myself. I started poor. I hadn't a single moral. There is hardly a man in this house that is poorer than I was then. Yes, I started like that—the world before me, not a moral in the slot. Not even an insurance moral.

His First Moral.

"I can remember the first one I ever got. I can remember the landscape, the weather, the—I can remember how everything looked. It was an old moral, an old second-hand moral, all out of repair, and didn't fit, anyway. But if you are careful with a thing like that, and keep it in a dry place, and save it for processions, and Chautauquas, and World's Fairs and so on, and disinfect it now and then, and give it a fresh coat of whitewash once in a while, you will be surprised to see how well she will last and how long she will keep sweet, or at least inoffensive. When I got that moldy old moral she had stopped growing, because she hadn't any exercise, but I worked her hard, I worked her Sundays and all. Under this cultivation she waxed in might and stature beyond belief, and served me well and was my pride and joy for sixty-three years; then she got to associating with insurance Presidents, and lost flesh and character, and was a sorrow to look at and no longer competent for business. She was a great loss to me.

"Yet not all loss. I sold her—ah, pathetic skeleton, as she was!—I sold her to Leopold, the pirate King of Belgium; he sold her to our Metropolitan Museum, and it was very glad to get her, for without a rag on, she stands fifty-seven feet long and sixteen feet high, and they think she's a brontosaur. Well, she looks it. They believe it will take nineteen geological periods to breed her match.

Joys of Being Moral.

"Morals are of inestimable value, for every man is born crammed with sin microbes, and the only thing that can extirpate these sin microbes is morals. Now you take a sterilized Christian—I mean, you take the sterilized Christian, for there's only one—Dear Sir, I wish you wouldn't look at me like that.

"Threescore years and ten!

"It is the Scriptural statute of limitations. After that you owe no active duties; for you the strenuous life is over. You are a time-expired man, to use Kipling's military phrase. You have served your term, well or less well, and you are mustered out.

"The Previous Engagement plea, which in forty years has cost you so many twinges, you can lay aside forever; on this side of the grave you will never need it again. If you shrink at thought of night, and winter, and the late home coming from the banquet and the lights and the laughter, through the deserted streets—a desolation which would not remind you now, as for a generation it did, that your friends are sleeping, and you must creep in a-tiptoe and not disturb them, but would only remind you that you need not tiptoe, you can never disturb them more—if you shrink at thought of these things, you need only reply:

"Your invitation honors me, and pleases me because you still keep me in your remembrance, but I am seventy; seventy, and would nestle in the chimney corner, and smoke my pipe, and read my book, and take my rest, wishing you well in all affection, and that when you in your turn shall arrive at pier No. 70 you may step aboard your waiting ship with a reconciled spirit, and lay your course toward the sinking sun with a contented heart."

New Year's

New Year's Day—Now is the accepted time to make your regular annual good resolutions. Next week you can begin paving hell with them as usual. Yesterday, everybody smoked his last cigar, took his last drink, and swore his last oath. Today, we are a pious and exemplary community. Thirty days from now, we shall have cast our reformation to the winds and gone to cutting our ancient shortcomings considerably shorter than ever. We shall also reflect pleasantly upon how we did the same old thing last year about this time. However, go in, community. New Year's is a harmless annual institution, of no particular use to anybody save as a scapegoat for promiscuous drunks, and friendly calls, and humbug resolutions, and we wish you to enjoy it with a looseness suited to the greatness of the occasion.

— Letter to Virginia City *Territorial Enterprise*, January 1863

~⁀

The *New York Times*, January 1, 1907

MARK TWAIN AND TWIN CHEER NEW YEAR'S PARTY

Humorist in a Siamese Twin Act at His House.

TWO JOINED BY A RIBBON

Twin Gets Drunk and the Joy of it Penetrates to Twain While Lecturing on Temperance.

The last thing Mark Twain did in 1906 was to get drunk and deliver a lecture on temperance, and the first thing he did in 1907 was to glory in the fact that he would be able to rejoice over other dead people when he died in having been the first man to have telharmonium music turned on in his house—"like gas."

Of course Mark Twain did not really get drunk any more than he delivered a real lecture on temperance. He imitated a drunken man and a temperance lecturer at one and the same time, and took all the glory for the lecture to himself while he blamed his Siamese brother for the jag.

Those who have never heard that Mr. Clemens has a Siamese brother, must be told that he only had such a relative for one night only, and the occasion was a party given to a few friends in honor of Miss Clemens, at the author's home,

21 Fifth Avenue, last night, or partially this morning, for all well-regulated cases of intoxication last more than fifteen minutes, even the imitations and the imitation given last night and given in such style that even the most ardent admirer had to admit that Mark was at least a close observer, resulted in what might be termed colloquilly [sic] a "hold over." During the hold over Mr. Clemens had something to say about politics.

The score or so of guests who had passed the evening playing charades and other games were surprised to see Mr. Clemens enter the drawing room on to the little stage at 11:30, dressed in the white suit he wore recently on Pennsylvania Avenue, Washington.

With him, in a similar white suit, came a young gentleman whom the author introduced to the company as his Siamese brother. The two had their arms about each other, and their suits were fastened together with a pink ribbon supposed to represent a ligature. Twain was rather short and broad and his hair was snow white. His brother was very tall and very slight and had black hair. It was easy to see that they were brothers. Mark remarked on the close resemblance almost as soon as he came into the room.

"We come from afar," said Mark. "We come from very far; very far, indeed—as far as New Jersey. We are the Siamese twins, but we have been in this country long enough to know something of your customs, and we have learned as much of your language as it is written and spoke as—well—as the newspapers."

"We are so much to each other, my brother and I, that what I eat nourishes him and what he drinks—ahem!—nourishes me. I often eat when I don't really want to because he is hungry, and, of course, I need hardly tell you that he often drinks when I am not thirsty.

"I am sorry to say that he is a confirmed consumer of liquor—liquor, that awful, awful curse—while I, from principle, and also from the fact that I don't like the taste, never touch a drop."

Mark then went on to say that he had been asked to take up the temperance cause and had done so with great success, taking his brother along as a horrible example.

"It has often been a source of considerable annoyance to me, when going about the country lecturing on temperance, to find myself at the head of a procession of white-ribbon people—so drunk I couldn't see," he said. "But I am thankful to say that my brother, has reformed."

At this point the Siamese brother surreptitiously took a drink out of a flask.

"He hasn't touched a drop in three years."

Another drink.

"He never will touch a drop."

"Thank God for that."

Several drinks.

"And if, by exhibiting my brother to you, I can save any of you people here from the horrible curse of the demon rum!" Mark fairly howled, "I shall be satisfied."

Just then apparently some of the rum or the influence of it, got through the pink ribbon. Mark hiccoughed several times.

"Zish is wonderful reform—"

Another drink.

"Wonder'l 'form we are 'gaged in."

"Glorious work—we doin' glorious work—glori-o-u-s work. Best work ever done, my brother and work of reform, reform work, glorious work. I don' feel jus' right."

The company by this time was hysterical was [sic] laughter. Mark was staggering about on the improvised stage, apparently horribly under the influence. His brother still held the bottle and was still putting it to the use for which it was made.

The laughter became so great that it was impossible for the old man to carry on the little farce any longer, and in a few minutes the Telharmonium music, played a mile and a half away up on Broadway, was turned on and it was playing "Auld Lang Syne" when the New Year was ushered in.

Religion

Illustration by Frank Carter Beard from the
American Publisher, July 1872.

Adam, the first man in the bible, in the book of Genesis, was one of Twain's favorite targets. In 1867, Twain wrote in his notebook:

It all began with Adam. He was the first man to tell a joke—or a lie. How lucky Adam was. He knew when he said a good thing, nobody had said it before. Adam was not alone in the Garden of Eden, however, and does not deserve all the credit; much is due to Eve, the first woman, and Satan, the first consultant." He later wrote again on Adam, making the point, "It was not that Adam ate the apple for the apple's sake, but because it was forbidden. It would have been better for us—oh infinitely better for us—if the serpent had been forbidden.

But Twain's penultimate nudge against man's forebearer was published in the New York Times*, on November 10, 1901, when he said in a speech:*

Adam and Noah were ancestors of mine. I never thought much of them. Adam lacked character. He couldn't be trusted with apples. Noah had an absurd idea that he could navigate without any knowledge of navigation, and he ran into the only shoal place on earth.

~୨

Adam is fading out. It is on account of Darwin and that crowd. I can see that he is not going to last much longer. There's a plenty of signs. He is getting belittled to a germ—a little bit of a speck that you can't see without a micro-scope powerful enough to raise a gnat to the size of a church. They take that speck and breed from it: first a flea; then a fly, then a bug, then cross these and get a fish, then a raft of fishes, all kinds, then cross the whole lot and get a reptile, then work up the reptiles till you've got a supply of lizards and spiders and toads and alligators and Congressmen and so on, then cross the entire lot again and get a plant of amphibiums, which are half-breeds and do business both wet and dry, such as turtles and frogs and ornithorhyncuses and so on, and cross-up again and get a mongrel bird, sired by a snake and dam'd by a bat, resulting in a pterodactyl, then they develop him, and water his stock till they've got the air filled with a million things that wear feathers, then they cross-up all the accumulated animal life to date and fetch out a mammal, and start-in diluting again till there's cows and tigers and rats and elephants and monkeys and everything you want down to the Missing Link, and out of him and a mermaid they propagate Man, and there you are! Everything ship-shape and finished-up, and nothing to do but lay low and wait and see if it was worth the time and expense.

— *"The Refuge of the Derelicts" published in* Fables of Man

~୨

San Francisco Call, April 29, 1901

MEETS INSULT WITH A JEST

Mark Twain Replies to Taunt That He Is Low Born.

Special Dispatch to the Call.

NEW YORK. April 28. —Mark Twain was a guest of the Brooklyn Clerical Union last night. It was "ladies' night," and President Rev. Dr. J. F. Carson welcomed the ladies with a eulogy of wives.

"All our best and noblest impulses and inspirations come from them," said he.

When Mark Twain's time came he said: "At just this time I am remarkably comforted by an invitation to meet a body of clergymen like this. Is it only in Brooklyn that I am appreciated. But what's the use of lugging that in about our wives? Don't you think that's extravagant?

"Mrs. Clemens was too tired to come, and I'm glad she was. I don't want her to hear things like that. Why don't you people, so far as your calling will allow, try to tell the truth? To be sure, you sometimes get out of practice, but one saying one thing and one another you produce confusion in the minds of people about religious matters.

"Rev. Dr. ___, oh, I won't mention his name, has just called me low born and ill bred. I don't mind that so much. Shakespeare was low born, too; and there was Adam—I believe he was born out in the woods. But I'm glad the doctor didn't say it about Adam. When such a thing is said about the head of the family it hurts. Anyhow, I think I would prefer to be low born—in a republic—like the rest. If I had been born on the other side, why, then I would have liked to be born a Duke, as I suppose Rev. Dr. ___ I won't mention his name—would have been, if he had been born there."

It was Rev. Dr. Wayland Spauldine, president of the Congregational Clerical Union, who, on Monday last, called Mark Twain low born and ill bred.

Clemens' parents family record from their Bible.

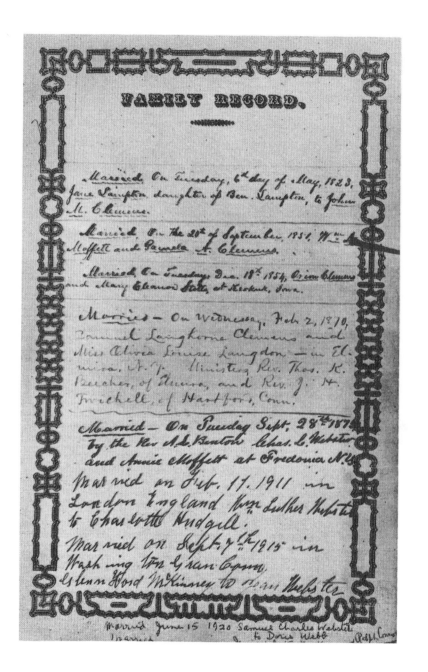

FAMILY RECORD.

Married, On Tuesday, 6th day of May, 1823, Jane Lampton, daughter of Ben. Lampton, to John M. Clemens.

Married, On the 20th of September, 1851, Wm. A. Moffett and Pamela A. Clemens.

Married, On Tuesday, Dec. 18th 1854, Orion Clemens and Mary Eleanor Stotts, at Keokuk, Iowa.

Married — On Wednesday, Feb 2, 1870, Samuel Langhorne Clemens and Miss Olivia Louise Langdon — in Elmira, N. Y. Ministers Rev. Thos. K. Beecher, of Elmira, and Rev. J. H. Twichell, of Hartford, Conn.

Married — On Tuesday Sept. 28th 187_ by the Rev A.S. Benton Chas. L. Webster and Annie Moffett at Fredonia N.Y.

Married on Feb. 17. 1911 in London England Wm. Luther Webster to Charlotte Hudgill.

Married on Sept. 7th 1915 in Washington Green Co. Glenn Ford McKinney to Jean Webster.

Married June 15 1920 Samuel Charles Webster
Married to Doris Webb   Ralph Conn.

Bible

It is full of interest. It has noble poetry in it; and some clever fables; and some blood-drenched history; and some good morals; and a wealth of obscenity; and upwards of a thousand lies.

—Mark Twain's *Letters from the Earth*, 1962

The two Testaments are interesting, each in its own way. The Old one gives us a picture of these people's Deity as he was before he got religion, the other one gives us a picture of him as he appeared afterward.

—Mark Twain's *Letters from the Earth*, 1962

The Christian's Bible is a drug store. Its contents remain the same; but the medical practice changes...The world has corrected the Bible. The church never corrects it; and also never fails to drop in at the tail of the procession—and take the credit of the correction. During many ages there were witches. The Bible said so. the Bible commanded that they should not be allowed to live. Therefore the Church, after eight hundred years, gathered up its halters, thumbscrews, and firebrands, and set about its holy work in earnest. She worked hard at it night and day during nine centuries and imprisoned, tortured, hanged, and burned whole hordes and armies of witches, and washed the Christian world clean with their foul blood.

Then it was discovered that there was no such thing as witches, and never had been. One does not know whether to laugh or to cry....There are no witches. The witch text remains; only the practice has changed. Hell fire is gone, but the text remains. Infant damnation is gone, but the text remains. More than two hundred death penalties are gone from the law books, but the texts that authorized them remain.

—"Bible Teaching and Religious Practice," *Europe and Elsewhere*, 1923

On Christianity

If Christ were here there is one thing he would not be--a Christian.

—Mark Twain's *Notebook*

~⁀

Christianity will doubtless still survive in the earth ten centuries hence--stuffed and in a museum.

—*Notebook*, 1898

~⁀

The so-called Christian nations are the most enlightened and progressive... but in spite of their religion, not because of it. The Church has opposed every innovation and discovery from the day of Galileo down to our own time, when the use of anesthetic in childbirth was regarded as a sin because it avoided the biblical curse pronounced against Eve. And every step in astronomy and geology ever taken has been opposed by bigotry and superstition. The Greeks surpassed us in artistic culture and in architecture five hundred years before Christian religion was born.

—Mark Twain, a Biography

~⁀

You can never find a Christian who has acquired this valuable knowledge, this saving knowledge, by any process but the everlasting and all-sufficient "people say." In all my seventy-two years and a half I have never come across such another ass as this human race is.

—Mark Twain's Autobiography

Missionaries

Mark Twain had little to no use for missionaries, even in his earliest days, dating back to his trips to the Sandwich Islands (now Hawaii), he lampooned the missionary work going on there. In his later years he became a staunch and vocal leader in the anti-imperialist movement in America. He strongly disapproved of American involvement in China and the Philippines.

During the Boxer Rebellion in China in 1900 Christians and foreigners were attacked. Many missionaries and their children, as well as native Chinese who had converted, were killed and much property was destroyed. Many missionaries refused any sort of payment for those loses, "in order to demonstrate the meekness of Christ to the Chinese," while the allied nations insisted on compensation from the Chinese government. In 1901 the missionary Rev. Dr. William Scott Ament, who had served in China since 1877, became embroiled in a controversy in the months and years following. He and others demanded reparations, but many thought it unseemly, including Twain.

Twain ridiculed Ament's work and his motives. Ament sought extremely high compensation, far beyond what many thought acceptable. The Chinese custom was to payback the lost sum with 33% interest to make up for such losses. Ament and his group demanded 13 times what he lost. Twain charged Ament with "extortion." The two became embroiled in a war of words in the press, with a great many journalists, politicians, and clergy joining the fray.

Many in the clergy demanded Twain make a public apology. Instead, Twain penned "To My Missionary Critics," which offered no apologies, although it ended by acknowledging that missionaries no doubt meant well. The essay, originally entitled "The Case of Rev. Dr. Ament, Missionary," was published in the North American Review *in April 1901.*

Twain wrote, "To Dr. Smith the 'thirteen-fold-extra' clearly stood for 'theft and extortion,' and he was right, distinctly right, indisputably right. He manifestly thinks that when it got scaled away down to a mere 'one-third' a little thing like that was some other than 'theft and extortion.' Why, only the board knows! I will try to explain this difficult problem so that the board can get an idea of it. If a pauper owes me a dollar and I catch him unprotected and make him pay me fourteen dollars, thirteen of it is "theft and extortion." If I make him pay only one dollar thirty-three and a third cents the thirty-three and a third cents are 'theft and extortion,' just the same."

Twain's article was submitted typewritten, which was rare for the author.

The Case of Rev. Dr. Ament, Missionary.

By Mark Twain.

I have received many newspaper cuttings; also letters from several clergymen; also a note from Rev. Judson Smith, secretary of the American Board of Foreign Missions---all of a like tenor; all saying substantially what is said in the cutting here copied:

"An Apology Due From Mr. Clemens.

"The evidence of the past day or two should induce Mark Twain to make for the amen corner, and formulate a prompt apology for his scathing attack on the Rev. Dr. Ament, the veteran Chinese missionary. The assault was based on a Pekin despatch to the New York Sun, which said that Dr. Ament had collected from the Chinese in various places damages thirteen times in excess of actual losses. So Mark Twain charged Mr. Ament with bullyragging, extortion and things. A Pekin despatch to the Sun yesterday, however, explains that the amount collected was not thirteen times the damage sustained but one-third in excess of the indemnities, and that the blunder was due to a cable error in transmission. The 1-3 got converted into 13. Yesterday, the Rev. Judson Smith, secretary of the American board, received a despatch from Dr. Ament, calling atten-

"To succeed in business, avoid my example."
—Mark Twain, *the New York Times*, 1901

"October: This is one of the peculiarly dangerous months to speculate in stocks in. The others are July, January, September, April, November, May, March, June, December, August, and February."
—*Pudd'nhead Wilson*, 1894

3. Business and Politics

THE PIRATE PUBLISHER.—AN INTERNATIONAL BURLESQUE THAT HAS HAD THE LONGEST RUN ON RECORD.

This Illustration shows a man, identified as the "Pirate Publisher," standing at the center with one foot on a large book labeled "Law." He is surrounded by authors from around the world, including Mark Twain on his left. They are accusing the Pirate Publisher of illegally publishing their work without compensating them, while the man maintains that he has a legal right to publish their books.

The Business
of Being Mark Twain

Copyright

Mark Twain spent much of his life fighting for copyright and other licensing infringements of which he was a common victim. Many products bore his name and/or likeness without him ever receiving a penny. Charles Dickens, too, fought many of these same battles a generation before.

The *New York Times*, June 12, 1873

Mark Twain's Suit—He Obtains a Permanent Injunction

In the case of Samuel L. Clemens, known as Mark Twain, against Benjamin J. Such, to restrain by injunction the publication of a book containing some of the former's sketches, and purporting to have been revised by him, the facts of which appeared in yesterday's *Times*, Chief Justice Ingraham has ordered a permanent injunction to issue against the defendant. In a brief memorandum indorsed on the papers in the case, the Chief Justice says: "The sketches were the property of plaintiff and he is entitled to an order restraining their publication without his consent. The agreement only contemplated the use of one sketch, and there was no authority to publish that one as revised by the author."

Twain, circa 1907.

COPYRIGHTED BY
A.F. BRADLEY.
NEW YORK. 1907.

The New York Times, *December 8, 1906*

MARK TWAIN IN WHITE AMUSES CONGRESSMEN

Advocates New Copyright Law and Dress Reform.

WEARS LIGHT FLANNEL SUIT

Says at 71 Dark Colors Depress Him—Talks Seriously of Author's Right to Profit

Special to the *New York Times.*

WASHINGTON, Dec. 7.—Mark Twain spent a busy afternoon at the Capitol today, and for half an hour entertained the newspaper correspondents with a characteristic talk. Despite the blustering wind which swept down Pennsylvania Avenue, the author wore a suit of white flannels. In the members' gallery, which he first visited to watch the proceedings of the House, he attracted general attention.

Later Mr. Clemens visited the Speaker's room, and while awaiting the arrival of "Uncle Joe," entertained a dozen Congressmen, including Governors, Payne, Daizell, and Foster, who hastened to pay him their respects. With the Speaker Mr. Clemens discussed briefly the pending Copyright bill. With William Dean Howells and a party of other authors and publishers, Mr. Clemens came here to be present at the hearings on this bill, which are now being conducted in the Senate reading room at the Congressional Library by the Committee on Patents of the Senate and the House.

With Mr. Howells, Edward Everett Hale, Thomas Nelson Page, and a number of other authors, he appeared before the committee this afternoon. The new Copyright bill extends the authors' copyright after the term of his life and for fifty years thereafter. It is also for the benefit of artists, musicians, and others, but the authors did most of the talking. F. D. Millet made a speech for the artists, and John Philip Sousa for the musicians.

Committee Enjoys Twain's Speech.

Mr. Clemens was the last speaker of the day, and its chief feature. He made a speech the serious parts of which created a strong impression, and the humorous parts set the Senators and Representatives in roars of laughter.

"I have read this bill," he began. "At least I have read such portions as I could understand. Nobody but a practiced legislator can read the bill and thoroughly understand it, and I am not a practiced legislator.

"I am interested particularly and especially in the part of the bill which concerns my trade. I like that extension of copyright life to the author's life and fifty years afterward. I think that would satisfy any reasonable author, because it would take care of his children. Let the grandchildren take care of themselves. That would take care of my daughters, and after that I am not particular. I shall then have long been out of this struggle, independent of it, indifferent to it.

"It isn't objectionable to me that all the trades and professions in the United States are protected by the bill. I like that. They are all important and worthy, and if we can take care of them under the copyright law I should like to see it done. I should like to see oyster culture added, and anything else.

"I am aware that copyright must have a limit, because that is required by the Constitution of the United States, which sets aside the earlier Constitution, which we call the decalogue. The decalogue says you shall not take away from any man his profit. I don't like," he explained, "to use the harsh term. What the decalogue really says is, 'Thou shalt not steal,' but I am trying to use more polite language.

"The laws of England and America do take it way, do select but one class, the people who create the literature of the land. They always talk handsomely about the literature of the land, always what a fine, great, monumental thing a great literature is, and in the midst of their enthusiasm they turnaround and do what then can to discourage it.

"I know we must have a limit, but forty-two years is too much of a limit. I am quite unable to guess why there should be a limit at all to the possession of the product of a man's labor. There is no limit to real estate.

"Dr. Hale has suggested that a man might just as well, after discovering a coal mine and working it forty-two years, have the Government step in and take it away."

Says Publishers Never Die.

"What is the excuse? It is that the author who produced that book has had the profit of it long enough, and therefore the Government takes a profit which does not belong to it and generously gives it to the 88,000,000 people. But it doesn't do anything of the kind. It merely takes the author's property, takes his children's bread and gives the publisher double profit. He goes on publishing the book and as many of his confederates as choose to go into the conspiracy do so, and they rear families in affluence.

"And they continue the enjoyment of those ill-gotten gains generation after generation forever, for they never die. In a few weeks or months or years I shall be out of it, I hope under a monument. I hope I shall not be entirely forgotten, and shall subscribe to the monument myself. But I shall not be caring what along; I know a lot of trades. But that goes to my daughters, who can't get along as well as I can because I have carefully raised them as young ladies, who don't know anything and can't do anything. I hope Congress will extend to them the charity which they have failed to get from me."

No Limit on Families.

"Why, if a man who is not even mad, but only strenuous—strenuous about race suicide—should come to me and try to get me to use my large political and ecclesiastical influence to get a bill passed by this Congress limiting families to twenty-two children by one mother, I should try to calm him down. I should reason with him. I should say to him, 'Leave it alone. Leave it alone and it will take care of itself. Only one couple a year in the United States can reach that limit. If they have reached that limit let them go right on. Let them have all the liberty they want. In restricting that family to twenty-two children you are merely conferring discomfort and unhappiness on one family per year in a nation of 88,000,000, which not worth while.'

"It is the very same with copyright. One author per year produces a book which can outlive the forty-two year limit; that's all. This Nation can't produce two authors a year that can do it; the thing is demonstrably impossible. All that the limited copyright can do is to take the bread out of the mouths of the children of that one author per year."

The Books That Live.

"I made an estimate some years ago, when I appeared before a committee for the House of Lords, that we had published in this country since the Declaration of Independence 220,00 [sic] books. They have all gone. They had all perished before they were ten years old. It is only one book in 1,000 that can outlive the forty-two year limit. Therefore why put a limit at all? You might as well limit the family to twenty-two children.

"If you recall the Americans in the nineteenth century who wrote books that lived forty-two years you will have to begin with Cooper; you can follow with Washington Irving, Harriet Beecher Stowe, Edgar Allan Poe, and there you have to wait a long time. You come to Emerson, and you have to stand still and look further. You find Howells and T. B. Aldrich, and then your numbers begin to run pretty thin, and you question if you can name twenty persons in the United States who in a whole century have written books that would live forty-two years. Why, you could take them all and put them on one bench there [pointing]. Add the wives and children and you could put the result in two or three more benches.

"One hundred persons—that is the little insignificant crowd whose bread and butter is to be taken away for what purpose, for what profit to anybody? You turn these few books into the hands of the pirate and of the legitimate publisher, too, and they get the profit that should have gone to the wife and children.

Property in Ideas.

"When I appeared before that committee of the House of Lords the Chairman asked me what limit I would propose. I said 'Perpetuity.' I could see some resentment in his manner, and he said the idea was illogical, for the reason that it has long ago been decided that there can be no such thing as property in ideas. I said there was property in ideas before Queen Anne's time; they had perpetual copyright. He said, 'What is a book? A book is just built from base to roof on ideas, and there can be no property in it.'

"I said I wished he could mention any kind of property on this planet that had a pecuniary value which was not derived from an idea or ideas. He said real estate. I put a suppositious case, a dozen Englishmen who travel through South African and camp out, and eleven of them see nothing at all; they are mentally blind. But there is one in the party who knows what this harbor means and what the lay of the land means. To him it means that some day a railway will go through here, and there on that harbor a great city will spring up. That is his idea. And he has another, which to go and trade his last bottle of Scotch whisky and his last horse blanket to the principal chief of that region and buy a piece of land the size of Pennsylvania. [Laughter.] That was the value of an idea that the day would come when the Cape to Cairo Railway would be built.

"Every improvement that is put upon the real estate is the result of an idea in somebody's head. The skyscraper is another idea; the railroad is another; the telephone and all those things are merely symbols which represent ideas. An andiron, a washtub, is the result of an idea that did not exist before.

"So if, as that gentleman said, a book does consist solely of ideas, that is the best argument in the world that it is property, and should not be under any limitation at all. We don't ask for that. Fifty years from now we shall ask for it."

And Then He Tells a Story.

"I hope the bill will pass without any deleterious amendments. I do seem to be extraordinarily interested in a whole lot of arts and things that I have got nothing to do with. It is a part of my generous, liberal nature; I can't help it. I feel the same sort of charity to everybody that was manifested by a gentleman who arrived at home at 2 o'clock in the morning from the club and was feeling so perfectly satisfied with life, so happy, and so comfortable, and there was his house weaving, weaving, weaving around. He watched his chance, and by and by when the steps got in his neighborhood he made a jump an climbed up and got on the portico.

"And the house went on weaving and weaving, but he watched the door, and when it came around his way he plunged through it. He got to the stairs, and when he went up on all fours the house was so unsteady that he could hardly make his way, but a last he got to the top and raised his foot and put it on the top step. But only the toe hitched on the step, and he rolled down and fetched up on the bottom step, with his arm around the newel post, and he said: 'God pity the poor sailors out at sea on a night like this.' "

∽

Thomas Nast Lampoon's Twain's Search for Justice in Canada

In the January 21, 1881 Mark Twain was lampooned by cartoonist Nast for Twain's complaints about the odd copyright laws in Canada. According to Harper's, "where [Twain] went in search of copyright on his new book, had created considerable amusement in the newspapers. Mr. NAST's cartoon is founded on the odd clause in the Canadian Copyright Act which provides that authors shall register their works in the office of the Minister of Agriculture."

Innocence Abroad (In Search of a Copyright), Thomas Nast's illustration in
Harper's Weekly, January 21, 1882

Elmira, July 22/76.

Friend Bliss:

Of course I can neither confess nor deny your underlings' New York gossip without knowing what it is. But come — we are all a good deal alike, I judge. I listen to a director of the company + others, + under irritated impulse, talk + act unwisely, + get sorry at leisure. You tell hard things about me to entertain a group (the worst of it being that they are mainly true, although not pleasant things to remember,) + for a day I am angry

Book Selling

Twain wrote the following letter to his publisher at the American Publishing Company regarding a dispute they were having over the publication of The Adventures of Tom Sawyer. *The first edition of the book did not appear in the United States until a year after the final version had been sent to the type-setters. Twain believed the delay had cost him $10,000.*

PRIVATE

Elmira, July 22/76.

Friend Bliss:

Of course I can neither confess nor deny your underlings' New York gossip without knowing what it is. But come—we are all a good deal alike, I judge. I listen to a director of the company & others, & under irritated impulse, talk & act unwisely, & get sorry at leisure. You tell hard things about me to entertain a group (the worst of it being that they are mainly true, although not pleasant things to remember,) & for a day I am angry & ready to do or say anything that comes handy; by that time I begin to imagine that I am fooling away time & tongue on a matter that is not very prodigious—& ~~I am~~ so there an end for the time being. As regards Williams, we will dismiss that with the single & simple remark that what I said to him occupied but short space & will bear repeating in any presence, since it was to no one's prejudice. But come—~~if I have said as injurious things about~~ a truce to this—if it is good matter to talk about together, but not to write about.

You write as if you supposed I was mightily concerned about the company & its ~~management~~ expenses. I was am concerned just this far, exactly: The business seems to be a great big unpaying thing, whereas the reverse would be the case if it were shrunk up, perhaps. I don't know it, I simply suggest it. And with the suggestion I stop. ~~I have~~ My duty as a director & stockholder ends there. I shall not lose any sleep about it one way or the other.

But there is a matter in which I am strongly interested. You told me, several times that a subscription house could not run two books at once & do justice

Mark Twain's letter to publisher Elisha Bliss, Jr. at the American Publishing Company in 1876.

to either of them. I saw no reason to disbelieve that, & I never have disbelieved it. Therefore I am solicitous about *Tom Sawyer*—more so than I would be about another book, because this is an experiment. I want it run by itself, if possible, & pushed like everything. Can this be done?—& when? Give me your ideas about it. What do you think of canvassing in September & October & issuing 1st Nov.? Shall you be canvassing any new book then?

You must not think that I never wanted to attend a director's meeting. It is a mistake. My notices always arrived too late. This is why I wrote twice requesting that my notice be mailed a day earlier.

I wouldn't have aggravated you if I had known you were going to be sick—I don't pick out such times purposely, but only by accident.

I think that if you offer a prize of $1000 (I to pay the money myself but not be known in it) for the canvasser who shall sell the largest number of *Tom Sawyers* in six months (putting it in the circulars but not in the newspapers,) it might have a good effect. Or make two $500-prizes of it—one for east of the east line of Ohio & the other for west of that line. What do you think of it?

I shall start the proofs back with this mail.

~~If~~ Confidentially, I shall have a business proposition to make to you individually in the fall when I return. ~~, if Tom Sawyer sells as well as I think it is going to.~~ I foresee advantage in it, & I think you will, also. I came near making it once before, but was restrained by a feeling which has well nigh ceased to exist, now, & seems likely to cease altogether & speedily. I think I was ~~a fool that~~ unwise that I did not make it when I first thought of it. If I chance to have occasion to run to Hartford in the meantime, I can get my data together & make the proposition then. I have figured upon it for hours, to-day, & if I had had any wit I would have done the same thing long ago. ~~I shall be ready to talk with you about it at any time that we can get together.~~

Meantime I hope you will say nothing about the matter to anybody—& I shall not. I mark my letter "Private" for this reason.

Ys Truly

Samuel. L. Clemens

Those chapters are a nice clean proof—please do it again.

All publishers are Columbuses. The successful author is their America. The reflection that they—like Columbus—didn't discover what they expected to discover, and didn't discover what they started out to discover, doesn't trouble them. All they remember is that they discovered America; they forget that they started out to discover some patch or corner of India.

—Mark Twain's Autobiography

Original salesman's dummy and presentation kit for *The Innocent's Abroad*, 1867.

Mark Twain's The Innocents Abroad *was not sold in bookstores but by a sales force of agents who went door-to-door. The above case was custom made by an agent, who carried the sample pages with him as he went. The agents sold to farmers, to outliers, and in towns where there were no book stores.*

According to Cornell University, "In November of 1867, publisher Elisha Bliss contacted Samuel Clemens about writing a book based on his travel correspondence from his 163-day tour of Europe and the Holy Land. That book, *The Innocents Abroad,* or *The New Pilgrim's Progress,* would be both a critical and a popular success, selling over 70,000 copies in its first year of publication. It would also be Mark Twain's best-selling work during his lifetime."

The book was "Issued by subscription only, and not for sale in the book-stores." *All of Mark Twain's major nineteenth-century titles were sold by salesmen door-to-door rather than as trade publications in bookstores.*

The subscription publication industry blossomed in post-Civil War America. Tens of thousands of sales agents, many of them veterans and war widows, canvassed small towns and rural areas armed with a sales prospectus and a "book" containing sample pages and illustrations, and offered multiple binding options to fit every décor and price range. Prospective buyers selected a binding and signed an agreement to pay for the book when it was delivered to their door.

In this way Samuel Clemens sold more Mark Twain books and attained a broader audience than he would have with regular trade publications, but he had to contend with the lower status that subscription authors were accorded. Disguised as popular entertainment, his books were bought by the masses "who never knew what good literature they were."

These notions were born to me in the fall of 1867, in Washington. That is to say, thirty-nine years ago. I had come back from the Quaker City excursion. I had gone to Washington to write *The Innocents Abroad*, but before beginning that book it was necessary to earn some money to live on meantime, or borrow it—which would be difficult, or to take it where it reposed unwatched—which would be unlikely. So I started the first Newspaper Correspondence Syndicate that an unhappy world ever saw. I started it in conjunction with William Swinton, a brother of the admirable John Swinton. William Swinton was a brilliant creature, highly educated, accomplished. He was such a contrast to me that I did not know which of us most to admire, because both ends of a contrast are equally delightful to me. A thoroughly beautiful woman and a thoroughly homely woman are creations which I love to gaze upon, and which I cannot tire of gazing upon, for each is perfect in her own line, and it is perfection, I think, in many things, and perhaps most things, which is the quality that fascinates us. A splendid literature charms us; but it doesn't charm me any more than its opposite does—"hog-wash" literature. At another time I will explain that word, "hog-wash" and offer an example of it which lies here on the bed--a book which was lately sent to me from England, or Ireland.

An advertisement recruiting salespeople for *The Innocents Abroad*.

Swinton kept a jug. It was sometimes full, but seldom as full as himself—and it was when he was fullest that he was most competent with his pen. We wrote a letter apiece once a week and copied them and sent them to twelve newspapers, charging each of the newspapers a dollar apiece. And although we didn't get rich, it kept the jug going and partly fed the two of us. We earned the rest of our living with magazine articles. My trade in that line was better than his, because I had written six letters for the *New York Tribune* while I was out on the Quaker City excursion, fifty-three for the *Alta Californian*, and one pretty breezy one for the *New York Herald* after I got back, and so I had a good deal of a reputation to trade on. Every now and then I was able to get twenty-five dollars for a magazine article.

He also wrote about Innocents Abroad:

"I wish to make a note upon the preface of the *Innocents*. In the last paragraph of that brief preface I speak of the proprietors of the *Daily Alta Californian* having "waived their rights" in certain letters which I wrote for that journal while absent on the Quaker City trip. I was young then, I am white-headed now, but the insult of that word rankles yet, now that I am reading that paragraph for the first time in many years, reading that paragraph for the first time since it was written, perhaps. There were rights, it is true—such rights as the strong are able to acquire over the weak and the absent. Early in '66 George Barnes invited me to resign my reportership on his paper, the *San Francisco Morning Call*, and for some months thereafter I was without money or work; then I had a pleasant turn of fortune. The proprietors of the *Sacramento Union*, a great and influential daily journal, sent me to the Sandwich Islands to write four letters a month at twenty dollars apiece. I was there four or five months, and returned to find myself about the best known man on the Pacific coast. Thomas McGuire, proprietor of several theaters, said that now was the time to make my fortune—strike while the iron was hot—break into the lecture field! I did it. I announced a lecture on the Sandwich Islands, closing the advertisement with the remark: "Admission one dollar; doors open at half past seven, the trouble begins at eight." A true prophecy. The trouble certainly did begin at eight, when I found myself in front of the only audience I had ever faced, for the fright which pervaded me from head to foot was paralyzing. It lasted two minutes and was as bitter as death; the memory of it is indestructible, but it had its compensations, for it made me immune from timidity before audiences for all time to come. I lectured in all the principal Californian towns and in Nevada, then lectured once or twice more in San Francisco, then retired from the field rich—for me—and laid out a plan to sail westward from San Francisco and go around the world. The proprietors of the *Alta* engaged me to write an account of the trip for that paper—fifty letters of a column and a half each, which would be about 2,000 words per letter, and the pay to be twenty dollars per letter.

I went east to St. Louis to say good-by to my mother, and then I was bitten by the prospectus of Captain Duncan of the *Quaker City* excursion, and I ended by joining it. During the trip I wrote and sent the fifty letters; six of them miscarried and I wrote six new ones to complete my contract. Then I put together a lecture on the trip and delivered it in San Francisco at great and satisfactory pecuniary profit; then I branched out into the country and was aghast at the result: I had been entirely forgotten, I never had people enough in my houses to sit as a jury of inquest on my lost reputation! I inquired into this curious condition of things and found that the thrifty owners of that prodigiously rich Alta newspaper had copyrighted all those poor little twenty-dollar letters and had threatened with prosecution any journal which should venture to copy a paragraph from them.

And there I was! I had contracted to furnish a large book, concerning the excursion, to the American Publishing Co. of Hartford, and I supposed I should need all those letters to fill it out with. I was in an uncomfortable situation—that is, if the proprietors of this stealthily acquired copyright should refuse to let me use the letters. That is what they did; Mr. MacCrelish said his firm were going to make a book out of the letters in order to get back the thousand dollars which they had paid for them. I said that if they had acted fairly and honorably, and had allowed the country press to use the letters or portions of them, my lecture skirmish on the coast would have paid me ten thousand dollars, whereas the *Alta* had lost me that amount. Then he offered a compromise: he would publish the book and allow me 10-per-cent royalty on it. The compromise did not appeal to me, and I said so. The book sale would be confined to San Francisco, and my royalty would not pay me enough to board me three months, whereas my Eastern contract, if carried out, could be profitable to me, for I had a sort of reputation on the Atlantic seaboard, acquired through the publication of six excursion letters in the *New York Tribune* and one or two in the *Herald*.

In the end Mr. Mac agreed to suppress his book, on certain conditions: in my preface I must thank the *Alta* for waiving its "rights" and granting me permission. I objected to the thanks. I could not with any large degree of sincerity thank the *Alta* for bankrupting my lecture raid. After considerable debate my point was conceded and the thanks left out.

CANVASS OF MARK TWAIN.

I have got specimen pages of Mark Twain's latest and greatest book. There is no occasion for me to talk to you about Mark Twain; there is not a man, woman or child in the United States that does not know him as AMERICA'S GREATEST HUMORIST. Probably there are MORE COPIES of is "Innocents Abroad" in the homes of the United States than there are of ANY OTHER SINGLE BOOK in existence with the exception of the Bible; Everybody has laughed with him hundreds of times.

We always have a warm place in our hearts for the man who can entertain us, who can make us laugh, who can make us FORGET the fret and worry of life, and help us to lengthen out our days by a little innocent enjoyment. There are nearly 700 pages in this book, and there is a laugh on every page.

The title of this work (open title page) is "Following the Equator" a journey around the world by Mark Twain. For frontispiece (opposite page) we have a picture of the great writer. He says he considers this the best photograph of himself ever taken. Underneath it you have a Mark Twainism "Be good and you will be lonesome." His inimitable humor crops out again in the dedication (read it.) Here we have another of the Pudd'nhead Maxims (read it.)

In this work Mark Twain carries us around the world visting such places as Hawaii, Australia, New Zealand, Ceylon, Fiji Islands, India, Indian Ocean, South Africa, etc. The book has been called forty thousand miles of fun; in this prospectus I can give you only the headings of a few of the chapters. You see our table of contents run only to Chapter 22 with a statement at the foot of the page that there are thirty more chapters to follow (read.)

(Turn back to page headed "Illustrations" and call attention of the customer to the statement in red type on the opposite page and the name of the illustrators. Tell him there will be several hundred illustrations in the book, the quality of which he can judge from the prospectus.)

"Canvass of Mark Twain." A leaflet given to subscription agents outlining how they could pitch Mark Twain's book *Following the Equator.*

Noah Brooks was editor of the *Alta* at the time, a man of sterling character and equipped with a right heart, also a good historian where facts were not essential. In biographical sketches of me written many years afterward (1902) he was quite eloquent in praises of the generosity of the *Alta* people in giving to me without compensation a book which, as history had afterward shown, was worth a fortune. After all the fuss, I did not levy heavily upon the *Alta* letters. I found that they were newspaper matter, not book matter. They had been written here and there and yonder, as opportunity had given me a chance working moment or two during our feverish flight around about Europe or in the furnace heat of my stateroom on board the *Quaker City*, therefore they were loosely constructed and needed to have some of the wind and water squeezed out of them. I used several of them—ten or twelve, perhaps. I wrote the rest of *The Innocents Abroad* in sixty days, and I could have added a fortnight's labor with the pen and gotten along without the letters altogether. I was very young in those days, exceedingly young, marvelously young, younger than I am now, younger than I shall ever be again, by hundreds of years. I worked every night from eleven or twelve until broad day in the morning, and as I did 200,000 words in the sixty days the average was more than 3,000 words a day—nothing for Sir Walter Scott, nothing for Louis Stevenson, nothing for plenty of other people, but quite handsome for me. In 1897, when we were living in Tedworth Square, London, and I was writing the book called *Following the Equator*, my average was 1,800 words a day; here in Florence (1904), my average seems to be 1,400 words per sitting of four or five hours.

I was deducing from the above that I have been slowing down steadily in these thirty-six years, but I perceive that my statistics have a defect: 3,000 words in the spring of 1868, when I was working seven or eight or nine hours at a sitting, has little or no advantage over the sitting of to-day, covering half the time and producing half the output. Figures often beguile me, particularly when I have the arranging of them myself; in which case the remark attributed to Disraeli would often apply with justice and force:

"There are three kinds of lies: lies, damned lies, and statistics."

—Mark Twain's Autobiography

Book Tours

For four months in the winter of 1884–1885, Clemens traveled with fellow southern writer George Washington Cable for a lecture tour. The two authors delivered readings from their works in over sixty cities across the United States and Canada. Cable wrote mostly of New Orleans and was famous for his novels The Grandissimes: A Story of Creole Life *(1880), portraying multiracial members and different classes of society in the early 1800s shortly after the Louisiana Purchase. His novella* Madame Delphine *(1881) explored more racial issues in the Creole south.*

Mark Twain wrote of Cable, "With Mr. Cable along to see for you, and describe and explain and illuminate, a jog through that old quarter is a vivid pleasure. And you have a vivid sense as of unseen or dimly seen things—vivid, and yet fitful and darkling; you glimpse salient features, but lose the fine shades or catch them imperfectly through the vision of the imagination: a case, as it were, of ignorant near-sighted stranger traversing the rim of wide vague horizons of Alps with an inspired and enlightened long-sighted native."

Twain wrote in 1907, "The man who recites without the book has all the advantage; when he comes to an old familiar remark in his tale which he has uttered nightly for a hundred nights—a remark preceded or followed by a pause—the faces of the audience tell him when to end the pause. For one audience the pause will be short, for another a little longer, for another a shade longer still; the

A newspaper advertisement of Twain's 1884–1885 book tour with fellow author George Washington Cable.

performer must vary the length of the pause to suit the shades of difference between audiences. These variations of measurement are so slight, so delicate, that they may almost be compared with the shadings achieved by Pratt and Whitney's ingenious machine which measures the five-millionth part of an inch. An audience is that machine's twin; it can measure a pause down to that vanishing fraction.

I used to play with the pause as other children play with a toy. In my recitals, when I went reading around the world for the benefit of Mr. Webster's creditors, I had three or four pieces in which the pauses performed an important part, and I used to lengthen them or shorten them according to the requirements of the case, and I got much pleasure out of the pause when it was accurately measured, and a certain discomfort when it wasn't. In the negro ghost story of "The Golden Arm" one of these pauses occurs just in front of the closing remark. Whenever I got the pause the right length, the remark that followed it was sure of a satisfactorily startling effect, but if the length of the pause was wrong by the five-millionth of an inch, the audience had had time in that infinitesimal fraction of a moment to wake up from its deep concentration in the grisly tale and foresee the climax, and be prepared for it before it burst upon them--and so it fell flat."

Mark Twain and George Washington Cable performed at the Wilgus Opera House in downtown Ithaca as part of their "Twins of Genius" lecture tour on December 3, 1884. The next day the student newspaper reported on its front page that: "a more thoroughly satisfactory entertainment has never before appeared in Ithaca..."

The Sunbeams section on page 3 noted: "The assembling of students at the 'resort' [the restaurant and bar, Zinck's] after the show last evening was a reminder of old times. Although the singing was not as spirited as usual, it is evident that the old songs are not forgotten. The remarks of Mr. Clemens were very brief but impressive and his excuse for not speaking longer, as he had 'worn out his voice in trying to reform the people of Ithaca,' was received with applause."

Mark Twain appeared at Steinway Hall in New York City on February 6, 1873, and repeated the same performance the next night at the Brooklyn Academy of Music in Brooklyn. On the day of his Brooklyn appearance, the review of his Steinway Hall performance appeared in the the New York Times.

Mark Twain's Lecture on the Sandwich Islands

The inimitable Mark Twain delivered his lecture on the Sandwich Islands last night at Steinway Hall, for the benefit of the Mercantile Library Association. The Hall and balconies were crowded to excess; every seat was occupied, and the centre and side passages were literally packed with persons who could not procure seats. The lecturer on being introduced assured the audience that he felt himself fully competent to speak of the interesting locality to which public attention has been lately directed, having spent several months on the islands. They were situated about 2,100 miles southwest of San Francisco, but why they were put in such an out-of-the-way locality he never could ascertain. The geological structure of the group of islands was described in the dry caustic style for which Twain is celebrated. The visit of the whites introduced civilization and education and killed out the natives. The latest reliable information fixes the population at 50,000, and when the benevolent foreigners start a few more seminaries, it is to be hoped that that event will materially help to kill off the remainder of the native population. The females wear a long robe, the gentlemen generally wear a smile and a pair of spectacles. The humorous description of the king and nobility kept the audience convulsed with laughter. It was not to be supposed that the natives were ignorant of scripture history; that they had some idea of the fall of Eve. Mr. Twain proved by stating that it was death for a woman to eat any fruit of the island, probably they did not wish to give woman a second chance. The American Missionary Society had started schools and introduced printing, and, owing to their exertions, there was not a single uneducated native above eighteen years old on the island, and the nation was about the best educated in the world. The expense of the mission was paid by the Sunday-school children of America, and Mr. Twain mentioned the fact that some thirty years ago he invested $2 in the speculation. Of course he did not mind the money, nor did he wish to "show off;" the incident was referred to as an instance of confiding humanity, and he hoped it would have its effect on the house. The natives are very hospitable, and feast their guests on roast dog and friccaseed cat—the ordinary American sausage

BROOKLYN ACADEMY OF MUSIC, FEB. 7th

Tickets at 244 Fulton St. and
172 Montague St.

stripped of its mystery. The dog was the pet of the household and the constant companion of the family, and when fit for the table was killed and served up. Mr. Twain had no decided objection to the dish, but he did not relish the idea of eating a personal friend. There were no cannibals in the Sandwich Islands. True, one addicted to that barbarous custom settled on one of the group, and getting tired of digesting natives, he resolved to try a white man with onions. This savage succeeded in capturing the captain of a whaling-ship, a tough old salt, who had spent fifty years at sea, living on shark steaks and blubber, but he proved too much for the digestive organs of the interesting native, and he died of the feast, with the crime on his conscience and the whaler in his stomach. The various peculiarities of the Kanacks were described by Mr. Twain, who interspersed his discourse with humorous sketches and witty allusions to the topics of the day, which kept his audience in a continuous roar of laughter. His attitudes, gestures, and looks, even his very silence were provocative of mirth. The lecture will be repeated on Monday evening.

Fundraising

In 1907, the Actors' Fund of America held a fundraiser in New York City. Twain lent his name to their promotional materials for the event and even sat in a booth signing autographs during the fair. Shown are a promotional letter with Twain's mimeographed endorsement, and a copy of The Adventures of Tom Sawyer *signed at the event by Twain, with the sticker still present. Mr. Clemens, in his white suit, formally declared the fair open. Mr. Daniel Frohman, in introducing Mr. Clemens, said:*

"We intend to make this a banner week in the history of the Fund, which takes an interest in every one on the stage, be he actor, singer, dancer, or workman. We have spent more than $40,000 during the past year. Charity covers a multitude of sins, but it also reveals a multitude of virtues. At the opening of the former fair we had the assistance of Edwin Booth and Joseph Jefferson. In their place we have to-day that American institution and apostle of wide humanity—Mark Twain."

As Mr. Frohman has said, charity reveals a multitude of virtues. This is true, and it is to be proved here before the week is over. Mr. Frohman has told you something of the object and something of the character of the work. He told me he would do this—and he has kept his word! I had expected to hear of it through the newspapers. I wouldn't trust anything between Frohman and the newspapers—except when it's a case of charity!

You should all remember that the actor has been your benefactor many and many a year. When you have been weary and downcast he has lifted your heart out of gloom and given you a fresh impulse. You are all under obligation to him. This is your opportunity to be his benefactor—to help provide for him in his old age and when he suffers from infirmities.

At this fair no one is to be persecuted to buy. If you offer a twenty-dollar bill in payment for a purchase of $1 you will receive $19 in change. There is to be no robbery here. There is to be no creed here—no religion except charity. We want to raise $250,000—and that is a great task to attempt.

The President has set the fair in motion by pressing the button in Washington. Now your good wishes are to be transmuted into cash.

By virtue of the authority in me vested I declare the fair open. I call the ball game. Let the transmuting begin!

—Speech to the *Actors' Fund of America*, 1907

Card Games

Portrait Authors (or The Game of Authors) card game is one of the longest selling card games that is still available to play today. It was first produced by G. M. Whipple & A. A. Smith of Salem, Massachusetts in 1861. Parker Brothers published a version in 1897. According to Cornell University, The West & Lee edition of this popular card game was patented in 1873, and was the first edition of the game to include Mark Twain. Parker Brothers produced their edition in 1897, and dominated the market. The game is still published today. According to collector Kevin Mac Donnell, the green deck dates from 1873 and the cards date from the 1880s to 1910.

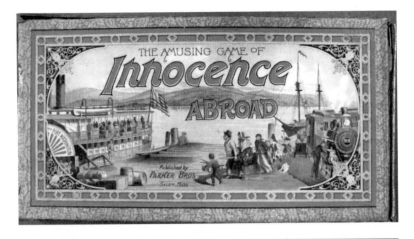

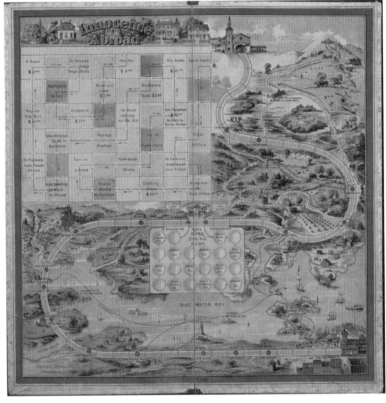

Innocence Abroad Board Game

According to the Museum of Play, "Parker Brothers' 1888 game The Amusing Game of Innocence Abroad is unique and groundbreaking in several ways. Most obviously, the game's title draws upon the huge popularity of Mark Twain's book The Innocents Abroad or the New Pilgrims' Progress, *published about 20 years prior. Parker cleverly changed innocents to innocence in the game title, to avoid a lawsuit. Innocence Abroad is also the first game designed under license to Parker Brothers. But nothing more is known about the game's designer, Mrs. Shepherd. And the game's play, simulating activities American tourists might encounter traveling through Europe, also follows a theme in the actual book. Players must guide two tokens apiece around the track, spending money wisely as they go. The first player to land both tokens on the finish wins, unless the second player lands there having spent less than half the money of the first. Parker Brothers advertised this game in the game instruction sheets to other popular games of the period."

Cigars

Twain was widely associated with cigar-smoking, and cigar makers found it profitable to use his image and name. The box below dates from 1889.

No one can tell me what is a good cigar—for me, I am the only judge. People who claim to know say that I smoke the worst cigars in the world. They bring their own cigars when they come to my house. They betray an unmanly terror when I offer them a cigar; they tell lies and hurry away to meet engagements which they have not made when they are threatened with the hospitalities of my box. Now then, observe what superstition, assisted by a man's reputation, can do.

I was to have twelve personal friends to supper one night. One of them was as notorious for costly and elegant cigars as I was for cheap and devilish ones. I called at his house and when no one was looking borrowed a double handful of his very choicest; cigars which cost him forty cents apiece and bore red-and-gold labels in sign of their nobility. I removed the labels and put the cigars into a box with my favorite brand on it—a brand which those people all knew, and which cowed them as

men are cowed by an epidemic. They took these cigars when offered at the end of the supper, and lit them and sternly struggled with them—in dreary silence, for hilarity died when the fell brand came into view and started around—but their fortitude held for a short time only; then they made excuses and filed out, treading on one another's heels with indecent eagerness; and in the morning when I went out to observe results the cigars lay all between the front door and the gate. All except one—that one lay in the plate of the man from whom I had cabbaged the lot. One or two whiffs was all he could stand. He told me afterward that some day I would get shot for giving people that kind of cigars to smoke.

～)

In his 1897 travelogue Following the Equator, *he mused*: I pledged myself to smoke but one cigar a day. I kept the cigar waiting until bedtime, then I had a luxurious time with it. But desire persecuted me every day and all day long. I found myself hunting for larger cigars...within the month my cigar had grown to such proportions that I could have used it as a crutch.

—The essay "Concerning Tobacco"

Insert cards were popular in tobacco products, and Twain was a popular subject.

Scrapbooks

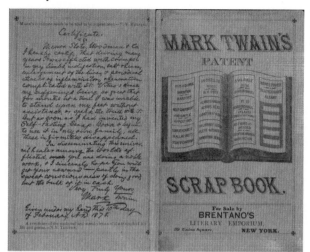

Twain's submission for a patent on his scrapbook.

Twain was an avid scrapbooker. However, he grew tired of hand gluing his life into books and figured his fellow scrapbookers felt the same way. In fact we received a patent for an invention that improved scrapbooking techniques, devising two possible self-adhesive systems.

The leaves of which the book A is composed are entirely covered, on one or both sides, with mucilage or other suitable adhesive substance, while the leaves of which the book B is composed have the mucilage or adhesive substance applied only at intervals, as represented in Fig. 1.

In either case the scrap-book is, so to say, self-pasting, as it is only necessary to moisten so much of the leaf as will contain the piece to be pasted in, and place such piece thereon, when it will stick to the leaf.

Works like an envelope. Moisten the gluey part and paste in your memories.

—Patent letter

After acquiring the patent, Twain successfully marketed and sold the invention. An 1885 St. Louis Post-Dispatch *article claimed that Twain's scrapbook made him $50,000 compared to $200,000 for all of his other books combined.*

Memory-Builder

Biographer Milton Meltzer, in Mark Twain Himself *wrote,* "On August 18, 1885 Mark Twain patented his Memory-Builder, a game board aimed at developing memory for dates and facts. The game board measured approximately 9 x 13 ¹/₂ inches and about ¹/₄ of an inch thick. The game and instructions (see below), which were written by Twain, were glued on the top front and back of the game board. The game came supplied with a package of straight pins of different colors. Several models were test marketed in 1891 but failed to capture the public's fancy, possibly because Twain's instructions were too complicated. According to one critic, 'The game looked like a cross between an income tax form and a table of logarithms.'

Mark Twain's Memory-Builder was a game for acquiring and retaining all sorts of facts and dates. The original three-piece game was written and designed by Mark Twain.

According to the Morgan Library: "By the nineteenth century, invention as a means of progress had become deeply rooted in the American consciousness, and individual entrepreneurial inventors were akin to folk heroes. Twain enjoyed the friendship of Thomas Edison, who recorded the author's voice on a wax cylinder and his image with a motion picture camera. Twain nurtured aspirations as an inventor and secured patents on a diverse range of products, including a self-pasting scrapbook, a perpetual calendar, a notebook with tear-away tabs, a self-adjusting garter, and this game. Only the scrapbook ever turned a profit, bringing him $50,000. Memory-Builder was a commercial disaster."

Flour

Mark Twain Flour was introduced in 1900, two years after this company began milling flour. It was made until just a few years before the company closed in 1955. According to the St. Paul Pioneer-Press, Mr. Kingsland Smith of the St. Paul roller mills sent a barrel of his flour to Mark Twain. This was Twain's reply.

HARTFORD, Conn., Oct. 12

My Dear Smith--A barrel of the best flour we ever had in our house arrived while we were away on summer vacation, and we are using it now. It came from St. Paul, but no bill came with it. Did you send it? Is this the ordinary price? Let me know right away, because I have got over one hundred people who want to trade with you and with nobody else. They want to give you all their custom.

Sincerely yours,

SAMUEL L. CLEMENS

—*Hartford Daily Courant*, November 2, 1882

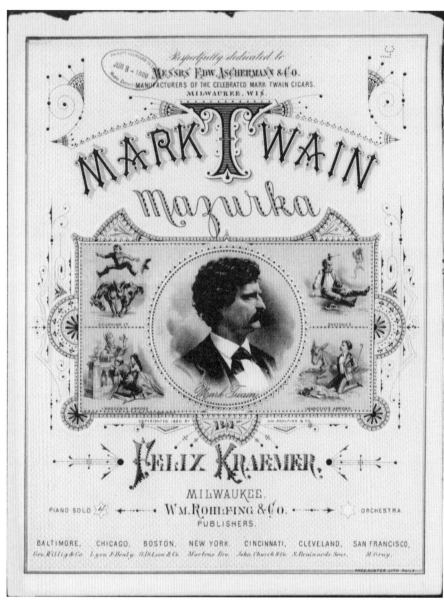

Mark Twain Mazurka

Sheet Music

Written in three-quarter time, with a very pronounced second beat, this song is very typical of mazurkas. Although it is certainly entertaining, the song itself really has very little to do with Mark Twain. It appears from the large picture of Mark Twain on the front that he is there merely for the purpose of selling more sheet music. This is significant because it shows that in 1880—several years before the publication of Adventures of Huckleberry Finn—*Mark Twain was already a household name and marketing tool. The cover art features Twain and scenes from Twain's bestsellers* Innocents Abroad *and* Roughing It.

When you want genuine music—music that will come right home to you like a bad quarter, suffuse your system like strychnine whisky, go right through you like Brandreth's pills, ramify your whole constitution like the measles, and break out on your hide like the pin-feather pimples on a picked goose,—when you want all this, just smash your piano, and invoke the glory-beaming banjo!

—"Enthusiastic Eloquence," *San Francisco Dramatic Chronicle*, June 29, 1865

Punch! Brothers Punch! music written by J.A. Kuren with supplementary words by R.E. O'Brien in 1876.

The cover art proclaims it to be "Mark Twain's Nightmare," which apparently led many people to believe that the words were written by Mark Twain himself. However, two editorials in the New York Times *were devoted to clarifying that Mark Twain never wrote—and never tried to say that he wrote—the jingle himself. Interestingly, the editorials appeared in 1915—on August 3 and August 8. This was five years after the death of Samuel Clemens, proving that the song and the story were still garnering the interest and enthusiasm of the public. The words of the jingle were actually written by Isaac Bromley, Noah Brooks, W.C. Wyckoff, and Moses W. Handy, according to Barbara Wheeler, author of "The Soundtrack*

of Mark Twain. *"The poem was not composed by Mark Twain, but by a group of people in 1876. It was the brainchild of Messrs. Isaac Bromley, Noah Brooks, W. C. Wyckoff, and Moses W. Handy. Bromley and Brooks, while riding a tram one night, had taken notice of a sign informing passengers about the fare:*

A Blue Trip Slip for an 8-cents fare.

A Buff Trip Slip for a 6-cents fare.

A Pink Trip Slip for a 3-cents fare.

For Coupon and Transfer, punch the Tickets.

Bromley had reportedly exclaimed, "Brooks, it's poetry. By George, it's poetry!"

Prospect Mining

HOW TO PROSPECT A MINE!

By watching the operations of miners in Washoe we are enabled to lay down the following rules: First, find a lead; no matter what it looks like, or how much bed-rock is mixed with it, so you have something that seems to be running somewhere. If you can't find something that has length, breadth and direction, drive a peg and stick up your notice on the first spot of ground you can see that looks red or yaller—them's indications, and there's nothing like indications in this county. In locating your claim put in as many stripes of men as you can get—"variety is the spice of life," as you will soon find. A mixture of Dutch,

French, Spanish, Irish, Scotch, American, English and Norwegian makes a very lively company. No matter how rich the prospect you may be able to get on the surface of your lead, go off about 2,000 feet and start a tunnel towards it—nothing like getting deep enough the first thing—nothing like a tunnel, especially a long one. 2,000 or 3,000 feet is about the distance most companies "kalkerlate" to run, but a company anxious to do the big thing might go further off from the lead.

Having got your claim located, and having decided upon a sufficiently long tunnel, organize. Nothing like organizing, as you will find, with a very little experience. You can't have too much of it. Get up by-laws; they are very useful, as all members of mining companies are greatly addicted to respecting them. No such thing as getting them too long; their great length will make them more binding. You want a number of officers; the more officers you have, the more plans will be found for prosecuting the work, and you can't have too many plans. Having a President makes you look weighty; it takes well with men from the Bay. All the men you see that are from the Bay believe in having Presidents. You may never have any use for a Treasurer, but it looks well, and men from the Bay will expect it; therefore, it is best to have one. Be sure to have a provision in your by-laws allowing each member to work out his assessments; then the work can go on, whether the company is rich or not, and it will give your foreman something to do, to see that each member does his share of the work. Let the members work two days each, by turns.

Have meetings every two or three days—nothing like meetings, you get to know each other so well, and the more you know of each other the better you will be apt to agree. Every time you make 5 feet in your tunnel is not too often to have meetings, you will soon become very fond of these "feasts of reason."

Having members representing a variety of nations gives you a splendid opportunity for gaining some insight into their languages; you are sure to hear them talk at ll the meetings. You cannot have too many meetings.

—*Territorial Enterprise*, May 18, 1862

∽ɔ

It was amazing how wild the people became all over the Pacific coast. In San Francisco and other large cities barbers, hack-drivers, servant-girls, merchants, and nearly every class of people would club together and send agents representing all the way from $5,000 to $500,000 or more to buy mines. They would buy anything in the shape of quartz, whether it contained any mineral value or not.

An extract from a letter of April is a fair exhibit:

Work not yet begun on the "Horatio and Derby"—haven't seen it yet. It is still in the snow. Shall begin on it within 3 or 4 weeks —strike the ledge in July: Guess it is good—worth from $30 to $50 a foot in California....

Man named Gebhart shot here yesterday while trying to defend a claim on Last Chance Hill. Expect he will die.

These mills here are not worth a d—n—except Clayton's—and it is not in full working trim yet.

Send me $40 or $50—by mail-immediately. I go to work to-morrow with pick and shovel. Something's got to come, by G—, before I let go here.

By the end of April work had become active in the mines, though the snow in places was still deep and the ground stony with frost. On the 28th he writes:

I have been at work all day blasting and digging, and d—ning one of our new claims—"Dashaway"—which I don't think a great deal of, but which I am willing to try. We are down, now, 10 or 12 a feet. We are following down under the ledge, but not taking it out. If we get up a windlass to-morrow we shall take out the ledge, and see whether it is worth anything or not.

In May it is the "Monitor" that is sure to bring affluence, though realization is no longer regarded as immediate.

To use a French expression, I have "got my d—-d satisfy" at last. Two years' time will make us capitalists, in spite of anything. Therefore we need fret and fume and worry and doubt no more, but just lie still and put up with privation for six months. Perhaps 3 months will "let us out." Then, if government refuses to pay the rent on your new office we can do it ourselves. We have got to wait six weeks, anyhow, for a dividend—maybe longer—but that it will come there is no shadow of a doubt. I have got the thing sifted down to a dead moral certainty. I own one-eighth of the new "Monitor Ledge, Clemens Company," and money can't buy a foot of it; because I know it to contain our fortune. The ledge is six feet wide, and one needs no glass to see gold and silver in it.... When you and I came out here we did not expect '63 or '64 to find us rich men—and if that proposition had been made we would have accepted it gladly. Now, it is made. I am willing, now, that "Neary's tunnel" or anybody else's tunnel shall succeed. Some of them may beat us a few months, but we shall be on hand in the fullness of time, as sure as fate. I would hate to swap chances with any member of the tribe....

It is the same man who twenty-five years later would fasten his faith and capital to a type-setting machine and refuse to exchange stock in it, share for share, with the Mergenthaler linotype. He adds:

But I have struck my tent in Esmeralda, and I care for no mines but those which I can superintend myself. I am a citizen here now, and I am satisfied, although Ratio and I are "strapped" and we haven't three days' rations in the house.... I shall work the "Monitor" and the other claims with my own hands. I prospected 3/4 of a pound of "Monitor" yesterday, and Raish reduced it with the blow-pipe, and got about 10 or 12 cents in gold and silver, besides the other half of it which we spilt on the floor and didn't get....

I tried to break a handsome chunk from a huge piece of my darling "Monitor" which we brought from the croppings yesterday, but it all splintered up, and I send you the scraps. I call that "choice"—any d—-d fool would.

There is much more of this, and other such letters, most of them ending with demands for money. The living, the tools, the blasting-powder, and the help eat it up faster than Orion's salary can grow.

"Send me $50 or $100, all you can spare; put away $150 subject to my call—we shall need it soon for the tunnel."

In another he wrote.

"The pick and shovel are the only claims I have any confidence in now," the miner concludes, after one fierce outburst. "My back is sore, and my hands are blistered with handling them to-day."

—*Mark Twain, A Biography*

Steamboats

When I was a boy, there was but one permanent ambition among my comrades in our village on the west bank of the Mississippi River. That was, to be a steamboatman. We had transient ambitions of other sorts, but they were only transient. When a circus came and went, it left us all burning to become clowns; the first negro minstrel show that came to our section left us all suffering to try that kind of life; now and then we had a hope that if we lived and were good, God would permit us to be pirates. These ambitions faded out, each in its turn; but the ambition to be a steamboatman always remained.

—Life on the Mississippi, 1883

Illustration from Twain's *Life on the Mississippi.*

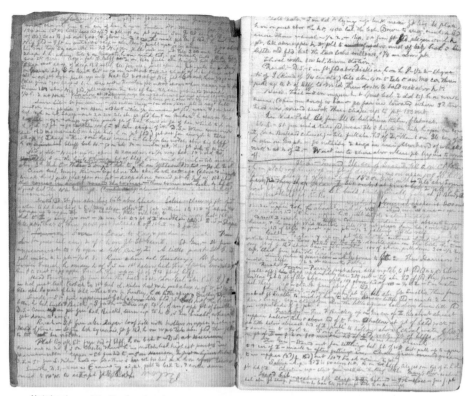

Notebook used by Twain when he was a cub pilot on the Mississippi River, April–July 1857.

The displayed pages show Twain's pilot notes on the waters surrounding St. Louis. It has been suggested by scholars that the book was probably acquired hastily by Twain, probably from a steam boat clerk, since it is a ledger book with ruled lines and it contains cargo records.

～

The face of the water, in time, became a wonderful book—a book that was a dead language to the uneducated passenger, but which told its mind to me without reserve, delivering its most cherished secrets as clearly as if it uttered them with a voice. And it was not a book to be read once and thrown aside, for it had a new story to tell every day. Throughout the long twelve hundred miles there was never a page that was void of interest, never one that you could leave unread without loss, never one that you would want to skip, thinking you could find higher enjoyment in some other thing. There never was so wonderful a book written by man; never one whose interest was so absorbing, so unflagging, so sparklingly renewed with every reperusal. The passenger who could not read it was charmed with a peculiar sort of faint dimple on its surface (on the rare occasions when he did not overlook it altogether); but to the pilot that was an italicized passage; indeed, it was more than that, it was a legend of the largest capitals, with a string of shouting exclamation points at the end of it, for it meant that a wreck or a rock was buried there that could tear the life out of the strongest vessel that ever floated. It is the faintest and simplest expression the water ever makes, and the most hideous to a pilot's eye. In truth, the passenger who could not read this book saw nothing but all manner of pretty pictures in it, painted by the sun and shaded by the clouds, whereas to the trained eye these were not pictures at all, but the grimmest and most dread-earnest of reading matter.

—Life on the Mississippi

The origin of the name Mark Twain came from his time as a cub pilot on a steamboat.

"I am going below a while. I suppose you know the next crossing?"

This was almost an affront. It was about the plainest and simplest crossing in the whole river. One couldn't come to any harm, whether he ran it right or not; and as for depth, there never had been any bottom there. I knew all this, perfectly well.

"Know how to run it? Why, I can run it with my eyes shut."

"How much water is there in it?"

"Well, that is an odd question. I couldn't get bottom there with a church steeple."

"You think so, do you?"

The very tone of the question shook my confidence. That was what Mr. Bixby was expecting. He left, without saying anything more. I began to imagine all sorts of things. Mr. Bixby, unknown to me, of course, sent somebody down to the forecastle with some mysterious instructions to the leadsmen, another messenger was sent to whisper among the officers, and then Mr. Bixby went into hiding behind a smoke-stack where he could observe results. Presently the

Published in the *New York Times* on August 18, 1900.

Mark Twain's Debut.

From "The Man Who Corrupted Hadleyberg."
By Mark Twain.

In my view, a person who published things in a mere newspaper could not properly claim recognition as a literary person; he must rise away above that; he must appear in a magazine. He would then be a literary person; also he would be famous—right away. These two ambitions were strong upon me. This was in 1866. I prepared my contribution, and then looked around for the best magazine to go up to glory in. I selected the most important one in New York. The contribution was accepted. I signed it " Mark Twain," for that name had some currency on the Pacific Coast, and it was my idea to spread it all over the world, at this one jump. The article appeared in the December number, and I sat up a month waiting for the January number, for that would contain the year's list of contributors, and my name would be in it, and I should be famous, and could give the banquet I was meditating.

I did not give the banquet. I had not written the " Mark Twain " distinctly; it was a fresh name to Eastern printers, and they put it " Mike Swain " or " Mac Swain," I do not remember which. At any rate, I was not celebrated, and I did not give the banquet. I was a literary person, but that was all—a buried one; buried alive.

captain stepped out on the hurricane deck; next the chief mate appeared; then a clerk. Every moment or two a straggler was added to my audience; and before I got to the head of the island I had fifteen or twenty people assembled down there under my nose. I began to wonder what the trouble was. As I started across, the captain glanced aloft at me and said, with a sham uneasiness in his voice—

"Where is Mr. Bixby?"

"Gone below, sir."

But that did the business for me. My imagination began to construct dangers out of nothing, and they multiplied faster than I could keep the run of them. All at once I imagined I saw shoal water ahead! The wave of coward agony that surged through me then came near dislocating every joint in me. All my confidence in that crossing vanished. I seized the bell-rope; dropped it, ashamed; seized it again; dropped it once more; clutched it tremblingly one again, and pulled it so feebly that I could hardly hear the stroke myself. Captain and mate sang out instantly, and both together—

"Starboard lead there! and quick about it!"

This was another shock. I began to climb the wheel like a squirrel; but I would hardly get the boat started to port before I would see new dangers on that side, and away I would spin to the other; only to find perils accumulating to starboard, and be crazy to get to port again. Then came the leadsman's sepulchral cry—

"D-e-e-p four!"

Deep four in a bottomless crossing! The terror of it took my breath away.

"M-a-r-k three!... M-a-r-k three... Quarter less three!... Half twain!"

This was frightful! I seized the bell-ropes and stopped the engines.

"Quarter twain! Quarter twain! Mark twain!"

I was helpless. I did not know what in the world to do. I was quaking from head to foot, and I could have hung my hat on my eyes, they stuck out so far.

"Quarter less twain! Nine and a half!"

We were drawing nine! My hands were in a nerveless flutter. I could not ring a bell intelligibly with them. I flew to the speaking-tube and shouted to the engineer—

"Oh, Ben, if you love me, back her! Quick, Ben! Oh, back the immortal soul out of her!"

I heard the door close gently. I looked around, and there stood Mr. Bixby, smiling a bland, sweet smile. Then the audience on the hurricane deck sent up a thundergust of humiliating laughter. I saw it all, now, and I felt meaner than the meanest man in human history. I laid in the lead, set the boat in her marks, came ahead on the engines, and said—

"It was a fine trick to play on an orphan, wasn't it? I suppose I'll never hear the last of how I was ass enough to heave the lead at the head of 66."

"Well, no, you won't, maybe. In fact I hope you won't; for I want you to learn something by that experience. Didn't you know there was no bottom in that crossing?"

"Yes, sir, I did."

"Very well, then. You shouldn't have allowed me or anybody else to shake your confidence in that knowledge. Try to remember that. And another thing: when you get into a dangerous place, don't turn coward. That isn't going to help matters any."

It was a good enough lesson, but pretty hardly learned.

—*Life on the Mississippi*

In due course I got my license. I was a pilot now, full fledged. I dropped into casual employments; no misfortunes resulting, intermittent work gave place to steady and protracted engagements. Time drifted smoothly and prosperously on, and I supposed— and hoped—that I was going to follow the river the rest of my days, and die at the wheel when my mission was ended. But by and by the war came, commerce was suspended, my occupation was gone.

A copy of Twain's steamboat pilot license that he received in 1859 at the age of twenty three.

I had to seek another livelihood. So I became a silver miner in Nevada; next, a newspaper reporter; next, a gold miner, in California; next, a reporter in San Francisco; next, a special correspondent in the Sandwich Islands; next, a roving correspondent in Europe and the East; next, an instructional torch-bearer on the lecture platform; and, finally, I became a scribbler of books, and an immovable fixture among the other rocks of New England.

—Life on the Mississippi

～〇

There is a great difference in boats, of course. For a long time I was on a boat that was so slow we used to forget what year it was we left port in. But of course this was at rare intervals. Ferryboats used to lose valuable trips because their passengers grew old and died, waiting for us to get by. This was at still rarer intervals. I had the documents for these occurrences, but through carelessness they have been mislaid. This boat, the "John J. Roe," was so slow that when she finally sunk in Madrid Bend, it was five years before the owners heard of it. That was always a confusing fact to me, but it is according to the record, any way. She was dismally slow; still, we often had pretty exciting times racing with islands, and rafts, and such things. One trip, however, we did rather well. We went to St. Louis in sixteen days. But even at this rattling gait I think we changed watches three times in Fort Adams reach, which is five miles long. A "reach" is a piece of straight river, and of course the current drives through such a place in a pretty lively way.

In so few words have I disposed of the twenty-one slow-drifting years that have come and gone since I last looked from the windows of a pilot-house.

—The Galaxy, November 1870

～〇

Horace Bixby, Twain's piloting mentor, told Twain's biographer, Albert Bigelow Paine, "It is the fashion to-day to disparage Sam's piloting. Men who were born since he was on the river and never saw him will tell you that Sam was never much of a pilot. Most of them will tell you that he was never a pilot at all. As a matter of fact, Sam was a fine pilot, and in a day when piloting on the Mississippi required a great deal more brains and skill and application than it does now. There were no signal-lights along the shore in those days, and no search-lights on the vessels; everything was blind, and on a dark, misty night in a river full of snags and shifting sand-bars and changing shores, a pilot's judgment had to be founded on absolute certainty."
—Mark Twain, a Biography

Politics

"Suppose you were an idiot. And suppose you were a member of Congress. But then I repeat myself," Twain said. He also opined, "Politicians are like diapers; they need to be changed often, and for the same reason."

~

The New York Times, October 30, 1901

MARK TWAIN AND SETH LOW SPEAK

The Humorist Compares Tammany to a Rotten Banana.

Says that Mr. Shephard is the White End of it—Mr. Low Speaks of Deveryism.

Mark Twain and Seth Low were the attractions at the noon meeting yesterday in the hall on the ground floor of 350 Broadway. A crowd of more than 2,000 jammed into the place, and was so thick that several times the management had to interrupt the speakers to prevent surging, and injury to many in the audience. Ten minutes before the opening of the meeting the rush of those trying to crowd into the already packed hall became so threatening that a half dozen policemen at the entrance were almost carried off their feet, and were forced, by way of precaution, to close the doors.

Within the hall every available inch of space was called into requisition. Men and boys climbed up the latticework surrounding the elevator at one side of the hall, and climbed up on window sills and wherever there was an inch to give a foothold above the heads of the rest of the men. In the opinion of many who have been identified with political meetings for years past, never was such a jam seen as the one that greeted the Fusion candidate and the man who had come to throw bombs of humor into the camp of Tammany.

Promptly at 11:55 o'clock Mark Twain appeared from the doorway of the New York Life Building. He was linked to the arm of Joseph Johnson, Jr., President of the Order of Acorns, and, followed by Mr. Low, the trio worked its way through the crowd of about 1,000 persons that had been locked out of the hall by the closing of the doors.

As Mark Twain and Seth Low stepped upon the platform the yell that arose was deafening, and it was many minutes before Mr. Johnson, assisted by the humorist, could restore order. President Johnson introduced Mark Twain. The latter arose immediately, and when, after several minutes effort, quiet had been restored, he began:

"In this campaign there is nothing very much simpler than to decide if we are to vote for the continuance of Crokerism and Tammany rule or whether we shall not. I think we have had enough of a system of American royalty residing in Europe. If we should have nothing but excellent and trusted men on the ticket of Mr. Croker, I think it would be doubtful if we would want to continue it. But it is not likely that we will continue it, and it is very likely that we will vote the Fusion ticket from top to bottom. [Cheers.]

"Of course, I cannot expect you all to know this, but it was only against my physician's advice that I came here. I have been on a sickbed for the past forty-eight hours. I told my physician that I must come, but he was obdurate. I explained to him that if I had only some reputable sort of an ailment I might be able to consider his advice, but that I did not see, under the circumstances, how I could explain a nursery ailment to the gentlemen who expected me to talk to them. The trouble was, gentlemen indiscriminate eating. I ate a banana, thinking that by doing so I might conciliate the Italians of this city to voting the Fusion ticket. But, as it turned out, it was not an Italian banana. It was a Tammany banana, as should have been easily detected. A Tammany banana is a strange thing. One end of it, or one part, here or there, is perfectly white. The rest of it is rotten.

"Now, I have the greatest respect for Mr. Shepard personally, but nine-tenths of the rest of the bananas on that ticket are rotten. Mr. Shepard is the white part of the banana. The best we can do is to throw the whole banana from us, for it is unfit. It will make us sick. It will make us feel as if we had swallowed whole bunches of Tammany tigers and as if they were all wrestling for the supremacy in our interiors.

"What we need is a doctor to handle the feeling within. I think I can introduce you to a very good doctor, too - Seth Low, who but lately was honored with a Yale LL.D.". . .

Washington

Twain wrote for the Virginia City, Nevada newspaper the Territorial Enterprise *in the 1860s. Here is one of his dispatches from Washington, DC.*

Territorial Enterprise, March 7, 1868

MARK TWAIN'S LETTERS FROM WASHINGTON.

NUMBER IX.

[SPECIAL CORRESPONDENCE OF THE ENTERPRISE.]

WASHINGTON, February, 1868

Washington Rascality.

Right here in this heart and home and fountain-head of law—in this great factory where are forged those rules that create good order and compel virtue and honesty in the other communities of the land, rascality achieves its highest perfection. Here rewards are conferred for conniving at dishonesty, but never for exposing it. I know several cases that come under this head; persons who have lived here longer and are better acquainted, know of a great many. I meet a man in the Avenue, sometimes, whose history most residents of the city are acquainted with. He was a clerk of high grade in one of the Departments; but he was a stranger and had no rules of action for his guidance except some effete maxims of integrity picked up in Sunday school—that snare to the feet of the unsophisticated!—and some unpractical moral wisdom instilled into him by his mother, who meant well, poor soul,, but whose teachings were morally bound to train up her boy for the poor-house. Well, nobody told this stranger how he ought to conduct himself, and so he went on following up those old maxims of his, and acting so strangely in consequence, that the other clerks began to whisper and nod, and exchange glances of commiseration—for they thought that his mind was not right—that his brain had been touched by sorrow, or hard fortune, or something. They observed that he never stole anything; by and by they noticed that people who came to bribe him went away with an expression of disappointment in their faces; finally it became apparent that he worked very had, and performed his tasks well, and never "shirked." Then they grew a little afraid of him. They said he was very quiet and peaceable, but then there was no telling when a lunatic was going to get one of those spells on him and scalp somebody. Finally the young man caught the high grand sachem of a great bureau perpetrating a flagrant swindle on the Government! What did he do?—call for a division of the proceeds, like an intelligent being? No! He went, like an ignorant, besotted ass, and told the Secretary of the Department! The Secretary of the Department said he would look into the matter; and added, "By the way, what business is it of yours?" And the next thing the foolish young man knew, he found himself discharged and the intelligent sachem promoted. Then he went and told the Senators from the State all about it and asked them to get him another place, and they told him very properly that he had ruined himself, and that the official doors would all be closed against him now. He soon found out that that was the truth. He soon found out that you can't educate a boy in a Sunday school so as to make him useful to his country. That young man is idle to this day. Nobody has tried harder to get employment than he, but they all know his story; and they always refuse him. Everybody shuns him because everybody knows he is afflicted with a loathsome leprosy—the strange, foreign leprosy of honesty—and they are afraid they might catch it. There isn't any danger, maybe, but then they don't like to take any chances.

Why, no one would ever imagine the absurdities that imbecile was guilty of before he discovered what a mistake his education had been. When he found out that they admit bad women into private rooms in one of the Departments at all hours of the night he went and told people about it, as if he had discovered some great thing. He was always carrying around some old stale piece of news like that. And when he found out that in the basement of another Department they feed and lodge and pay salaries to 120 New York election sharps who do nothing in the world, and that their names are set down in the record books, not as Michael O'Flaherty, Dennis O'Flannigan, Patrick O'Dougherty, and so on, but always simply as "FIRE AND LIGHTS," he went and told that also. And when he learned that one of the heads of the Printing Bureau hires bindery girls with especial reference to their unchastity, and that it was proved by Government investigation and duly published in a book that he sometimes sleeps with two of them at a time and has the free run of his harem to choose from, and that he flourishes around Washington, now, the best dressed and gallantest officer the Government has, he even thought that trifle a matter of sufficient importance to run around and talk about. Why, when the Tice meter was covertly foisted upon the public by the Government, and every distiller in America peremptorily commanded to come forward and buy one at from $600 to $1,500, when a better machine could have been furnished for just half the money, he said he believed there was a ten million dollar swindle behind all that, and that certain high officials were privy to it and reaping a vast profit from it—which was no doubt true as gospel, but where is the wisdom in talking about these dangerous topics?

I stopped in at a fine boarding-house last night to see a friend, and the land lady came in to collect her bill. She mentioned the fact that she had two hand-somely furnished apartments which she would like to rent to some one. I said I knew of several Senators and Congressmen who would be glad to have them. She said she would not venture to risk that kind of people! I thought she was jesting, but she was not. An agent of a Senator had called and engaged those rooms for him two months before he was to arrive—with the understanding that he was to occupy them during the whole session. He came, and said they were perfectly satisfactory. After a while he wanted some more furniture added—which was done, at a cost of two hundred dollars. He staid two months, said he was still perfectly satisfied with the apartments, and could have no desire to leave them, but for the fact that some friends had taken up their residence in another part of the town, and he wished to be near them—so he was going to move. He did not deny that the agent's contract was duly authorized, but he said, "Have you any writing to show for it?" She hadn't. He said, "Well"—and left. The law does not permit members of Congress to be sued. So there was no redress. The breached contract had to remain breached.

She rented the rooms to a Territorial delegate, but refused to let him have them unless he would take them for the remainder of the session, because she had a chance at the moment to rent them to a gentleman for a month or two, and she would rather have a gentleman than a Congressman because Congressmen kept such late hours and burned so much fuel and gas. He occupied the rooms twenty-four hours, expressed himself entirely pleased with them, but had found lodgings which were cheaper and would do him as well. And he moved. He moved first, when nobody was watching, and said that afterward. He did not deny his contract either, but refused to fulfill it or give any redress. The law cannot touch the delegate. Isn't this a curious state of things? Isn't it refreshing to see men break laws so coolly whose sole business is law-making? I wonder if all the Congressmen are so unreliable? If they are, I think I could subscribe to this landlady's suggestive remark that it is pleasanter to have a "gentleman" around than a Congressman.

I said I would be glad to have her general opinion of Washington probity; and she said her opinion was that it did not exist in a very great degree. She believe that the whole city was polluted with peculation and all other forms of rascality— debauched and demoralized by the wholesale dishonesty that prevails in every single department of the Washington Government, great and small. She said that false weights were used in the market, the grocery stores, the butcher shops and all such places. The meat a butcher sells you for seven pounds can never persuaded to weight more than five and a half in your kitchen scales at home; a grocer's pound of butter usually weights only three-quarters in scales that are unconscious and have no motive to deceive. They paint rocks and add them to your coal; they put sand in your sugar; lime in your flour; water in your milk; turpentine in your whisky; clothespins in your sausages; turnips in your canned peaches; they will rather cheat you out of ten cents than make a dollar out of you by honest dealing. That was her opinion. What little I have seen of Washington in the short time I have been here, leads me to think it must be correct.

Ulysses S. Grant

This is the simple soldier, who, all untaught of the silken phrase-makers, linked words together with an art surpassing the art of the schools and put into them a something which will still bring to American ears, as long as America shall last, the roll of his vanished drums and the tread of his marching hosts.

—Twain's notebook, 1866

~

I can't rise to General Grant's lofty place in the estimation of this nation, but it is a deep happiness to me to know that when it comes to epistolary literature, he can't sit in the front seat along with me.

—Mark Twain's Autobiography, 1924

Women's Suffrage

Mark Twain wrote several satirical letters about women's suffrage that were printed in newspapers in 1867.

The Iniquitous Crusade Against Man's Regal Birthright Must Be Crushed

Another Letter From Mark Twain

Dear Cousin Jennie,

I did not know I had a cousin named Jennie, but I am proud to claim such a relationship with you. I have no idea who you are, but you talk well—you talk exceedingly well. You seem inclined to treat the question of female suffrage seriously, and for once I will drop foolishness, and speak with the gravity the occasion demands. You fully understand the difference between justice and expediency? I am satisfied you do. You know very well that it would have been a just and righteous act if we had rescued struggling Poland four or five years

This illustration by Frederick Gruger for the *Sunday Magazine*, December 1, 1907 shows Twain with his daughter Suzy and Ulysses S. Grant. Twain assisted in writing Grant's memoirs.

ago, but you also know it would not have been good policy to do it. No one will say that it is not just and right that women should vote; no one will say that an educated American woman would not vote with fifty times the judgment and independence exercised by stupid, illiterate newcomers from foreign lands; I will even go so far as myself as to say that in my experience only third-rate intelligence is sent to Legislatures to make laws, because he first-rate article will not leave important private interests go unwatched to go and serve the public for a beggarly four or five dollars a day, and a miserably trivial distinction, while it is possible that a matron , unencumbered with children, might go with no detriment to the affairs of her household. We also know that between constable and United States Senator, the one thousand offices of mere honor (though burdened with high responsibilities) are held by third-rate ability because first-rate ability can only afford to hold offices of great emolument—and we know that first-rate female talent could afford to hold those offices of mere honor without making business sacrifices. You see I have made a very strong argument for your side; and I repeat that no one will deny the truth of any of the above propositions; but behold that matter of expediency comes in here—policy!

Now, you think I am going to string out a long argument on my own side, but I am not. I only say this: The ignorant foreign women would vote with the ignorant foreign men—the bad women would vote with the bad men—the good women would vote with the good men. The same candidate who would be elected now would be elected then, the only difference being that there might be twice as many votes polled then as now. Then in what respect is the condition of things improved? I cannot see.

So, I conceive that if nothing is to be gained by it, it is expedient to extend the suffrage to women. That must be a benefit beyond the power of figures to estimate, which can make us consent to take the High Priestess we reverence at the sacred fireside and send her forth to electioneer for votes among the mangy mob who are unworthy to touch the hem of her garment. A lady of my acquaintance came very near putting my feeling in this matter into words the other day, Jennie, when she said she was opposed to female suffrage, because she was not willing to see her sex reduced to a level with negroes and men!

Female suffrage, would do harm, my dear—it would actually do harm. A very large proportion of our best and wisest women would still cling to the holy ground of the home circle, and refuse to either vote or hold office—but every grand rascal among your sex would work, bribe, and vote with all her might; and, behold, mediocrity and dishonesty would be appointed to conduct the affairs of government more surely than ever before. You see the policy of the thing is bad, very bad. It would augment the strength of the bad vote. I consider it a very strong point on your side of the question.

I think I could write a pretty strong argument in favor of female suffrage, but I do not want to do it. I never want to see women voting, and gabbling about politics, and electioneering. There is something revolting in the thought. It would shock me inexpressibly for an angel to come down from above and ask me to drink with him (thought I should doubtless consent); but it would shock me still more to see one of our blessed earthly angels peddling election tickets among a mob of shabby scoundrels she never saw before.

The is one insuperable obstacle in the way of female suffrage, Jennie; I approach the subject with fear and trembling, but it must be out: A woman would never vote, because she would have to tell her age at the polls. And even if she did dare to vote once or twice, when she was just of age, you know what ire results would flow from "putting this and that together" in after times. For instance, in an un-guarded moment, Miss A. says she voted for Mr. Smith. Her auditor, who knows it has been seven year since Smith ran for anything, easily ciphers out that he is at least seven years over age, instead of the tender young pullet she has been making herself out to be. No, Jennie, this new fashion of registering the name, age, residence and occupation of every voter, is a fatal bar to female suffrage.

Women will never be permitted to vote or hold office, Jennie, and it is a lucky thing for me, and for many other men, that such is the decree of fate. Because, you see, there are some few measures they would all unite on—there are one or two measures that would bring out their entire voting strength, in site of their antipathy to making themselves conspicuous; and there being vastly more women than men in this State, they would trot those measures through the Leg-islature with a velocity that woul be appalling. For instance, they would enact:

1. That all men should be home by 10pm, without fail.
2. That married men bestow considerable attention on their own wives.
3. That it should be a hanging offense to sell whiskey in saloons, and that fine and disenfranchisement should follow the drinking of it in those places.
4. That the smoking of cigars in excess should be forbidden, and the smoking of pipes utterly abolished.
5. That the wife should have a little of her own property when she mar-ried a man who hadn't any.

Jennie, such tyranny as this, we could never stand. Our free souls could never endure such degrading thralldom. Women, go your ways! Seek not to beguile us of our imperial privileges. Content yourself with your little feminine trifles—your babies, your benevolent societies and your knitting—and let your natural bosses do the voting. Stand back—you will be wanting to go to war next. We will let you teach school as much as you want to, and we will pay you half wages for it too, but beware! We don't want you to crowd us too much.

If I get time, cousin Jennie, I will furnish you a picture of a female legislature that will distress you – I know it will, because you cannot disguise form me that fact that you are no more in favor of female suffrage, really, than I am.

In conclusion, honesty compels me to tell you that I have been highly complimented a dozen times on my articles signed "Cousin Jennie" and "A.L." The same honesty, though, compelled me to confess that I did not write either of those articles.

Mark Twain

p.s. That tiresome old goose, my wife, is prancing around like a lunatic, up stairs, rehearsing a speech in favor of female suffrage which she is going to deliver before a mass meeting of seditious old maid sin my back parlor tonight. (She is a vigorous speaker, but you can smell her eloquence further than you can hear it; it is on a account of gin, I think.) It is a pity those old skeletons have chosen my back parlor, because I have concluded to touch off a keg of powder under there tonight, and I am afraid the noise may disturb their deliberations some.

～う

FEMALE SUFFRAGE.
A VOLLEY FROM THE DOWN-TRODDEN.
A DEFENSE.

Editors Missouri Democrat:
I should think you would be ashamed of yourselves. I would, anyway—to publish the vile, witless drivelings of that poor creature who degrades me with his name. I say you ought to be ashamed of yourselves. Two hundred noble, Spartan women cast themselves into the breach to free their sex from bondage, and instead of standing with bowed heads before the majesty of such a spectacle, you permit this flippant ass, my husband, to print a weak satire on it.

The wretch! I combed him with a piano stool for it. And I mean to comb every newspaper villain I can lay my hands on. They are nothing but villains anyhow. They published our names when nobody asked them to, and therefore they are low, mean and depraved, and fit for any crime however black and infamous.

Mr. Editor, I have not been appointed the champion of my sex in this matter; still, if I could know that any argument of mine in favor of female suffrage which has been presented in the above communication will win over any enemy to our cause, it would soften and soothe my dying hour; ah, yes, it would soothe it as never another soother could soothe it.

MRS. MARK TWAIN,
President Affghanistan Aid Association, Secretary of the Society for introducing the Gospel into New Jersey, etc., etc., etc.

FEMALE SUFFRAGE.

A VOLLEY FROM THE DOWN-TRODDEN.

A DEFENSE.

Editors Missouri Democrat:
I should think you would be ashamed of yourselves. I would, anyway—to publish the vile, witless drivelings of that poor creature who degrades me with his name. I say you ought to be ashamed of yourselves. Two hundred noble, Spartan women cast themselves into the breach to free their sex from bondage, and instead of standing with bowed heads before the majesty of such a spectacle, you permit this flippant ass, my husband, to print a weak satire upon it. The wretch! I combed him with a piano stool for it. And I mean to comb every newspaper villain I can lay my hands on. They are nothing but villains anyhow. They published our names when nobody asked them to, and therefore they are low, mean and depraved, and fit for any crime however black and infamous.
Mr. Editor, I have not been appointed the champion of my sex in this matter; still, if I could know that any argument of mine in favor of female suffrage which has been presented in the above communication will win over any enemy to our cause, it would soften and soothe my dying hour; ah, yes, it would soothe it as never another soother could soothe it.
MRS. MARK TWAIN,

[The old woman states a case well, don't she? She states a case mighty well, for a woman of her years? She even soars into moving eloquence in that place where she says: "two hundred noble Spartan women cast themselves into the breeches", etc. And those "arguments" of her's afford her a prodigious satisfaction, don't they? She may possibly die easy on account of them, but she won't if I am able to stir her up in her last moments. That woman has made my life a burthen to me, and I mean to have a hand in soothing her myself when her time is up.—MARK TWAIN]

MORE DEFENSE.

Editors Missouri Democrat:
I have read the article in your paper on female suffrage, by the atrocious scoundrel Mark Twain. But do not imagine that such a thing as that will deter us from demanding and enforcing our rights. Sir, we will have our rights, though the heavens fall. And as for this wretch, he had better find something else to do than meddling with matters he is incapable of understanding. I suppose he votes—such is the law!—such is justice!—he is allowed to vote, but women a thousand times his superiors in intelligence are ruled out!—he!—a creature who don't know enough to follow the wires and find the telegraph office. Comment is unnecessary. If I get my hands on that whelp I will snatch hair out of his head till he is as bald as a phrenological bust.
Mr. Editor, I may not have done as much good for my species as I ought, in my time, but if any of the arguments I have presented in this article in favor of female suffrage shall aid in extending the privileges of woman, I shall die happy and content.
MRS. ZEB. LEAVENWORTH.
Originator and President of the Association for the Establishment of a Female College in Kamschatka.

[I perceive that I have drawn the fire of another heavy gun. I feel as anxious as any man could to answer this old Kamschatkan, but I do not know where to take hold. Her "arguments" are too subtle for me. If she can die happy and content on that mild sort of gruel, though, let her slide.—MARK TWAIN.]

At home, a standing argument against woman suffrage has always been that women could not go to the polls without being insulted. The arguments against woman suffrage have always taken the easy form of prophecy. The prophets have been prophesying ever since the woman's rights movement began in 1848—and in forty-seven years they have never scored a hit.

—Following the Equator

∼

I know that since the women started out on their crusade they have scored in every project they undertook against unjust laws. I would like to see them help make the laws and those who are to enforce them. I would like to see the whiplash in women's hands.

—quoted in the *New York Times*, January 21, 1901

Race

This piece has largely been attributed to Mark Twain over the years. During the time of the publication of this piece, he was the editor of the Buffalo Express. "He was an outspoken anti-slavery activist. The term "nigger" here is used sarcastically. It is not meant to be derogatory toward anyone except those "chivalrous whites" who formed the lunch mob in Memphis that killed innocent people" according to local historians of *The Buffalonian.*

ONLY A NIGGER

A dispatch from Memphis mentions that, of two Negro's lately sentenced to death for murder in that vicinity, on named woods has just confessed to having ravished a young lady during the war, for which deed another Negro was hung at the time by an avenging mob, the evidence that doomed the guilt-less wretch being a hat which Woods now relates that he stole from its owner and left behind, for the purpose of misleading. Ah, well! Too bad to be sure! A little blunder in the administration of justice by Southern mob-law, but nothing to speak of.

Only "a nigger" killed by mistake—that is all. Of course, every high toned gentleman whose chivalric impulses were so unfortunately misled in this

THE BUFFALO EXPRESS

THURSDAY, AUGUST 26, 1869.

ONLY A NIGGER.

A dispatch from Memphis mentions that, of two negroes lately sentenced to death for murder in that vicinity, one named Woods has just confessed to having ravished a young lady during the war, for which deed another negro was hung at the time by an avenging mob, the evidence that doomed the guiltless wretch being a hat which Woods now relates that he stole from its owner and left behind, for the purpose of misleading. Ah, well! Too bad, to be sure! A little blunder in the administration of justice by Southern mob-law; but nothing to speak of. Only "a nigger" killed by mistake—that is all. Of course, every high toned gentleman whose chivalric im-

Buffalo Express, August 26, 1869

affair, by the cunning of the miscreant. Woods, is as sorry about it as a high toned gentleman can be expected to be about the unlucky fate of "a nigger." But mistakes will happen, even in the best regulated and most high toned mobs, and surely there is no good reason why southern gentlemen should worry themselves with useless regrets, so long as only an innocent "nigger" is hanged, or toasted or knonted [sic] to death, now and then. What if the blunder of lynching the wrong man does happen once in four or five cases! Is that any fair argument against the cultivation and indulgence of those fine chivalric passions and that noble Southern spirit which will not brook the slow and cold formalities of regular law, when outraged white womanhood appeals for vengeance! Perish the thought so unworthy of a Southern soul! Leave it to the sentimentalism and humanitarianism of cold-blooded Yankee civilization! What are the lives of a few "niggers" in comparison with the preservation of the impetuous instincts of a proud and fiery race! Keep ready in the halter, therefore, oh chivalry of Memphis! Keep the lash knotted; keep the brand and the faggots in waiting, for prompt work with the next "nigger" who may be suspected of any damnable crime! Wreak a swift vengeance upon him, for the satisfaction of noble impulses that intimidate knightly hearts, and then have time and accidentally to discover, if they will, whether he was guilty or no.

~

We had a little slave boy whom we had hired from some one, there in Hannibal. He was from the Eastern Shore of Maryland, and had been brought away from his family and his friends, half way across the American continent, and sold. He was a cheery spirit, innocent and gentle, and the noisiest creature that ever was, perhaps. All day long he was singing, whistling, yelling, whooping, laughing—it was maddening, devastating, unendurable. At last, one day, I lost all my temper, and went raging to my mother, and said Sandy had been singing for an hour without a single break, and I couldn't stand it, and wouldn't she please shut him up.

The tears came into her eyes, and her lip trembled, and she said something like this—'Poor thing, when he sings, it shows that he is not remembering, and that comforts me; but when he is still, I am afraid he is thinking, and I cannot bear it. He will never see his mother again; if he can sing, I must not hinder it, but be thankful for it. If you were older, you would understand me; then that friendless child's noise would make you glad.' It was a simple speech, and made up of small words, but it went home, and Sandy's noise was not a trouble to me any more.

—*The Autobiography of Mark Twain*

~

The blunting effects of slavery upon the slaveholder's moral perceptions are known and conceded the world over; and a privileged class, an aristocracy, is but a band of slaveholders under another name.

—*A Connecticut Yankee in King Arthur's Court*

"Familiarity breeds
contempt—and children."
—*Notebook, 1894*

"If man could be crossed with a cat,
it would improve the man, but it
would deteriorate the cat."
—*Notebook, 1894*

4. Family, Friends, and Animals

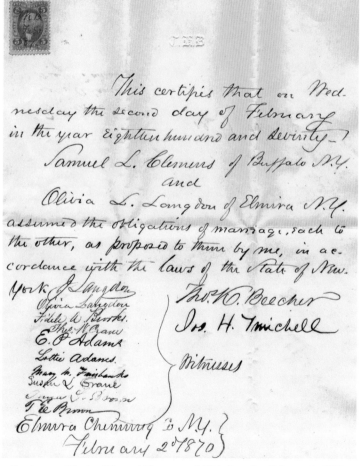

Marriage certificate of Samuel Clemens and Olivia Langdon, February 2, 1870.

Marriage

Wedding

A letter from Mark Twain to his family informing them of his engagement, 1869.

My dear Mother & Brother & Sisters & Nephew & Niece, & Margaret:

This is to inform you that on yesterday, the 4th of February, I was duly & solemnly & irrevocably engaged to be married to Miss Olivia L. Langdon, of Elmira, New York. Amen. She is the best girl in all the world, & the most sensible, & I am just as proud of her as I can be.

It may be a good while before we are married, for I am not rich enough to give her a comfortable home right away, & I don't want anybody's help. I can get an eighth of the Cleveland Herald for $25,000, & have it so arranged that I can pay for it as I earn the money with my unaided hands. I shall look around a little more, & if I can do no better elsewhere, I shall take it.

I am not worrying about whether you will love my future wife or not—if you know her twenty-four hours & then don't love her, you will accomplish what nobody else has ever succeeded in doing since she was born. She just naturally drops into everybody's affections that comes across her. My prophecy was correct. She said she never could or would love me—but she set herself the task of making a Christian of me. I said she would succeed, but that in the meantime she would unwittingly dig a matrimonial pit & end up tumbling into it—& lo! the prophecy is fulfilled. She was in New York a day or two ago, & George Wiley & his wife Clara know her now. Pump them, if you want to. You shall see her before very long.

Love to all. Affect'ly

Sam.

P.S. Shall be here a week.

～

Harford, Nov. 27/88

Livy Darling, I am grateful—gratefuler than ever before—that you were born, and that your love is mine and our two lives woven and welded together!

SLC.

Birthday wishes from Samuel Clemens to Livy Clemens.

~⁀

Hartford, November 27, 1875

Livy darling,

Six years have gone by since I made my first great success in life and won you, and thirty years have passed since Providence made preparation for that happy success by sending you into the world.

Every day we live together adds to the security of my confidence that we can never any more wish to be separated than that we can ever imagine a regret that we were ever joined. You are dearer to me to-day, my child, than you were upon the last anniversary of this birth-day; you were dearer then than you were a year before—you have grown more and more dear from the first of those anniversaries, and I do not doubt that this precious progression will continue on to the end.

Let us look forward to the coming anniversaries, with their age and their gray hairs without fear and without depression, trusting and believing that the love we bear each other will be sufficient to make them blessed.

So, with abounding affection for you and our babies, I hail this day that brings you matronly grace and dignity of three decades!

Always Yours,
S.L.C.

~⁀

Anniversaries

What ought to be done to the man who invented the celebrating of anniversaries? Mere killing would be too light. Anniversaries are very well up to a certain point, while one's babies are in the process of growing up: they are joy-flags that make gay the road and prove progress; and one looks down the fluttering rank with pride. Then presently one notices that the flagstaffs are in process of a mysterious change of some sort—change of shape. Yes, they are turning into milestones. They are marking something lost now, not gained. From that time on it were best to suppress taking notice of anniversaries.

—Notebook, 1896

Livy's Death

June 5, 1904, Italy

In his notebook that night he wrote:

At a quarter past 9 this evening she that was the life of my life passed to the relief & the peace of death after as months of unjust & unearned suffering. I first saw her near 37 years ago, & now I have looked upon her face for the last time.

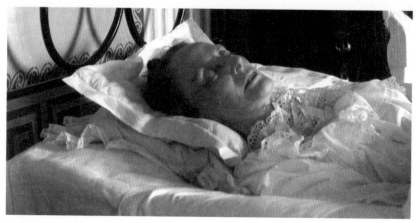

Olivia "Livy" Langdon Clemens on her deathbed. Photograph by daughter Jean Clemens.

Oh, so unexpected! . . . I was full of remorse for things done & said in these 34 years of married life that hurt Livy's heart.

~

Twain wrote to friends William Dean Howells and Joseph Twichell:

How sweet she was in death, how young, how beautiful, how like her dear girlish self of thirty years ago, not a gray hair showing!

This rejuvenescence was noticeable within two hours after her death; & when I went down again (2.30) it was complete. In all that night & all that day she never noticed my caressing hand—it seemed strange.

~

To Howells he recalled the closing scene:

I bent over her & looked in her face & I think I spoke—I was surprised & troubled that she did not notice me. Then we understood & our hearts broke. How poor we are to-day!

But how thankful I am that her persecutions are ended! I would not call her back if I could.

Family

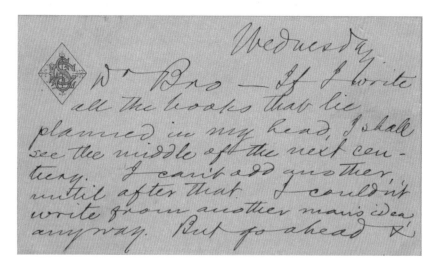

Orion Clemens

To his brother Orion:

Wednesday

Dear Bro

If I write all the books planed in my head, I shall see the middle of the next century. I can't add another, until after that. I couldn't write from another man's idea, anyway. But you go ahead.

Jane Clemens

To Jane Lampton Clemens

Hartford, 23d.

My Dear Mother:

Orion wrote me that he was writing a story—& sent me 3 or 4 disconnected paragraphs bitten out of it here & there, as specimens. I wrote him that this story seemed to promise quite fairly. So it did—but from a lot of extracts which I have since received I begin to fear it is going to be only a wandering, object-less, motiveless imitation of the rampaging French lunatic, Jules Verne.

I *saw*, in the first place, that he was walking gaily along, *exactly* in the French-man's footsteps, & with the air of a man who wasn't aware that there was anything to be ashamed of about it,—but I didn't make any objection, since the thing was but a sketch. But behold, it is to be a book, as I understand you! Well, even now I won't object, provided he either does one of two things: publish it anonymously, or make it a satire upon Verne & his frenzies.

To imitate an author, even in a sketch, is not an elevated thing to do; to imitate him to the extent of an entire book is such an offense against good morals, good taste & good manners,—I might say even decency—that I should very much hate to see the family name to such a production.

Twain's letter to his mother, Jane Clemens.

Orion sends his hero down Symmes's Hole into the interior of the earth; their his compass is wonderfully reversed; they he meets & talks with a very gentlemanly gorilla; he sees & elaborately describes a pterodactyl, &c &c. Orion writes me that one of *Verne's* heroes visits the interior of the earth, (through a volcano;) his compass is wonderfully reversed; he meets a gorilla; he sees a pterodactyl, &c/ &c.

Can you imagine a sane man deliberately proposing to retain these things & print them, while they already exist in another man's book?—his justification being that he treats them differently & more elaborately than the other man did!

Well, Orion is absolutely destitute of originality, wherefore he must imitate; there is no help for it; so, let him go ahead & imitate Verne/. But mind you, he has an opportunity to do a very delicious & bran-new thing—an original thing, a thing credentialed with a *raison d'etre*, & a very welcome thing to a Verne-cursed world waithal—i.e., *burlesque Verne & his writings.*

I have so written him. If he does this (& does it well), his book will deserve life & respect; but if it remains as it now is, a mere servile imitation of Verne, it will deserve only to be burned by the hangman.

Orion can't do either book *well*; but it would be better to fail in the burlesque than succeed in the imitation. But mind you, a rather poor travesty of Verne ought to be kindly received; & goodness knows ~~that~~ there are few easier tasks in the world than to travesty M. Verne.

Our going to Europe is decidedly uncertain; but we expect to sail 11th April; in which case I shall expect to see you in Fredonia ~~a week or so befo~~ before that—I don't know just what date.

With love to you all—

Affly

Sam

All well here.

Children

Babies

A baby is an inestimable blessing and bother.

—Letter to Annie Webster, 1876

∽

At a banquet in Chicago given by the army of the Tennessee to their first commander, General U. S. Grant, November, 1879 on the fifteenth regular toast was "The Babies—as they comfort us in our sorrows, let us not forget them in our festivities." Twain responded:

I like that. We have not all had the good fortune to be ladies. We have not all been generals, or poets, or statesmen; but when the toast works down to the babies, we stand on common ground. It is a shame that for a thousand years the world's banquets have utterly ignored the baby, as if he didn't amount to anything. If you will stop and think a minute—if you will go back fifty or one hundred years to your early married life and recontemplate your first baby—you will remember that he amounted to a great deal, and even something over. You soldiers all know that when the little fellow arrived at family headquarters you had to hand in your resignation. He took entire command. You became his lackey, his mere body servant, and you had to stand around, too. He was not a commander who made allowances for time, distance, weather, or anything else. You had to execute his order whether it was possible or not. And there was only one form of marching in his manual of tactics, and that was the double-quick. He treated you with every sort of insolence and disrespect, and the bravest of you didn't dare to say a word. You could face the death-storm at Donelson and Vicksburg, and give back blow for blow; but when he clawed your whiskers, and pulled your hair, and twisted your nose, you had to take it. When the thunders of war were sounding in your ears you set your faces toward the batteries, and advanced with steady tread; but when he turned on the terrors of his war-whoop you advanced in the other direction, and mighty glad of the chance, too. When he called for soothing-syrup, did you venture to throw out any side remarks about certain services being unbecoming an officer and a gentleman? No. You got up and got it. When he ordered his pap-bottle and it was not warm, did you talk back? Not you. You went to work and warmed it. You even descended so far in your menial office as to take a suck at that warm, insipid stuff yourself, to see if it was right—three parts water to one of milk, a touch of sugar to modify the colic, and a drop of peppermint to kill those hiccoughs. I can taste that stuff yet. And how many things you learned as you went along! Sentimental young folks still take stock in that beautiful old saying that when the baby smiles in his sleep, it is because the angels are whispering to him. Very pretty, but too thin—simply wind on the stomach, my friends. If the baby proposed to take a walk at his usual hour, two o'clock in the morning, didn't you rise up promptly and remark, with a mental addition which would not improve a Sunday-school book much, that that was the very thing you were about to propose yourself? Oh! you were under good discipline, and as you went fluttering up and down the room in your undress uniform, you not only prattled undignified baby-talk, but even tuned up your martial voices and tried to sing!—"Rock-a-by baby in the treetop," for instance. What a spectacle for an Army of the Tennessee! And what an affliction for the neighbors, too; for it is not everybody within a mile around that likes military music at three in the morning. And when you had been keeping this sort of thing up two or three hours, and your little velvet-head intimated that nothing suited him like exercise and noise, what did you do? ["Go on!"] You simply went on until you dropped in the last ditch. The idea that a baby doesn't amount to anything! Why, one baby is just a house and a front yard full by itself. One baby can furnish more business than you and your whole Interior Department can attend to. He is enterprising, irrepressible, brimful of lawless activities. Do what you please, you can't make him stay on the reservation. Sufficient unto the day is one baby. As long as you are in your right mind don't you ever pray for twins. Twins amount to a permanent riot. And there ain't any real difference between triplets and an insurrection.

Yes, it was high time for a toast-master to recognize the importance of the babies. Think what is in store for the present crop! Fifty years from now we shall all be dead, I trust, and then this flag, if it still survive (and let us hope it may), will be floating over a Republic numbering 200,000,000 souls, according to the settled laws of our increase. Our present schooner of State will have grown into a political leviathan—a Great Eastern. The cradled babies of to-day will be on deck. Let them be well trained, for we are going to leave a big contract on their hands. Among the three or four million cradles now rocking in the land are some which this nation would preserve for ages as sacred things, if we could know which ones they are. In one of them cradles the unconscious Farragut of the future is at this moment teething—think of it!—and putting in a world of dead earnest, unarticulated, but perfectly justifiable profanity over it, too. In another the future renowned astronomer is blinking at the shining Milky Way with but a languid interest—poor little chap!—and wondering what has become of that other one they call the wet-nurse. In another the future great historian is lying—and doubtless will continue to lie until his earthly mission is ended. In another the future President is busying himself with no profounder problem of state than what the mischief has become of his hair so early; and in a mighty array of other cradles there are now some 60,000 future office-seekers, getting ready to furnish him occasion to grapple with that same old problem a second time. And in still one more cradle, somewhere under the flag, the future illustrious commander-in-chief of the American armies is so little burdened with his approaching grandeurs and responsibilities as to be giving his whole strategic mind at this moment to trying to find out some way to get his big toe into his mouth—an achievement which, meaning no disrespect, the illustrious guest of this evening turned his entire attention to some fifty-six years ago; and if the child is but a prophecy of the man, there are mighty few who will doubt that he succeeded.

Susy Clemens

Susy wrote of her father, when she was 13 years old, "Papa's appearance has been described many times, but very incorrectly. He has beautiful gray hair, not any too thick or any too long, but just right; a Roman nose, which greatly improves the beauty of his features; kind blue eyes and a small mustache. He has a wonderfully shaped head and profile. He has a very good figure—in short, he is an extraordinarily fine looking man. All his features are perfect, except that he hasn't extraordinary teeth. His complexion is very fair, and he doesn't ware a beard. He is a very good man and a very funny one. He has got a temper, but we all of us have in this family. He is the loveliest man I ever saw or ever hope to see—and oh, so absent-minded. He does tell perfectly delightful stories. Clara and I used to sit on each arm of his chair and listen while he told us stories about the pictures on the wall.

Twain with his daughter Susy playing playing Hero and Leander.

~⌒

Twain wrote this many years after Susy had passed away while still a young woman.

When Susy was thirteen, and was a slender little maid with plaited tails of copper-tinged brown hair down her back, and was perhaps the busiest bee in the household hive, by reason of the manifold studies, health exercises, and recreations she had to attend to, she secretly, and of her own motion, and out of love, added another task to her labors—the writing of a biography of me. She did this work in her bedroom at night, and kept her record hidden. After a little, the mother discovered it and filched it, and let me see it; then told Susy what she had done, and how pleased I was and how proud. I remember that time with a deep pleasure. I had had compliments before, but none that touched me like this; none that could approach it for value in my eyes. It has kept that place always since. I have had no compliment, no praise, no tribute from any source, that was so precious to me as this one was and still is. As I read it now, after all these many years, it is still a king's message to me, and brings me the same dear surprise it brought me then—with the pathos added of the thought that the eager and hasty hand that sketched it and scrawled it will not touch mine again—and I feel as the humble and unexpectant must feel when their eyes fall upon the edict that raises them to the ranks of the noble."

~⌒

She was a magazine of feelings, & they were of all kinds & of all shades of force; & she was so volatile, as a little child, that sometimes the whole battery came into play in the short compass of a day. She was full of life, full of activity, full of fire, her waking hours were a crowding & hurrying procession of enthusiasms . . . Joy, sorrow, anger, remorse, storm, sunshine, rain, darkness—they were all there: They came in a moment, & they were gone as quickly.

In all things she was intense: in her this characteristic was not a mere glow, dispensing warmth, but a consuming fire.

—From Twain's unpublished manuscript, *A Family Sketch*. His eldest daughter and muse, Susy died from spinal meningitis at age twenty four in 1896.

Clara Clemens, the second of Twain's three daughters, was born in 1874.

Clara Clemens

Below is Twain's letter to Reverend Joseph Twitchell and his wife announcing the birth of daughter Clara Clemens. Twitchell married Twain and Olivia and was Twain's closest friend for over 40 years.

ELMIRA, June 11

My Dear Old Joe and Harmony,—The baby is here and is the great American Giantess—weighing 7 ³/₄ pounds. We had to wait a good long time for her, but she was full compensation when she did come.

The labor pains fooled along during the evening, after a fashion; became more pronounced at midnight & so continued till 7 AM; then very severe for 15 minutes, & the trouble was over. Mrs. Gleason & Della came up early in the evening & went to bed right away, up stairs, & neither of them were ever called till 15 minutes before the babe was born. Livy don't call for people till she needs them. She waltzed through this ordeal, walking the floor & sewing baby clothes in the bravest possible way. And even I was cool—slept a good part of the time. I am ashamed of that, but I couldn't keep my eyes open. And besides, this baby has fooled along so much that I hadn't much confidence in it. It is an admirable child, though, & has intellect. It puts its fingers against its brow & thinks. It was born with a caul, & so of course possesses the gift of second sight.

The Modoc was delighted with it, and gave it her doll at once. There is nothing selfish about the Modoc. She is fascinated with the new baby.

The Modoc rips and tears around out doors, most of the time, and consequently is as hard as a pine knot and as brown as an Indian. She is bosom friend to all the ducks, chickens, turkeys and guinea hens on the place. Yesterday as she marched along the winding path that leads up the hill through the red clover beds to the summer-house, there was a long procession of these fowls stringing contentedly after her, led by a stately rooster who can look over the Modoc's head. The devotion of these vassals has been purchased with daily largess of Indian meal, and so the Modoc, attended by her bodyguard, moves in state wherever she goes.

Susie Crane has built the loveliest study for me, you ever saw. It is octagonal, with a peaked roof, each octagon filled with a spacious window, and it sits perched in complete isolation on top of an elevation that commands leagues of valley and city and retreating ranges of distant blue hills. It is a cosy nest, with just room in it for a sofa and a table and three or four chairs—and when the storms sweep down the remote valley and the lightning flashes above the hills beyond, and the rain beats upon the roof over my head, imagine the luxury of it! It stands 500 feet above the valley and 2 $1/_2$ miles from it.

However one must not write all day. We send continents of love to you and yours.

Affectionately

MARK.

∽

Clara Clemens.

The *New York Times*, June 14, 1908

TWAIN'S DAUGHTER TALKS ABOUT HIM

Miss Clara Clemens Says It Is Hard to Have a Genius for a Father.

TAKEN FOR BUFFALO BILL

"Father Wears White Suit to Remind Him of Bed," Says Miss Clara.

Special Correspondence.

LONDON, June 6.—Miss Clara Clemens, daughter of Mark Twain, who is the possessor of a rich contralto voice, has made her debut in this country as a concert singer at the Queen's Hall. She will give a recital, with Miss Marie Nichols, violinist, and Mr. Wark, pianist, at the Bechstein Hall on June 16.

Miss Clemens inherits her father's sense of humor, and in an article published in the *London Express* she tells of the tribulations which face the daughter of a celebrity.

Miss Clemens writes as follows:

"I have just come to the conclusion that things want readjusting in this old world of ours.

"Need I mention the fact that I refer to the glaring injustice of having to go about labeled 'Mark Twain's daughter' when I am doing my best to pursue a musical career?

"Father, is, of course, a genius—and that is what makes me so tired. My fatigue is directly caused by the incessant strain—prolonged over some years and induced by trying to find a secret hiding place when I can shroud my identity and be sure of a really comfortable bed.

"I have a mind to scour Europe for such a place, and when I have found it to take to bed for, say, a couple of years, and arise—a genius. For the bed habit is the recipe of father's success.

"While I have been tiring myself out in an endeavor to rise to the heights as anybody else's daughter he has just lain in bed and thought things and got out of bed now and then to loaf around on a lecture tour or tramp lazily through Europe. That's why I'm looking for a really comfortable bed. Genius is the art of taking—to bed.

"Father called me a genius once when I was about 15, and, although I guess he was just fooling me, I am not likely to forget the occasion. He had gone on a lecture tour with Mr. George W. Cable, the Southern writer, and during his absence we girls—my two sisters and myself—arranged some theatricals as a surprise for him on his return to our home at Hartford, Conn.

"The piece we selected was 'The Prince and the Pauper,' and father pretended to enjoy it just as much as we did, and, as I said before, he informed me that I was a genius. Shortly after that memorable night I came over to Europe.

"Then my troubles began. They began in Berlin, where father, thanks to no violent physical efforts on his part, is wonderfully popular. When I was not studying hard at my music I would go out occasionally to little functions, where I would sit in a corner and be completely ignored by all assembled until some foolish person whispered to another: 'I believe that's Mark Twain's daughter in the corner.'

"Then the guests would arise as one man and swoop down upon me, and expect me to be 'bright' and amusing after a hard day's work. These, of course, were the occasions when my august parent was not present. At social gatherings graced by his presence my existence was on the level of a footstool—always unnecessary object in a crowded room. Father, fresh from bed, would completely flood the place with his talk. And yet the secret of his popularity never occurred to me at the time.

"But father has had much to endure, too. The last time he was in London he was assailed in Regent Street by a venerable old lady, who shook him cordially by the hand and repeated fervently: 'I have always wanted to shake hands with you.' My father, who was feeling particularly brilliant after a long day's rest, was much moved, and responded gratefully: 'So you know who I am, madam?' 'Of course I do,' answered the old lady with enthusiasm, 'You're Buffalo Bill!'

"Father's white suit is another of my trials. I have always believed that the reason he took to wearing it is that it soothed him and reminded him of bed. His white hair, too, can be explained scientifically. The explanation can be found in any well-equipped natural history museum. The hares and the bird and the foxes in the arctic regions are of a dazzling whiteness when the snow covers their haunts. Father is, therefore, a striking example of what is known as sympathetic coloration. His hair has gradually assumed the color of his pillow.

"But I must do father bare justice. In spite of his lying-in-bed habit he can be impetuous both in speech and action. When he gets too impetuous in speech I rise to the occasion and answer him back.

"Last Winter I was to sing at an important evening concert on the other side, and the entire family had been invited to attend a function in the afternoon, Father, being unmusical, could not understand that I should have been unfit to sing if I had chattered after his own fashion all the afternoon. And so I coaxed him to go and represent the family. At first he objected strongly, but finally, in a burst of impetuosity, he said: 'Yes, Clara, I'll go to that reception. I'd go to _____ for you.'

"To which I thoughtfully replied: 'If ever, father, you should be called upon to go there, please go labeled "I'm for Clara." "

STORMFIELD
REDDING
CONNECTICUT

Hamilton, Feb. 21/10

Clara dear, your darling letter of the 3d reached me a couple of hours ago & gave me peace & deep pleasure. Yesterday I dictated a scrawl to you, for I couldn't very well write, for I had been laid up a few days with bronchitis & was just out of bed & feeling rusty and incompetent! I caught that cold from a person

An excerpt from a letter from Twain to his daughter Clara in 1910, a few months before his death. Clara was his only surviving daughter; Jean had died a month before.

Hamilton, Feb. 21/10

Clara dear, your darling letter of the 3rd reached me a couple of hours ago + gave me peace + deep pleasure. Yesterday I dictated a scrawl to you, for I couldn't very well write for I had been laid up a few days with bronchitis + was just out of bed + feeling rusty and incompetent! I caught that cold from a person who had just brought it from America. I knew I was in danger, still I took the risk.

Don't you be afraid of making your letters too long—I love to read them: the longer they are, the better. But you must never tire yourself to write me; for that would distress me if I discovered it.

Indeed I *don't* "(*illegible*)" with you because you are married—no, you are nearer + dearer to me now more than ever; of my fair fleet all my ships have gone lent you; you are all my wealth; but while I have you I am still rich.

Twain's youngest daughter, Jean, surrounded by her
older sisters Clara and Susy, 1880.

~

Jean Clemens

Jean was so full of life and energy that she was constantly is danger of over
taxing her strength. Every morning she was in the saddle by half past seven,
and off to the station for her mail. She examined the letters and I distributed
them: some to her, some to Mr. Paine, the others to the stenographer and
myself. She dispatched her share and then mounted her horse again and went
around superintending her farm and her poultry the rest of the day. Sometimes
she played billiards with me after dinner, but she was usually too tired to play,
and went early to bed.

—*Mark Twain, A Biography*

Jean Clemens passed away tragically at the age of 29. The New York Times *reported the event.*

The *New York Times,* December 25, 1909

MISS JEAN CLEMENS FOUND DEAD IN BATH

She Was Overcome by an Epileptic Seizure an Hour Before Her Body Was Discovered.
HAD PLANNED A HAPPY XMAS
On Wednesday Her Father Helped Her Trim a Christmas Tree—Mark Twain Now All Alone.

Special to the *New York Times.*

REDDING, Conn., Dec. 24.—Miss Jean Clemens, youngest daughter of Mark Twain, was found dead in the bathtub at Stormfield, Mr. Clemens's country home near here, early this morning. Her body lay submerged in water when the young woman's maid discovered it, shortly after sunrise.

An attack of epilepsy, to which Miss Clemens had been subject for many years, is believed to have rendered her unconscious while she was taking her morning bath, with the result that she drowned in the water of the bath.

Mark Twain, her father, while heartbroken at the blow which has taken away the one daughter who had remained single to be his mainstay in his declining years, is bearing up bravely under the shock, and says that, in spite of his sorrow, he cannot help feeling glad that death came to his daughter at home.

He had feared for many months that she might be stricken while on horseback, far away on the lonely country roads, and that she might be mangled beneath the horse's hoofs. He had

Twain with his secretary, Isabel Lyon (left), his daughter Jean (center), and Jean's dog, Propsero.

many warnings that his daughter might be stricken down. Less than a month ago she suffered a violent attack of epilepsy, and for several years she had been under the constant care of an attendant.

For several months Miss Clemens was in a sanitarium, but in April last had come to Stormfield in order to be her father's housekeeper and to help him in his literary work as his secretary.

Had Prepared for a Jolly Christmas.

Miss Clemens herself had no thought of death. Several days ago she invited one of her girl friends in New York to come to Stormfield to spend the holidays and elaborate plans had been made for a jolly Christmas.

This friend had been instructed to come today on the Pittsfield express, and Mark Twain had arranged with the New York, New Haven & Hartford officials to have the train stop at Redding, which is a flag station, at 5:19 this afternoon. A telegram was sent to her this morning informing her of what had happened and telling her not to come, but she evidently did not get the message, for she arrived according to arrangement, and was driven at once to Stormfield.

Miss Clemens and her father were up late last night discussing plans for Christmas Day and talking of the future. This morning about 6:30 o'clock Katie, one of the maids at Stormfield, who usually accompanied Miss Clemens wherever she went, rapped on her door and asked if she were ready to dress.

"No, Katie, you can wait an hour, for I am going to lie in bed and read," said Miss Clemens through the door. She often did this in the morning before aris-ing, so the maid went away. An hour later she returned to the bedroom, which is on the second floor of Stormfield. Miss Clemens was not there.

Her Father Hears the News.

Katie went at once to the bathroom. One glance inside and the maid screamed in terror. She ran to the door of Mr. Clemens's room, who was still in bed, and told him that he had better come at once. Mr. Clemens hastily donned a bathrobe.

The servants were grouped around the bathroom door uncertain what to do. In a few minutes the body had been lifted from the tub, and a telephone call brought Dr. Ernest H. Smith, the family physician and County Medical Examiner, to the Clemens home. For a long time the doctor tried by artificial respiration to bring the young woman back to life, but it was useless. She had been dead at least an hour before he arrived, said the doctor later.

Soon after Dr. Smith arrived Mr. Clemens telephoned to Alfred [sic] Bigelow Paine, who has been assisting the author in writing his biography and who lives not far from Stormfield.

Mr. Paine and his wife were soon at the house and did what they could for Mr. Clemens. The news of Miss Clemens's death spread rapidly through the countryside, and there were many messages of sympathy and offers of help over the telephone. Many of Mark Twain's neighbors also called in person, and soon the reporters arrived. Mr. Clemens met them and told the sad story of his daughter's death.

"My daughter, Jean Clemens, passed from this life suddenly this morning at 7:30 o'clock," he said.

"All the last half of her life she was an epileptic, but she grew better latterly. For the past two years we considered her practically well, but she was not allowed to be entirely free. Her maid, who has served us twenty-eight years, was always with her when she went to New York on shopping excursions and such things. She had very few convulsions in the past two years and those she had were not violent.

"At 7:30 this morning a maid went to her room to see why she did not come down to her breakfast, and found her in her bathtub drowned. It means that she had a convulsion and could not get out.

"She had been leading a very active life.

"She spent the greater part of her time looking after a farm which I bought for her, and she did much of my secretarial work besides.

Her Last Talk With Her Father.

"Last night she and I chatted later than usual in the library, and she told me all her plans about the housekeeping, for she was also my housekeeper. I said everything was going so smoothly that I thought I would make another trip to Bermuda in February, and she said put it off till March and she and her maid would go with me. So we made that arrangement.

"But she is gone, poor child.

"She was all I had left, except Clara, who married Mr. Gabrilowitsch lately, and has just arrived in Europe."

On Boys

We think boys are rude, unsensitive animals but it is not so in all cases. Each boy has one or two sensitive spots, and if you can find out where they are located you have only to touch them and you can scorch him as with fire.

—Mark Twain's Autobiography

Original illustration of the characters Tom Sawyer, Huck Finn, and Joe Harper from *The Adventures of Tom Sawyer.*

This letter to an unnamed neighbor differs slightly from the version published by Albert Bigelow Paine in Mark Twain's Letters, *Vol. 2, p. 702.*

14 West 10th Street.

Nov. 30 [1900]

Dear Madam:

I know I ought to respect my duty & perform it, but I am weak & faithless where boys are concerned, & I can't help secretly approving pretty bad & noisy ones, though I do object to the kind that ring door-bells. My family try to get me to stop the boys from holding conventions on the front steps, but I basely shirk out of it, because I think the boys enjoy it. And I believe I enjoy it a little, too, because it pesters the family.

My wife has been complaining to me this evening about the boys on the front steps, & under compulsion I have made some promises. But I am very forgetful, now that I am older & my sense of duty getting spongy.

Very truly yours,

S. L. Clemens

Books for Children

In January 1887, Charles D. Crane, pastor of the Methodist Episcopal Church in Maine, wrote to Twain asking for book recommendations for a boy and a girl. He also asked Twain to name his favorite authors.

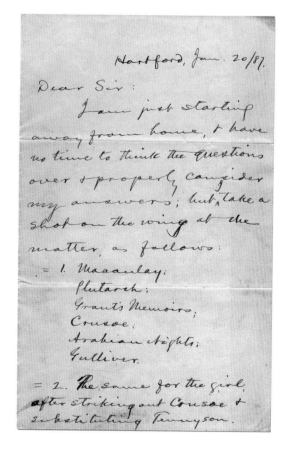

Hartford, Jan. 20/87.

Dear Sir:

I am just starting away from home, & have no time to think the questions over & properly consider my answers; but I take a shot on the wing at the matter, as follows:

1. Macaulay;
   Plutarch;
   Grant's Memoirs;
   Crusoe;
   Arabian Nights;
   Gulliver.

2. The same for the girl,
   after striking out out Crusoe
   & substituting Tennyson.

I can't answer No. 3 in this sudden way. When one is going to choose twelve authors, for better for worse, forsaking fathers & mothers to cling unto them & unto them alone, until death shall them part, there is an awfulness about the responsibility that makes marriage with one mere individual & divorcible woman a sacrament sodden with levity by comparison.

In my list I know I should put Shakspeare [sic]; & Browning; & Carlyle (French Revolution only); Sir Thomas Malory (King Aurthur); Parkman's Histories (a hundred of them if there were so many); Arabian Nights; Johnson (Boswell's), because I like to see that complacent old gasometer listen to himself talk; Jowett's Plato; & "B.B." (a book which I wrote some years ago, not for publication but just for my own private reading.)

I should be sure of these; & I could add the other three—but I should want to hold the opportunity open a few years, so as to make no mistake.

Truly Yours

S. L. CLEMENS

How to Make History Dates Work for Children

This essay stemmed from the summer of 1883—when Twain was trying to create an easy way for his daughters to remember the English monarchs and the dates they ruled which also happens to be when he was working on Huckleberry Finn. *He frequently used pictorial devices in place of notes when he delivered his platform speeches and thought the same methods could be used when teaching children history. Written in 1889, it first appeared in* Harper's Monthly Magazine *in December 1914 with Twain's own illustrations.*

These chapters are for children, and I shall try to make the words large enough to command respect. In the hope that you are listening, and that you have confidence in me, I will proceed. Dates are difficult things to acquire; and after they are acquired it is difficult to keep them in the head. But they are very valuable. They are like the cattle-pens of a ranch—they shut in the several brands of historical cattle, each within its own fence, and keep them from getting mixed together. Dates are hard to remember because they consist of figures;

figures are monotonously unstriking in appearance, and they don't take hold, they form no pictures, and so they give the eye no chance to help. Pictures are the thing. Pictures can make dates stick. They can make nearly anything stick—particularly IF YOU MAKE THE PICTURES YOURSELF. Indeed, that is the great point—make the pictures YOURSELF. I know about this from experience. Thirty years ago I was delivering a memorized lecture every night, and every night I had to help myself with a page of notes to keep from getting myself mixed. The notes consisted of beginnings of sentences, and were eleven in number, and they ran something like this:

"IN THAT REGION THE WEATHER—"

"AT THAT TIME IT WAS A CUSTOM—"

"BUT IN CALIFORNIA ONE NEVER HEARD—"

Eleven of them. They initialed the brief divisions of the lecture and protected me against skipping. But they all looked about alike on the page; they formed no picture; I had them by heart, but I could never with certainty remember the order of their succession; therefore I always had to keep those notes by me and look at them every little while. Once I mislaid them; you will not be able to imagine the terrors of that evening. I now saw that I must invent some other protection. So I got ten of the initial letters by heart in their proper order—I, A, B, and so on—and I went on the platform the next night with these marked in ink on my ten finger-nails. But it didn't answer. I kept track of the figures for a while; then I lost it, and after that I was never quite sure which finger I had used last. I couldn't lick off a letter after using it, for while that would have made success certain it also would have provoked too much curiosity. There was curiosity enough without that. To the audience I seemed more interested in my fingernails than I was in my subject; one or two persons asked me afterward what was the matter with my hands.

It was now that the idea of pictures occurred to me; then my troubles passed away. In two minutes I made six pictures with a pen, and they did the work of the eleven catch-sentences, and did it perfectly. I threw the pictures away as soon as they were made, for I was sure I could shut my eyes and see them any time. That was a quarter of a century ago; the lecture vanished out of my head more than twenty years ago, but I would rewrite it from the pictures—for they remain. Here are three of them:

The first one is a haystack—below it a rattlesnake—and it told me where to begin to talk ranch-life in Carson Valley. The second one told me where to begin the talk about a strange and violent wind that used to burst upon Carson City from the Sierra Nevadas every afternoon at two o'clock and try to blow the town away. The third picture, as you easily perceive, is lightning; its duty was to remind me when it was time to begin to talk about San Francisco weather, where there IS no lightning—nor thunder, either—and it never failed me.

I will give you a valuable hint. When a man is making a speech and you are to follow him don't jot down notes to speak from, jot down PICTURES. It is awkward and embarrassing to have to keep referring to notes; and besides it breaks up your speech and makes it ragged and non-coherent; but you can tear up your pictures as soon as you have made them—they will stay fresh and strong in your memory in the order and sequence in which you scratched them down. And many will admire to see what a good memory you are furnished with, when perhaps your memory is not any better than mine.

Sixteen years ago when my children were little creatures the governess was trying to hammer some primer histories into their heads. Part of this fun—if you like to call it that—consisted in the memorizing of the accession dates of the thirty-seven personages who had ruled England from the Conqueror down. These little people found it a bitter, hard contract. It was all dates, and all looked alike, and they wouldn't stick. Day after day of the summer vacation dribbled by, and still the kings held the fort; the children couldn't conquer any six of them.

With my lecture experience in mind I was aware that I could invent some way out of the trouble with pictures, but I hoped a way could be found which would let them romp in the open air while they learned the kings. I found it, and they mastered all the monarchs in a day or two.

The idea was to make them SEE the reigns with their eyes; that would be a large help. We were at the farm then. From the house-porch the grounds sloped gradually down to the lower fence and rose on the right to the high ground where my small work-den stood. A carriage-road wound through the grounds and up the hill. I staked it out with the English monarchs, beginning with the Conqueror, and you could stand on the porch and clearly see every reign and its length, from the Conquest down to Victoria, then in the forty-sixth year of her reign—EIGHT HUNDRED AND SEVENTEEN YEARS OF English history under your eye at once!

English history was an unusually live topic in America just then. The world had suddenly realized that while it was not noticing the Queen had passed Henry VIII., passed Henry VI. and Elizabeth, and gaining in length every day. Her reign had entered the list of the long ones; everybody was interested now—it was watching a race. Would she pass the long Edward? There was a possibility of it. Would she pass the long Henry? Doubtful, most people said. The long George? Impossible! Everybody said it. But we have lived to see her leave him two years behind.

I measured off 817 feet of the roadway, a foot representing a year, and at the beginning and end of each reign I drove a three-foot white-pine stake in the turf by the roadside and wrote the name and dates on it. Abreast the middle of the porch-front stood a great granite flower-vase overflowing with a cataract of bright-yellow flowers—I can't think of their name. The vase of William the Conqueror. We put his name on it and his accession date, 1066. We started from that and measured off twenty-one feet of the road, and drove William Rufus's state; then thirteen feet and drove the first Henry's stake; then thirty-five feet and drove Stephen's; then nineteen feet, which brought us just past the summer-house on the left; then we staked out thirty-five, ten, and seventeen for the second Henry and Richard and John; turned the curve and entered upon just what was needed for Henry III.—a level, straight stretch of fifty-six feet of road without a crinkle in it. And it lay exactly in front of the house, in the middle of the grounds. There couldn't have been a better place for that long reign; you could stand on the porch and see those two wide-apart stakes almost with your eyes shut. (Fig. 2.)

That isn't the shape of the road—I have bunched it up like that to save room. The road had some great curves in it, but their gradual sweep was such that they were no mar to history. No, in our road one could tell at a glance who was who by the size of the vacancy between stakes— with LOCALITY to help, of course.

[2]

Although I am away off here in a Swedish village [Summer of 1899] and those stakes did not stand till the snow came, I can see them today as plainly as ever; and whenever I think of an English monarch his stakes rise before me of their own accord and I notice the large or small space which he takes up on our road. Are your kings spaced off in your mind? When you think of Richard III. and of James II. do the durations of their reigns seem about alike to you? It isn't so to me; I always notice that there's a foot's difference. When you think of Henry III. do you see a great long stretch of straight road? I do; and just at the end where it joins on to Edward I. I always see a small pear-bush with its green fruit hanging down. When I think of the Commonwealth I see a shady little group of these small saplings which we called the oak parlor; when I think of George III. I see him stretching up the hill, part of him occupied by a flight of stone steps; and I can locate Stephen to an inch when he comes into my mind, for he just filled the stretch which went by the summer-house. Victoria's reign reached almost to my study door on the first little summit; there's sixteen feet to be added now; I believe that that would carry it to a big pine-tree that was shattered by some lightning one summer when it was trying to hit me.

We got a good deal of fun out of the history road; and exercise, too. We trotted the course from the conqueror to the study, the children calling out the names, dates, and length of reigns as we passed the stakes, going a good gait along the long reigns, but slowing down when we came upon people like Mary and Edward VI., and the short Stuart and Plantagenet, to give time to get in the statistics. I offered prizes, too—apples. I threw one as far as I could send it, and the child that first shouted the reign it fell in got the apple.

The children were encouraged to stop locating things as being "over by the arbor," or "in the oak parlor," or "up at the stone steps," and say instead that the things were in Stephen, or in the Commonwealth, or in George III. They got the habit without trouble. To have the long road mapped out with such exactness was a great boon for me, for I had the habit of leaving books and other articles lying around everywhere, and had not previously been able to definitely name the place, and so had often been obliged to go to fetch them myself, to save time and failure; but now I could name the reign I left them in, and send the children.

Next I thought I would measure off the French reigns, and peg them alongside the English ones, so that we could always have contemporaneous French history under our eyes as we went our English rounds. We pegged them down to the Hundred Years' War, then threw the idea aside, I do not now remember why. After that we made the English pegs fence in European and American history as well as English, and that answered very well. English and alien poets, statesmen, artists, heroes, battles, plagues, cataclysms, revolutions—we shoveled them all into the English fences according to their dates. Do you understand? We gave Washington's birth to George II.'s pegs and his death to George III.'s; George II. got the Lisbon earthquake and George III. the Declaration of Independence. Goethe, Shakespeare, Napoleon, Savonarola, Joan of Arc, the French Revolution, the Edict of Nantes, Clive, Wellington, Waterloo, Plassey, Patay, Cowpens, Saratoga, the Battle of the Boyne, the invention of the logarithms, the microscope, the steam-engine, the telegraph—anything and everything all over the world—we dumped it all in among the English pegs according to it date and regardless of its nationality.

If the road-pegging scheme had not succeeded I should have lodged the kings in the children's heads by means of pictures—that is, I should have tried. It might have failed, for the pictures could only be effective WHEN MADE BY THE PUPIL; not the master, for it is the work put upon the drawing that makes the drawing stay in the memory, and my children were too little to make drawings at that time. And, besides, they had no talent for art, which is strange, for in other ways they are like me.

But I will develop the picture plan now, hoping that you will be able to use it. It will come good for indoors when the weather is bad and one cannot go outside and peg a road. Let us imagine that the kings are a procession, and that they have come out of the Ark and down Ararat for exercise and are now starting back again up the zigzag road. This will bring several of them into view at once, and each zigzag will represent the length of a king's reign.

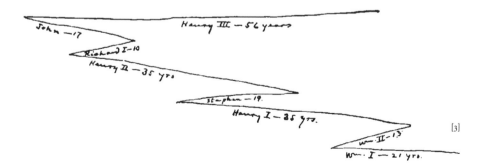

[3]

And so on. You will have plenty of space, for by my project you will use the parlor wall. You do not mark on the wall; that would cause trouble. You only attach bits of paper to it with pins or thumb-tacks. These will leave no mark.

Take your pen now, and twenty-one pieces of white paper, each two inches square, and we will do the twenty-one years of the Conqueror's reign. On each square draw a picture of a whale and write the dates and term of service. We choose the whale for several reasons: its name and William's begin with the same letter; it is the biggest fish that swims, and William is the most conspicuous figure in English history in the way of a landmark; finally, a whale is about the easiest thing to draw. By the time you have drawn twenty-one wales [sic] and written "William I.—1066–1087– twenty-one years" twenty-one times, those details will be your property; you cannot dislodge them from your memory with anything but dynamite. I will make a sample for you to copy: (Fig. 4).

William I
1066 —1087
21 years

[4]

I have got his chin up too high, but that is no matter; he is looking for Harold. It may be that a whale hasn't that fin up there on his back, but I do not remember; and so, since there is a doubt, it is best to err on the safe side. He looks better, anyway, than he would without it.

Be very careful and ATTENTIVE while you are drawing your first whale from my sample and writing the word and figures under it, so that you will not need to copy the sample any more. Compare your copy with the sample; examine closely; if you find you have got everything right and can shut your eyes and see the picture and call the words and figures, then turn the sample and copy upside down and make the next copy from memory; and also the next and next, and so on, always drawing and writing from memory until you have finished the whole twenty-one. This will take you twenty minutes, or thirty, and by that time you will find that you can make a whale in less time than an unpracticed person can make a sardine; also, up to the time you die you will always be able to furnish William's dates to any ignorant person that inquires after them.

You will now take thirteen pieces of BLUE paper, each two inches square, and do William II. (Fig. 5.)

Make him spout his water forward instead of back-
ward; also make him small, and stick a harpoon in him
and give him that sick look in the eye. Otherwise you
might seem to be continuing the other William, and
that would be confusing and a damage. It is quite right
to make him small; he was only about a No. 11 whale,

or along there somewhere; there wasn't room in him for his father's great spirit.
The barb of that harpoon ought not to show like that, because it is down inside
the whale and ought to be out of sight, but it cannot be helped; if the barb were
removed people would think some one had stuck a whip-stock into the whale.
It is best to leave the barb the way it is, then every one will know it is a harpoon
and attending to business. Remember—draw from the copy only once; make
your other twelve and the inscription from memory.

Now the truth is that whenever you have copied a picture and its inscription
once from my sample and two or three times from memory the details will stay
with you and be hard to forget. After that, if you like, you may make merely the
whale's HEAD and WATER-SPOUT for the Conqueror till you end his reign,
each time SAYING the inscription in place of writing
it; and in the case of William II. make the HARPOON
alone, and say over the inscription each time you do it.
You see, it will take nearly twice as long to do the first set
as it will to do the second, and that will give you a marked
sense of the difference in length of the two reigns.

Next do Henry I. on thirty-five squares of RED paper.
(Fig. 6.)

That is a hen, and suggests Henry by furnishing the first
syllable. When you have repeated the hen and the inscription
until you are perfectly sure of them, draw merely the hen's
head the rest of the thirty-five times, saying over the inscription each time. Thus: (Fig. 7).

You begin to understand how how this procession is going to look when
it is on the wall. First there will be the Conqueror's twenty-one whales and
water-spouts, the twenty-one white squares joined to one another and making
a white stripe three and one- half feet long; the thirteen blue squares of William II. will be joined to that—a blue stripe two feet, two inches long, followed
by Henry's red stripe five feet, ten inches long, and so on. The colored divisions

[8]

will smartly show to the eye the difference in the length of the reigns and impress the proportions on the memory and the understanding. (Fig. 8.)

[9]

Stephen of Blois comes next. He requires nineteen two-inch squares of YELLOW paper. (Fig. 9.)

That is a steer. The sound suggests the beginning of Stephen's name. I choose it for that reason. I can make a better steer than that when I am not excited. But this one will do. It is a good-enough steer for history. The tail is defective, but it only wants straightening out.

Next comes Henry II. Give him thirty-five squares of RED paper. These hens must face west, like the former ones. (Fig. 10.)

This hen differs from the other one. He is on his way to inquire what has been happening in Canterbury.

[10]

Now we arrive at Richard I., called Richard of the Lion-heart because he was a brave fighter and was never so contented as when he was leading crusades in Palestine and neglecting his affairs at home. Give him ten squares of WHITE paper. (Fig. 11).

[11]

That is a lion. His office is to remind you of the lion-hearted Richard. There is something the matter with his legs, but I do not quite know what it is, they do not seem right. I think the hind ones are the most unsatisfactory; the front ones are well enough, though it would be better if they were rights and lefts.

Next comes King John, and he was a poor circumstance. He was called Lackland. He gave his realm to the Pope. Let him have seventeen squares of YELLOW paper. (Fig. 12.)

[12]

That creature is a jamboree. It looks like a trademark, but that is only an accident and not intentional. It is prehistoric and extinct. It used to roam the earth in the Old Silurian times, and lay eggs and catch fish and climb trees and live on fossils; for it was of a mixed breed, which was the fashion then. It was very fierce, and the Old Silurians were afraid of it, but this is a tame one. Physically it has no representative now, but its mind has been transmitted. First I drew it sitting down, but have turned it the other way now because I think it looks more attractive and spirited when one end of it is galloping. I love to think that in this attitude it gives us a pleasant idea of John coming all in a happy excitement to see what the barons have been arranging for him at Runnymede, while the other one gives us an idea of him sitting down to wring his hands and grieve over it.

We now come to Henry III.; RED squares again, of course—fifty-six of them. We must make all the Henrys the same color; it will make their long reigns show up handsomely on the wall. Among all the eight Henrys there were but two short ones. A lucky name, as far as longevity goes. The reigns of six of the Henrys cover 227 years. It might have been well to name all the royal princes Henry, but this was overlooked until it was too late. (Fig. 13.)

[13]

[14]

This is the best one yet. He is on his way (1265) to have a look at the first House of Commons in English history. It was a monumental event, the situation in the House, and was the second great liberty landmark which the century had set up. I have made Henry looking glad, but this was not intentional.

Edward I. comes next; LIGHT-BROWN paper, thirty-five squares. (Fig. 14.)

That is an editor. He is trying to think of a word. He props his feet on a chair, which is the editor's way; then he can think better. I do not care much for this one; his ears are not alike; still, editor suggests the sound of Edward, and he will do. I could make him better if I had a model, but I made this one from memory. But is no particular matter; they all look alike, anyway. They are conceited and troublesome, and don't pay enough. Edward was the first really English king that had yet occupied the throne. The editor in the picture probably looks just as Edward looked when it was first borne in upon him that this was so. His whole attitude expressed gratification and pride mixed with stupefaction and astonishment.

Edward II. now; twenty BLUE squares. (Fig. 15.)

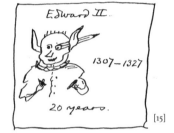

Another editor. That thing behind his ear is his pencil. Whenever he finds a bright thing in your manuscript he strikes it out with that. That does him good, and makes him smile and show his teeth, the way he is doing in the picture. This one has just been striking out a smart thing, and now he is sitting there with his thumbs in his vest-holes, gloating. They are full of envy and malice, editors are. This picture will serve to remind you that Edward II. was the first English king who was DEPOSED. Upon demand, he signed his deposition himself. He had found kingship a most aggravating and disagreeable occupation, and you can see by the look of him that he is glad he resigned. He has put his blue pencil up for good now. He had struck out many a good thing with it in his time.

Edward III. next; fifty RED squares. (Fig. 16.)

This editor is a critic. He has pulled out his carving-knife and his tomahawk and is starting after a book which he is going to have for breakfast. This one's arms are put on wrong. I did not notice it at first, but I see it now. Somehow he has got his right arm on his left shoulder, and his left arm on his right shoulder, and this shows us the back of his hands in both instances. It makes him left-handed all around, which is a thing which has never happened before, except perhaps in a museum. That is the way with art, when it is not acquired but born to you: you start in to make some simple little thing, not suspecting that your genius is beginning to work and swell and strain in secret, and all of a sudden there is a convulsion and you fetch out something astonishing. This is called inspiration. It is an accident; you never know when it is coming. I might have tried as much as a year to think of such a strange thing as an all-around left-handed man and I could not have done it, for the more you try to think of an unthinkable thing the more it eludes you; but it can't elude inspiration; you have only to bait with inspiration and you will get it every time. Look at Botticelli's "Spring." Those snaky women were unthinkable, but inspiration secured them for us, thanks to goodness. It is too late to reorganize this editor-critic now; we will leave him as he is. He will serve to remind us.

[17]

Richard II. next; twenty-two WHITE squares. (Fig. 17.)

We use the lion again because this is another Richard. Like Edward II., he was DEPOSED. He is taking a last sad look at his crown before they take it away. There was not room enough and I have made it too small; but it never fitted him, anyway.

Now we turn the corner of the century with a new line of monarchs—the Lancastrian kings.

[18]

Henry IV.; fourteen squares of YELLOW paper. (Fig. 18.)

This hen has laid the egg of a new dynasty and realizes the magnitude of the event. She is giving notice in the usual way. You notice I am improving in the construction of hens. At first I made them too much like other animals, but this one is orthodox. I mention this to encourage you. You will find that the more you practice the more accurate you will become. I could always draw animals, but before I was educated I could not tell what kind they were when I got them done, but now I can. Keep up your courage; it will be the same with you, although you may not think it. This Henry died the year after Joan of Arc was born.

Henry V.; nine BLUE squares. (Fig. 19)

There you see him lost in meditation over the monument which records the amazing figures of the battle of Agincourt. French history says 20,000 Englishmen routed 80,000 Frenchmen there; and English historians say that the French loss, in killed and wounded, was 60,000.

Henry VI.; thirty-nine RED squares. (Fig. 20)

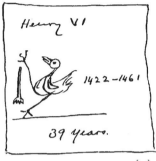

This is poor Henry VI., who reigned long and scored many misfortunes and humiliations. Also two great disasters: he lost France to Joan of Arc and he lost the throne and ended the dynasty which Henry IV had started in business with such good prospects. In the picture we see him sad and weary and downcast, with the scepter falling from his nerveless grasp. It is a pathetic quenching of a sun which had risen in such splendor.

Edward IV.; twenty-two LIGHT-BROWN squares. (Fig. 21.)

That is a society editor, sitting there elegantly dressed, with his legs crossed in that indolent way, observing the clothes the ladies wear, so that he can describe them for his paper and make them out finer than they are and get bribes for it and become wealthy. That flower which he is wearing in his buttonhole is a rose—a white rose, a York rose—and will serve to remind us of the War of the Roses, and that the white one was the winning color when Edward got the throne and dispossessed the Lancastrian dynasty.

Edward V.; one-third of a BLACK square. (Fig. 22.)

His uncle Richard had him murdered in the tower. When you get the reigns displayed upon the wall this one will be conspicuous and easily remembered. It is the shortest one in English history except Lady Jane Grey's, which was only nine days. She is never officially recognized as a monarch of England, but if you

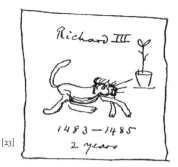

Richard III

1483—1485
2 years

or I should ever occupy a throne we should like to have proper notice taken of it; and it would be only fair and right, too, particularly if we gained nothing by it and lost our lives besides.

Richard III.; two WHITE squares. (Fig. 23.)

That is not a very good lion, but Richard was not a very good king. You would think that this lion has two heads, but that is not so; one is only a shadow. There would be shadows for the rest of him, but there was not light enough to go round, it being a dull day, with only fleeting sun-glimpses now and then. Richard had a humped back and a hard heart, and fell at the battle of Bosworth. I do not know the name of that flower in the pot, but we will use it as Richard's trade-mark, for it is said that it grows in only one place in the world—Bosworth Field—and tradition says it never grew there until Richard's royal blood warmed its hidden seed to life and made it grow.

Henry VII.; twenty-four BLUE squares. (Fig. 24.)

Henry VII. had no liking for wars and turbulence; he preferred peace and quiet and the general prosperity which such conditions create. He liked to sit on that kind of eggs on his own private account as well as the nation's, and hatch them out and count up their result. When he died he left his heir 2,000,000 pounds, which was a most unusual fortune for a king to possess in those days. Columbus's great achievement gave him the discovery-fever, and he sent Sebastian Cabot to the New

Henry VII.

1485—1509
24 years.

World to search out some foreign territory for England. That is Cabot's ship up there in the corner. This was the first time that England went far abroad to enlarge her estate—but not the last.

Henry VIII

1509—1547
38 years.

Henry VIII.; thirty-eight RED squares. (Fig. 25.)

That is Henry VIII. suppressing a monastery in his arrogant fashion.

Edward VI.; six squares of YELLOW paper. (Fig. 26.)

He is the last Edward to date. It is indicated by that thing over his head, which is a LAST— shoemaker's last.

[26]

Mary; five squares of BLACK paper. (Fig. 27.)

The picture represents a burning martyr. He is in back of the smoke. The first three letters of Mary's name and the first three of the word martyr are the same. Martyrdom was going out in her day and martyrs were becoming scarcer, but she made several. For this reason she is sometimes called Bloody Mary.

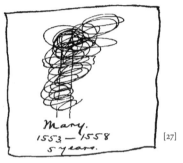

[27]

This brings us to the reign of Elizabeth, after passing through a period of nearly five hundred years of England's history—492 to be exact. I think you may now be trusted to go the rest of the way without further lessons in art or inspirations in the matter of ideas. You have the scheme now, and something in the ruler's name or career will suggest the pictorial symbol. The effort of inventing such things will not only help your memory, but will develop originality in art. See what it has done for me. If you do not find the parlor wall big enough for all of England's history, continue it into the dining-room and into other rooms. This will make the walls interesting and instructive and really worth something instead of being just flat things to hold the house together.

Friendship

The universal brotherhood of man is our most precious possession—what there is of it.

—*Mark Twain's Notebook*

The proper office of a friend is to side with you when you are in the wrong. Nearly anybody will side with you when you are in the right.

—Notebook, 1898

When we think of friends, and call their faces out of the shadows, and their voices out of the echoes that faint along the corridors of memory, and do it without knowing why save that we love to do it, we content ourselves that that friendship is a Reality, and not a Fancy—that it is builded upon a rock, and not upon the sands that dissolve away with the ebbing tides and carry their monuments with them.

—Letter to friend and confidant Mary Mason Fairbanks

William Dean Howells

William Dean Howells, editor of *Atlantic Monthly*, was a close friend to Mark Twain.

Is it true that the sun of a man's mentality touches noon at forty and then begins to wane toward setting? Doctor Osler is charged with saying so. Maybe he said it, maybe he didn't; I don't know which it is. But if he said it, I can point him to a case which proves his rule. Proves it by being an exception to it. To this place I nominate Mr. Howells.

I read his *Venetian Days* about forty years ago. I compare it with his paper on Machiavelli in a late number of *Harper*, and I cannot find that his English has suffered any impairment. For forty years his English has been to me a continual delight and astonishment. In the sustained exhibition of certain great qualities—clearness, compression, verbal exactness, and unforced and seemingly unconscious felicity of phrasing—he is, in my belief, without his peer in the English-writing world. *Sustained.* I entrench myself behind that protecting word. There are others who exhibit those great qualities as greatly as he does, but only by intervaled distributions of rich moonlight, with stretches of veiled and dimmer landscape between; whereas Howells's moon sails cloudless skies all night and all the nights.

In the matter of verbal exactness Mr. Howells has no superior, I suppose. He seems to be almost always able to find that elusive and shifty grain of gold, the *Right Word*. Others have to put up with approximations, more or less frequently; he has better luck. To me, the others are miners working with the gold-pan—of necessity some of the gold washes over and escapes; whereas, in my fancy, he is quicksilver raiding down a riffle—no grain of the metal stands much chance of eluding him. A powerful agent is the right word: it lights the reader's way and makes it plain; a close approximation to it will answer, and much traveling is done in a well-enough fashion by its help, but we do not welcome it and applaud it and rejoice in it as we do when the right one blazes out on us. Whenever we come upon one of those intensely right words in a book or a newspaper the resulting effect is physical as well as spiritual, and electrically prompt: it tingles exquisitely around through the walls of the mouth and tastes as tart and crisp and good as the autumn-butter that creams the sumac-berry. One has no time to examine the word and vote upon its rank and standing, the automatic recognition of its supremacy is so immediate. There is a plenty of acceptable literature which deals largely in approximations, but it may be likened to a fine landscape seen through the rain; the right word would dismiss the rain, then you would see it better. It doesn't rain when Howells is at work.

And where does he get the easy and effortless flow of his speech? and its cadenced and undulating rhythm? and its architectural felicities of construction, its graces of expression, its pemmican quality of compression, and all that? Born to him, no doubt. All in shining good order in the beginning, all extraordinary; and all just as shining, just as extraordinary today, after forty years of diligent wear and tear and use. He passed his fortieth year long and long ago; but I think his English of today—his perfect English, I wish to say—can throw down the glove before his English of that antique time and not be afraid.

—Mark Twain, on his friend William Dean Howells

John T. Lewis

Mark Twain with his friend John T. Lewis.

John T. Lewis was a free man born in 1835 in Carroll County, Maryland and worked as a coachman for Clemens's in-laws, the Langdons. Lewis and Clemens became good friends and it is believed Twain used Lewis as one of the model for the character Jim in The Adventures of Huckleberry Finn.

While looking at a photograph of himself and Lewis, Twain said:

"The colored man. . . is John T. Lewis, a friend of mine. These many years— thirty-four in fact. He was my father-in-law's coachman forty years ago; was many years a farmer of Quarry Farm, and is still my neighbor. I have not known an honester man nor a more respect-worthy one. Twenty-seven years ago, by the prompt and intelligent exercise of his courage, presence of mind and extraordinary strength, he saved the lives of three relatives of mine, whom a runaway horse was hurrying to destruction. Naturally I hold him in high and grateful regard."

Twain wrote the story of the runaway horse in a letter to his friend, William Dean Howells.

ELMIRA, Aug. 25 '77.

MY DEAR HOWELLSES,—I thought I ought to make a sort of record of it for further reference; the pleasantest way to do that would be to write it to some-body; but that somebody would let it leak into print and that we wish to avoid. The Howellses would be safe—so let us tell the Howellses about it.

Day before yesterday was a fine summer day away up here on the summit. Aunt Marsh and Cousin May Marsh were here visiting Susie Crane and Livy at our farmhouse. By and by mother Langdon came up the hill in the "high carriage" with Nora the nurse and little Jervis (Charley Langdon's little boy)— Timothy the coachman driving. Behind these came Charley's wife and little girl in the buggy, with the new, young, spry, gray horse—a high-stepper. Theodore Crane arrived a little later.

The Bay and Susy were on hand with their nurse, Rosa. I was on hand, too. Susy Crane's trio of colored servants ditto—these being Josie, house-maid; Aunty Cord, cook, aged 62, turbaned, very tall, very broad, very fine every way (see her portrait in "A True Story just as I Heard It" in my *Sketches*;) Chocklate (the laundress) (as the Bay calls her—she can't say Charlotte,) still taller, still more majestic of proportions, turbaned, very black, straight as an

Indian—age 24. Then there was the farmer's wife (colored) and her little girl, Susy.

Wasn't it a good audience to get up an excitement before? Good excitable, inflammable material?

Lewis was still down town, three miles away, with his two-horse wagon, to get a load of manure. Lewis is the farmer (colored). He is of mighty frame and muscle, stocky, stooping, ungainly, has a good manly face and a clear eye. Age about 45—and the most picturesque of men, when he sits in his fluttering work-day rags, humped forward into a bunch, with his aged slouch hat mashed down over his ears and neck. It is a spectacle to make the broken-hearted smile. Lewis has worked mighty hard and remained mighty poor. At the end of each whole year's toil he can't show a gain of fifty dollars. He had borrowed money of the Cranes till he owed them $700 and he being conscientious and honest, imagine what it was to him to have to carry this stubborn, helpless load year in and year out.

Well, sunset came, and Ida the young and comely (Charley Langdon's wife) and her little Julia and the nurse Nora, drove out at the gate behind the new gray horse and started down the long hill—the high carriage receiving its load under the porte cochere. Ida was seen to turn her face toward us across the fence and intervening lawn—Theodore waved good-bye to her, for he did not know that her sign was a speechless appeal for help.

The next moment Livy said, "Ida's driving too fast down hill!" She followed it with a sort of scream, "Her horse is running away!"

We could see two hundred yards down that descent. The buggy seemed to fly. It would strike obstructions and apparently spring the height of a man from the ground.

Theodore and I left the shrieking crowd behind and ran down the hill bare-headed and shouting. A neighbor appeared at his gate—a tenth of a second too late! the buggy vanished past him like a thought. My last glimpse showed it for one instant, far down the descent, springing high in the air out of a cloud of dust, and then it disappeared. As I flew down the road my impulse was to shut my eyes as I turned them to the right or left, and so delay for a moment the ghastly spectacle of mutilation and death I was expecting.

I ran on and on, still spared this spectacle, but saying to myself: "I shall see it at the turn of the road; they never can pass that turn alive." When I came in sight of that turn I saw two wagons there bunched together—one of them full of people. I said, "Just so—they are staring petrified at the remains."

But when I got amongst that bunch, there sat Ida in her buggy and nobody hurt, not even the horse or the vehicle. Ida was pale but serene. As I came tearing down, she smiled back over her shoulder at me and said, "Well, we're alive yet, aren't we?" A miracle had been performed—nothing else.

You see Lewis, the prodigious, humped upon his front seat, had been toiling up, on his load of manure; he saw the frantic horse plunging down the hill toward him, on a full gallop, throwing his heels as high as a man's head at every jump. So Lewis turned his team diagonally across the road just at the "turn," thus making a V with the fence—the running horse could not escape that, but must enter it. Then Lewis sprang to the ground and stood in this V. He gathered his vast strength, and with a perfect Creedmoor aim he seized the gray horse's bit as he plunged by and fetched him up standing!

It was down hill, mind you. Ten feet further down hill neither Lewis nor any other man could have saved them, for they would have been on the abrupt "turn," then. But how this miracle was ever accomplished at all, by human strength, generalship and accuracy, is clean beyond my comprehension—and grows more so the more I go and examine the ground and try to believe it was actually done. I know one thing, well; if Lewis had missed his aim he would have been killed on the spot in the trap he had made for himself, and we should have found the rest of the remains away down at the bottom of the steep ravine.

—from Twain's letter to William Dean Howells

Laura Hawkins

Anna Laura (Elizabeth) Hawkins Frazier was the model for Becky Thatcher, featured in Tom Sawyer *and* Huckleberry Finn.

"Sam and I started going to school the same year; he was seven and I was six. We lived opposite each other on Hill street. Sam had long golden curls hanging over his shoulders at that time. He used to carry my books to school every morning, bring them home for me in the afternoon, and occasionally he would treat me to apples, oranges and such things, or divide his candy with me," *Hawkins said of Twain.*

"In the winter when the creeks or the river were frozen, Sam spent a greater part of his time on the ice. I couldn't skate, but he always arranged for me to go along in the crowd. He used to push me along on the ice in a split-bottom chair. He was a fine skater, too, in fact, he was good at anything he undertook. I remember the last time I saw Sam when he was a boy. It was just before he left

Hannibal for the last time. We were skating on Bear creek and I can distinctly recall that I had trouble in getting on one of my skates and Sam performed the services very beautifully.

"The first time I ever saw Sam was on a hot summer day. He came out of his home, opposite mine, and started showing off, turning handsprings and cutting capers just as described in *Tom Sawyer*. I remember one time when we were riding saplings, and I was thrown to the ground and knocked unconscious. I recall hearing the children talking about how badly scared Sam was."

Sam immortalized his boyhood love for Hawkins in Tom Sawyer:

"Say, Becky, was you ever engaged?"

"What's that?"

"Why, engaged to be married."

"No."

"Would you like to?"

"I reckon so. I don't know. What is it like?"

"Like? Why it ain't like anything. You only just tell a boy you won't ever have anybody but him, ever ever ever, and then you kiss and that's all. Anybody can do it."

"Kiss? What do you kiss for?"

"Why, that, you know, is to—well, they always do that."

"Everybody?"

"Why, yes, everybody that's in love with each other. Do you remember what I wrote on the slate?"

"Ye—yes."

"What was it?"

"I sha'n't tell you."

"Shall I tell you?"

"Ye—yes—but some other time."

"No, now."

"No, not now—to-morrow."

"Oh, no, now. Please, Becky—I'll whisper it, I'll whisper it ever so easy."

Becky hesitating, Tom took silence for consent, and passed his arm about her waist and whispered the tale ever so softly, with his mouth close to her ear. And then he added:

"Now you whisper it to me—just the same."

She resisted, for a while, and then said:

"You turn your face away so you can't see, and then I will. But you mustn't ever tell anybody—will you, Tom? Now you won't, will you?"

"No, indeed, indeed I won't. Now, Becky."

He turned his face away. She bent timidly around till her breath stirred his curls and whispered, "I—love—you!"

Then she sprang away and ran around and around the desks and benches, with Tom after her, and took refuge in a corner at last, with her little white apron to her face. Tom clasped her about her neck and pleaded:

"Now, Becky, it's all done—all over but the kiss. Don't you be afraid of that—it ain't anything at all. Please, Becky." And he tugged at her apron and the hands.

By and by she gave up, and let her hands drop; her face, all glowing with the struggle, came up and submitted. Tom kissed the red lips and said:

"Now it's all done, Becky. And always after this, you know, you ain't ever to love anybody but me, and you ain't ever to marry anybody but me, ever never and forever. Will you?"

"No, I'll never love anybody but you, Tom, and I'll never marry anybody but you—and you ain't to ever marry anybody but me, either."

"Certainly. Of course. That's part of it. And always coming to school or when we're going home, you're to walk with me, when there ain't anybody looking— and you choose me and I choose you at parties, because that's the way you do when you're engaged."

"It's so nice. I never heard of it before."

Animals

On Cats

"As far as I can see, he showed up best in naming animals. Considering that he hadn't ever seen any animals before, I am of the opinion that he did it very well indeed, as far as he got. He had a sure touch, on the common ones— named them with insight and judacity, and the names stick, to this day, after all the wear and tear they've been through; it was when he struck the big ones and the long ones that he couldn't cash-in. Take, the ornithorhyncus, for instance. . . As we know, he skipped the ornithorhyncus. Left him out of the invoice. Why? . . . In my judgment the alphabet was just beginning to accumulate, in that early day, and there wasn't much of it yet, and so it seems reasonable that he had to skip it because he couldn't spell it . . . Adam skipped a lot of the creatures. This has been the astonishment of the world for—well, from away back. Ages, as you may say. But you can see, now how it was. He didn't want to skip, he wanted to do his honest duty, but there he was—he hadn't the ammunition. He was equipped for short names, but not the others. If a bear came along—all right, he was loaded for bear. There was no embarrassment. The same if a cow came along; or a cat, or a horse, or a lion, or a tiger, or a hog, or a frog, or a worm, or a bat, or a snipe, or an ant, or a bee, or a trout, or a shark, or a whale, or a tadpole—anything that didn't strain his alphabet, you know: they would find him on post and tranquil; he would register them and they would pass on, discussing their names, most of them pleased—such as leopards and scarlet tanagers and such, some of them pained—such as buzzards, and alligators, and so on, the others ashamed— such as squids, and polecats, and that kind; but all resigned, in a way, and reconciled, recognizing that he was new to the business and doing the best he could. Plain sailing, and satisfactory, you see. But in the course of trade, along comes the pterodactyl— . . . Could he spell that? No, sir. Solomon couldn't. Nor no other early Christian—not in that early time . . . in those old early geological times the alphabet hadn't even got up to the Old Red Sandstone period yet, and it was worse in Adam's time, of course; so, as he didn't want to let on that he couldn't spell it, he just said, 'Call again, office hours over for to-day,' and pulled down the shades and locked up and went home, the same as if nothing had happened.

"It was natural, I think, and right enough, too. I would have done it; most people would. Well, he had a difficult time, limited the way he was, and it is only fair for us to take that into account. Every few days along would come an animal as big as a house—grazing along, eating elephants and pulling down the synagogues and things: 'Dinosauriumiguanodon,' says Adam; 'tell him to come Sunday;' and would close up and take a walk. And the very next day, like enough, along comes a creation a mile long, chewing rocks and scraping the hills away with its tail, and lightening and thundering with its eyes and its lungs, and Eve scoops up her hair over her arm and takes to the woods, and Adam says 'Megatheriomylodonticoplesiosauriasticum—give him his first syllable and get him to take the rest on the instalment plan,' which it seems to me was one of the best ideas Adam ever had, and in every way creditable to him. He had to save some of the alphabet, he couldn't let one animal have it all, it would not have been fair, anyway.

"I will say it again, I think Adam was at his level best when he was naming the creatures, and most to be praised. If you look up your fossiliferous paleontology, I acknowledge you will have to admit that where he registered one creature he skipped three hundred and fifty, but that is not his fault, it was the fault of his alphabet-plant. You can't build a battleship out of a scrap-heap. Necessarily he couldn't take the whole of one of those thirteen-syllabers and pay spot cash; the most he could do was to put up a margin. Well, you know what happens to that kind of financing."

—"The Refuge of the Derelicts" published in *Fables of Man*, 1972

Testimonial from Col. George Harvey, Mark Twain's publisher:

I think that perhaps the funniest thing about Mark Twain now is not his writing, but his bed. He lies in bed a good deal; he says he has formed the habit. His bed is the largest one I ever say, and on it is the weirdest collection of objects you ever saw, enough to furnish a Harlem

flat—books, writing materials, clothes, any and everything that could foregather in his vicinity.

He looks quite happy rising out of the mass, and over all prowls a huge black cat of a very unhappy disposition. She snaps and snarls and claws and bites, and Mark Twain takes his turn with the rest; when she gets tired of tearing up manuscript she scratches him and he bears it with a patience wonderful to behold.

—An interview subtitled "Mark Twain's Bed,"
for the *Washington Post*, March 26, 1905

Testimonial from Clara Clemens,
Mark Twain's daughter:

In the early autumn Father rented a house on Fifth Avenue, corner of Ninth Street, number 21, where he, Jean, the faithful Katie, and the secretary settled down for the winter. I was taken to a sanatorium for a year. During the first months of my cure I was completely cut off from friends and family, with no one to speak to but the doctor and nurse. I must modify this statement, however, for I had smuggled a black kitten into my bedroom, although it was against the rules of the sanatorium to have any animals in the place. I called the cat Bambino and it was permitted to remain with me until the unfortunate day when it entered one of the patient's rooms who hated cats. Bambino came near giving the good lady a cataleptic fit, so I was invited to dispose of my pet after that. I made a present of it to Father, knowing he would love it, and he did. A little later I was allowed to receive a limited number of letters, and Father wrote that Bambino was homesick for me and refused all meat and milk, but contradicted his statement a couple of days later saying: "It has been discovered that the reason your cat declines milk and meat and lets on to live by miraculous intervention is, that he catches mice privately.

—*My Father, Mark Twain* by Clara Clemens, 1931

"I simply can't resist a cat, particularly a purring one. They are the cleanest, cunningest, and most intelligent things I know, outside of the girl you love, of course," *Twain once wrote.*

He also opined: "If man could be crossed with the cat it would improve man, but it would deteriorate the cat."

~♪

The Clemens had a black cat named Satan, that gave birth to a similarly very dark kitten that Sam respectively named Sin.

"He is very fond of animals particularly cats," Susy Clemens stated in Papa, her biography of her father that she wrote when she was in her teens. "He had a dear little gray kitten once, that he named "Lazy" (Papa always wears grey to match his gray hair and eyes) and he would carry him around on his shoulder, it was a mighty pretty sight! the gray cat sound asleep against Papa's gray coat and hair. The names he has given our different cats, are remarkably funny, they are namely "Stray Kit," "Abner," "Motly," "Freulein," "Lazy," "Buffalo Bill," and "Soapy Sal," "Cleveland," "Sour Mash," and "Famine.""

~♪

To Mrs. Mabel Larkin Patterson, in Chicago:
Redding, Connecticut, Oct. 2, '08.
DEAR MRS. PATTERSON,—The contents of
your letter are very pleasant and very welcome,
and I thank you for them, sincerely. If I can find
a photograph of my "Tammany" and her kittens,
I will enclose it in this. One of them likes to be
crammed into a corner-pocket of the billiard
table—which he fits as snugly as does a finger in a
glove and then he watches the game (and ob-
structs it) by the hour, and spoils many a shot by
putting out his paw and changing the direction of
a passing ball. Whenever a ball is in his arms, or so

close to him that it cannot be played upon without risk of hurting him, the player
is privileged to remove it to any one of the 3 spots that chances to be vacant.
Ah, no, my lecturing days are over for good and all.
Sincerely yours,
S. L. CLEMENS.

On Raising Poultry

The Black Spanish is an exceedingly fine bird and a costly one. Thirty-five dollars is the usual figure, and fifty a not uncommon price for a specimen. Even its eggs are worth from a dollar to a dollar and a half apiece, and yet are so unwholesome that the city physician seldom or never orders them for the workhouse. Still I have once or twice procured as high as a dozen at a time for nothing, in the dark of the moon. The best way to raise the Black Spanish fowl is to go late in the evening and raise coop and all. The reason I recommend this method is that, the birds being so valuable, the owners do not permit them to roost around promiscuously, but put them in a coop as strong as a fireproof safe and keep it in the kitchen at night. The method I speak of is not always a bright and satisfying success, and yet there are so many little articles of vertu about a kitchen, that if you fail on the coop you can generally bring away something else. I brought away a nice steel trap one night, worth ninety cents.

—"To Raise Poultry" from *Sketches New and Old*

On Oysters

God first had to make the oyster. You can't make an oyster out of nothing, nor you can't do it in a day. You've got to start with a vast variety of invertebrates, belemnites, trilobites, jebusites, amalekites, and that sort of fry, and put them into soak in a primary sea and observe and wait what will happen. Some of them will turn out a disappointment; the belemnites and the amalekites and such will be failures, and they will die out and become extinct in the course of the nineteen million years covered by the experiment; but all is not lost, for the amalekites will develop gradually into encrinites and stalactites and blatherskites, and one thing and another, as the mighty ages creep on and the periods pile their lofty crags in the primordial seas, and at last the first grand stage in the preparation of the world for man stands completed; the oyster is done. Now an oyster has hardly any more reasoning power than a man has, so it is probable this one jumped to the conclusion that the nineteen million years was a preparation for him. That would be just like an oyster...

—*Mark Twain, a Biography*

Twain in a cart drawn by a horse and a cow, 1897

On Horses

While I am speaking of animals, I will mention that I have a horse now by the name of "Jericho." He is a mare. I have seen remarkable horses before, but none so remarkable as this. I wanted a horse that could shy, and this one fills the bill. I had an idea that shying indicated spirit. If I was correct, I have got the most spirited horse on earth. He shies at every thing he comes across, with the utmost impartiality. He appears to have a mortal dread of telegraph poles, especially; and it is fortunate that these are on both sides of the road, because as it is now, I never fall off twice in succession on the same side. If I fell on the same side always, it would get to be monotonous after a while. This creature has scared at every thing he has seen to-day, except a haystack. He walked up to that with an intrepidity and a recklessness that were astonishing. And it would fill any one with admiration to see how he preserves his self-possession in the presence of a barley sack. This dare-devil bravery will be the death of this horse some day.

He is not particularly fast, but I think he will get me through the Holy Land. He has only one fault. His tail has been chopped off or else he has sat down on it too hard, some time or other, and he has to fight the flies with his heels. This is all very well, but when he tries to kick a fly off the top of his head with his hind foot, it is too much variety. He is going to get himself into trouble that way some day. He reaches around and bites my legs too. I do not care particularly about that, only I do not like to see a horse too sociable.

—Innocents Abroad

When the landlord learned that I and my agents were artists, our party rose perceptibly in his esteem; we rose still higher when he learned that we were making a pedestrian tour of Europe.

He told us all about the Heidelberg road, and which were the best places to avoid and which the best ones to tarry at; he charged me less than cost for the things I broke in the night; he put up a fine luncheon for us and added to it a quantity of great light-green plums, the pleasantest fruit in Germany; he was so anxious to do us honor that he would not allow us to walk out of Heilbronn, but called up Goetz von Berlichingen's horse and cab and made us ride.

I made a sketch of the turnout.

A sketch by Mark Twain from *A Tramp Abroad* of he and "Harris" (a pseudonym for Rev. Joseph Twichell), among others, leaving Heilbronn by carriage.

It is not a Work, it is only what artists call a "study"—a thing to make a finished picture from. This sketch has several blemishes in it; for instance, the wagon is not traveling as fast as the horse is. This is wrong. Again, the person trying to get out of the way is too small; he is out of perspective, as we say. The two upper lines are not the horse's back, they are the reigns; there seems to be a wheel missing—this would be corrected in a finished Work, of course. This thing flying out behind is not a flag, it is a curtain. That other thing up there is the sun, but I didn't get enough distance on it. I do not remember, now, what that thing is that is in front of the man who is running, but I think it is a haystack or a woman. This study was exhibited in the Paris Salon of 1879, but did not take any medal; they do not give medals for studies.

—A Tramp Abroad

Animal Testing

Mark Twain on Vivisection in a letter to Sidney G. Trist (Editor of the Animals' Friend *Magazine), in his capacity as Secretary of the London Anti-Vivisection Society.*

DEAR SIR,—I believe I am not interested to know whether Vivisection produces results that are profitable to the human race or doesn't. To know that the results are profitable to the race would not remove my hostility to it. The pains which it inflicts upon unconsenting animals is the basis of my enmity towards it, and it is to me sufficient justification of the enmity without looking further. It is so distinctly a matter of feeling with me, and is so strong and so deeply-rooted in my make and constitution, that I am sure I could not even see a vivisector vivisected with anything more than a sort of qualified satisfaction. I do not say I should not go and look on; I only mean that I should almost surely fail to get out of it the degree of contentment which it ought, of course, to be expected to furnish.

I find some very impressive paragraphs in a paper which was read before the National Individualist Club (1898) by a medical man. I have read and re-read these paragraphs, with always augmenting astonishment, and have tried to understand why it should be considered a kind of credit and a handsome thing to belong to a human race that has vivisectors in it. And I have also tried to imagine what would become of a race if it had to be saved by my practising vivisection on the French plan. Let me quote:—

"Vivisectors possess a drug called curare, which, given to an animal, effectually prevents any struggle or cry. A horrible feature of curare is that it has no anæsthetic effect, but, on the contrary, it intensifies the sensibility to pain. The animal is perfectly conscious, suffers doubly, and is able to make no sign. Claude Bernard, the notorious French vivisector, thus describes the effect of curare: 'The apparent corpse before us hears and distinguishes all that is done. In this motionless body, behind that glazing eye, sensitiveness and intelligence persist in their entirety. The apparent insensibility it produces is accompanied by the most atrocious suffering the mind of man can conceive.' It has been freely admitted by vivisectors that they have used curare alone in the most horrible experiments, that these admissions are to be found multiplied to any extent in the report of the Royal Commission. And though it is illegal at the present day to dispense with anæsthetics, experiments are going on in which curare is the real means of keeping the animals quiet while a pretence is made of anæsthetising them.

I am not desirous of shocking you by reciting the atrocities of vivisection, but since the apologists try to deceive the public by vague statements that vivisectors would not, and do not, perpetrate cruelty, I wish to say sufficient to disprove their assertions.

There is unfortunately abundant evidence that innumerable experiments of the following character have been performed on sensitive animals. They have been boiled, baked, scalded, burnt with turpentine, frozen, cauterized; they have been partly drowned and brought back to consciousness to have the process repeated; they have been cut open and mangled in every part of the body and have been kept alive in a mutilated state for experiments lasting days or weeks. If I wished, I could pile up mountains of evidence, to be found in the publications of physiologists and in the report of the Royal Commission.

Here are some by Dr. Drasch in 1889 (du Bois-Reymond's archives), 'The frogs, curarised or not, are prepared in the following manner. The animal is placed on its back on a piece of cork fastened by a needle through the end of the nose, the lower jaw drawn back and also fastened with pins. Then the mucous membrane is cut away in a circular form, the right eye-ball which protrudes into the back of the throat is seized, and the copiously bleeding vessels are tied. Next a tent hook is introduced into the cavity of the eye drawing out the muscles and optic nerves, which are also secured by a ligature. The eyeball is then split with a needle near the point where the optic nerve enters, a circular piece cut away from the sclerotic, and the crystalline lens, etc., removed from the eyeball. I may remark that my experiments lasted a whole year, and I have therefore tried frogs at all seasons.' He calmly gives directions for keeping the animals still. 'If the frog is not curarised the sciatic and crual nerves are cut through. It is, however, sufficient to fasten the head completely to the cork to immobilise the animal.'

I could quote still more shameful vivisection records from this paper, but I lack the stomach for it.

Very truly yours,

Mark Twain

Dogs

By what right has the dog come to be regarded as a "noble" animal? The more brutal and cruel and unjust you are to him the more your fawning and adoring slave he becomes; whereas, if you shamefully misuse a cat once she will always maintain a dignified reserve toward you afterward—you will never get her full confidence again.

—Mark Twain, a Biography

If you pick up a starving dog and make him prosperous, he will not bite you. This is the principal difference between a dog and a man.

—Pudd'nhead Wilson's Calendar

Heaven goes by favor. If it went by merit, you would stay out and your dog would go in.

—Mark Twain, a Biography

Twain, his wife, Olivia, and their three daughters with an unidentified dog.

He wa'n't no common dog, he wa'n't no mongrel; he was a composite. A composite dog is a dog that is made up of all the valuable qualities that's in the dog breed—kind of a syndicate; and a mongrel is made up of all riffraff that's left over.

—Mark Twain, "His Grandfather's Old Ram"

$\sim$

Twains first wrote A Dog's Tale *as a short story for Harper's Magazine and it was expanded and published as a book by Harper & Brothers in 1904. The story is written from the perspective of a household dog.*

My father was a St. Bernard, my mother was a collie, but I am a Presbyterian. This is what my mother told me, I do not know these nice distinctions myself. To me they are only fine large words meaning nothing. My mother had a fondness for such; she liked to say them, and see other dogs look surprised and envious, as wondering how she got so much education. But, indeed, it was not real education; it was only show: she got the words by listening in the dining-room and drawing-room when there was company, and by going with the children to Sunday-school and listening there; and whenever she heard a large word she said it over to herself many times, and so was able to keep it until there was a dogmatic gathering in the neighborhood, then she would get it off, and surprise and distress them all, from pocket-pup to mastiff, which rewarded her for all her trouble. If there was a stranger he was nearly sure to be suspicious, and when he got his breath again he would ask her what it meant. And she always told him. He was never expecting this but thought he would catch her; so when she told him, he was the one that looked ashamed, whereas he had thought it was going to be she. The others were always waiting for this, and glad of it and proud of her, for they knew what was going to happen, because they had had experience. When she told the meaning of a big word they were all so taken up with admiration that it never occurred to any dog to doubt if it was the right one; and that was natural, because, for one thing, she answered up so promptly that it seemed like a dictionary speaking, and for another thing, where could they find out whether it was right or not? for she was the only cultivated dog there was. By and by, when I was older, she brought home the word Unintellectual, one time, and worked it pretty hard all the week at different gatherings, making much unhappiness and despondency;

The first edition cover of *A Dog's Tale*.

and it was at this time that I noticed that during that week she was asked for the meaning at eight different assemblages, and flashed out a fresh definition every time, which showed me that she had more presence of mind than culture, though I said nothing, of course. She had one word which she always kept on hand, and ready, like a life-preserver, a kind of emergency word to strap on when she was likely to get washed overboard in a sudden way—that was the word Synonymous. When she happened to fetch out a long word which had had its day weeks before and its prepared meanings gone to her dump-pile, if there was a stranger there of course it knocked him groggy for a couple of minutes, then he would come to, and by that time she would be away down wind on another tack, and not expecting anything; so when he'd hail and ask her to cash in, I (the only dog on the inside of her game) could see her canvas flicker a moment—but only just a moment—then it would belly out taut and full, and she would say, as calm as a summer's day, "It's synonymous with supererogation," or some godless long reptile of a word like that, and go placidly about and skim away on the next tack, perfectly comfortable, you know, and leave that stranger looking profane and embarrassed, and the initiated slatting the floor with their tails in unison and their faces transfigured with a holy joy.

"… nothing so liberalizes a man and expands the kindly instincts that nature put in him as travel and contact with many kinds of people."

—*Letter to San Francisco Alta California, dated May 18, 1867; published June 23, 1867*

"There is no unhappiness like the misery of sighting land (and work) again after a cheerul, careless voyage."

—*Letter to Will Bowen (prior to sailing on Quaker City)*

5. Travel and Foreign Lands

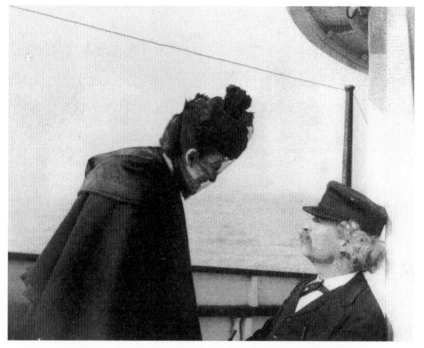

Olivia 'Livy' Clemens and Mark Twain aboard a steamship to Europe.

The gentle reader will never, never know what a consummate ass he can become until he goes abroad. I speak now, of course, in the supposition that the gentle reader has not been abroad, and therefore is not already a consummate ass. If the case be otherwise, I beg his pardon and extend to him the cordial hand of fellowship and call him brother.

—*Innocents Abroad*

It liberates the vandal to travel—you never saw a bigoted, opinionated, stubborn, narrow-minded, self-conceited, almighty mean man in your life but he had stuck in one place since he was born and thought God made the world and dyspepsia and bile for his especial comfort and satisfaction.

—The American Abroad speech, 1868

On San Francisco

Twain became a traveling correspondent for the newspaper Alta California *in 1866. In December of that year, he wrote the following article before leaving San Francisco.*

San Francisco Alta California, December 15, 1866

"MARK TWAIN'S" FAREWELL.

My Friends and Fellow-Citizens: I have been treated with extreme kindness and cordiality by San Francisco, and I wish to return my sincerest thanks and acknowledgments. I have also been treated with marked and unusual generosity, forbearance and good-fellowship, by my ancient comrades, my brethren of the Press—a thing which has peculiarly touched me, because long experience in the service has taught me that we of the Press are slow to praise but quick to censure each other, as a general thing—wherefore, in thanking them I am anxious to convince them, at the same time, that they have not lavished their kind offices upon one who cannot appreciate or is insensible to them.

I am now about to bid farewell to San Francisco for a season, and to go back to that common home we all tenderly remember in our waking hours and fondly revisit in dreams of the night—a home which is familiar to my recollection, but will be an unknown land to my unaccustomed eyes. I shall share the fate of many another longing exile who wanders back to his early home to find gray hairs where he expected youth, graves where he looked for firesides, grief where he had pictured joy—everywhere change! remorseless change where he had heedlessly dreamed that desolating Time had stood still!—to find his cherished anticipations a mockery,

San Francisco in the 1860s.

and to drink the lees of disappointment instead of the beaded wine of a hope that is crowned with its fruition!

And while I linger here upon the threshold of this, my new home, to say to you, my kindest and my truest friends, a warm good-bye and an honest peace and prosperity attend you, I accept the warning that mighty changes will have come over this home also when my returning feet shall walk these streets again.

I read the signs of the times, and I, that am no prophet, behold the things that are in store for you. Over slumbering California is stealing the dawn of a radiant future! The great China Mail Line is established, the Pacific Railroad is creeping across the continent, the commerce of the world is about to be revolutionized. California is Crown Princess of the new dispensation! She stands in the centre of the grand highway of the nations; she stands midway between the Old World and the New, and both shall pay her tribute. From the far East and from Europe, multitudes of stout hearts and willing hands are preparing to flock hither; to throng her hamlets and villages; to till her fruitful soil; to unveil the riches of her countless mines; to build up an empire on these distant shores that shall shame the bravest dreams of her visionaries. From the opulent lands of the Orient, from India, from China, Japan, the Amoor; from tributary regions that stretch from the Arctic circle to the equator, is about to pour in upon her the princely commerce of a teeming population of four hundred and fifty million souls. Half the world stands ready to lay its contributions at her feet! Has any other State so brilliant a future? Has any other city a future like San Francisco?

This straggling town shall be a vast metropolis; this sparsely populated land shall become a crowded hive of busy men; your waste places shall blossom like the rose, and your deserted hills and valleys shall yield bread and wine for unnumbered thousands; railroads shall be spread hither and thither and carry he invigorating blood of commerce to regions that are languishing now; mills and workshops, yea, and factories shall spring up everywhere, and mines that have neither name nor place to-day shall dazzle the world with their affluence. The time is drawing on apace when the clouds shall pass away from your firmament, and a splendid prosperity shall descend like a glory upon the whole land!

I am bidding the old city and my old friends a kind, but not a sad farewell, for I know that when I see this home again, the changes that will have been wrought upon it will suggest no sentiment of sadness; its estate will be brighter, happier and prouder a hundred fold than it is this day. This is its destiny, and in all sincerity I can say, So mote it be!

l.

MORTON.

─────

he Journal.

─────

er, who signs
bjects to being
the following
rietors of the

l attention to
come out and
creeter," and
ull and cross
r.

the above is
the Courier,
o produce the
he "*creeter*?"
ey are taking
Is it true?
r rather, are
orthy citizens
here two more
on over and
applying the
Law to this
il and attempt
just entering
ng against ad-
What would

quainted with
r this attack?
is community
Has it one

The free and easy impudence of the writer of
the following letter will be appreciated by those
who recognize him. We should be pleased to
have more of his letters :

NEW YORK, }
Wednesday, August 24th, 1853. }

MY DEAR MOTHER: you will doubtless be
a little surprised, and somewhat angry when you
receive this, and find me so far from home; but
you must bear a little with me, for you know I
was always the best boy you had, and perhaps
you remember the people used to say to their
children—"Now don't do like O. and H. C—
but take S. for your guide!"

Well, I was out of work in St. Louis, and
did'nt fancy loafing in such a dry place, where
there is no pleasure to be seen without paying
well for it, and so I thought I might as well go
to New York. I packed up my "duds" and left
for this village, where I arrived, all right, this
morning.

It took a day, by steamboat and cars, to go
from St. Louis to Bloomington, Ill; another day
by railroad, from there to Chicago, where I laid
over all day Sunday; from Chicago to Monroe,
in Michigan, by railroad, another day; from
Monroe, across Lake Erie, in the fine Lake
palace, "Southern Michigan," to Buffalo, another day; from Buffalo to Albany, by railroad,
another day; and from Albany to New York,
by Hudson river steamboat, another day—an
awful trip, taking five days, where it should
have been only three. I shall wait a day or so
for my insides to get settled, after the jolting
they received, when I shall look out for a sit;
for they say there is plenty of work to be had
for *sober* compositors.

---

incr

W
the
chee
have
sipp
Wh
inte
othe

ded
ing
on
(ne
for
stat
of t
his
sum
the

19

On St. Louis

Letter from New York

New York

Wednesday, August 24, 1853

My Dear Mother: you will doubtless be a little surprised, and somewhat angry when you receive this, and find me so far from home; but you must bear a little with me, for you know I was always the best boy you had, and perhaps you remember people used to say to their children – "Now, don't do like O. and H. C.—but take S. for your guide."

Well, I was out of work in St. Louis and didn't fancy loafing in such a dry place, where there is no pleasure to be seen without paying well for it, and so I thought I might as well go to New York. I packed up my "duds" and left for this village, all right, this morning.

It took a day, by steamboat and cars, to go from St. Louis to Bloomington, Ill; another day by railroad from there to Chicago, where I laid over all day Sunday; from Chicago to Monroe, in Michigan, across Lake Erie, in the fine lake palace "Southern Michigan" to Buffalo, another day; and from Buffalo to Albany, by railroad, another day; and from Albany to New York, by Hudson river steamboat, another day—an awful trip taking five days, where it should have only been three. I shall wait a day or so for my insides to get settled, after the jolting they received, when I shall look out for a sit; for they say there is plenty of work to be had for *sober* compositors.

Letter from Twain to his mother that was reprinted in the *Hannibal* newspaper by Orion Clemens.

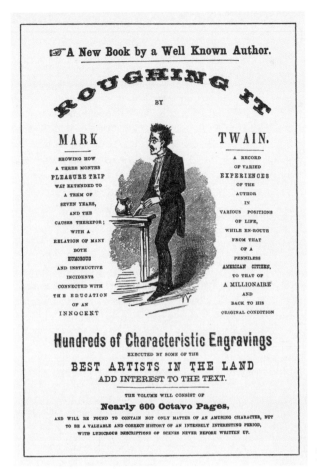

Advertisement
for *Roughing It.*

I dreamed all night about Indians, deserts, and silver bars, and in due time, next day, we took shipping at the St. Louis wharf on board a steamboat bound up the Missouri River.

We were six days going from St. Louis to "St. Jo."—a trip that was so dull, and sleepy, and eventless that it has left no more impression on my memory than if its duration had been six minutes instead of that many days. No record is left in my mind, now, concerning it, but a confused jumble of savage-looking snags, which we deliberately walked over with one wheel or the other; and of reefs which we butted and butted, and then retired from and climbed over in some softer place; and of sand-bars which we roosted on occasionally, and rested, and then got out our crutches and sparred over.

In fact, the boat might almost as well have gone to St. Jo. by land, for she was walking most of the time, anyhow—climbing over reefs and clambering over snags patiently and laboriously all day long. The captain said she was a "bully" boat, and all she wanted was more "shear" and a bigger wheel. I thought she wanted a pair of stilts, but I had the deep sagacity not to say so.

—*Roughing It*

On Nevada

Mark Twain's semi-autobiographical book Roughing It *follows the travels of young Twain through the Wild West during the years 1861– 1867. His brother Orion Clemens had been appointed Secretary of the Nevada Territory on a stagecoach journey west.*

My brother had just been appointed Secretary of Nevada Territory—an office of such majesty that it concentrated in itself the duties and dignities of Treasurer, Comptroller, Secretary of State, and Acting Governor in the Governor's absence. A salary of eighteen hundred dollars a year and the title of "Mr. Secretary," gave to the great position an air of wild and imposing grandeur. I was young and ignorant, and I

First edition of *Roughing It*, 1872.

envied my brother. I coveted his distinction and his financial splendor, but particularly and especially the long, strange journey he was going to make, and the curious new world he was going to explore. He was going to travel! I never had been away from home, and that word "travel" had a seductive charm for me. Pretty soon he would be hundreds and hundreds of miles away on the great plains and deserts, and among the mountains of the Far West, and would see buffaloes and Indians, and prairie dogs, and antelopes, and have all kinds of adventures, and may be get hanged or scalped, and have ever such a fine time, and write home and tell us all about it, and be a hero. And he would see the gold mines and the silver mines, and maybe go about of an afternoon when his work was done, and pick up two or three pailfuls of shining slugs, and nuggets of gold and silver on the hillside. And by and by he would become very rich, and return home by sea, and be able to talk as calmly about San Francisco and the ocean, and "the isthmus" as if it was nothing of any consequence to have seen those marvels face to face.

—Roughing It

What I suffered in contemplating his happiness, pen cannot describe. And so, when he offered me, in cold blood, the sublime position of private secretary under him, it appeared to me that the heavens and the earth passed away, and the firmament was rolled together as a scroll! I had nothing more to desire. My contentment was complete.

At the end of an hour or two I was ready for the journey. Not much packing up was necessary, because we were going in the overland stage from the Missouri frontier to Nevada, and passengers were only allowed a small quantity of baggage apiece. There was no Pacific railroad in those fine times of ten or twelve years ago—not a single rail of it. I only proposed to stay in Nevada three months—I had no thought of staying longer than that. I meant to see all I could that was new and strange, and then hurry home to business. I little thought that I would not see the end of that three-month pleasure excursion for six or seven uncommonly long years!

—Roughing It

… the Great Seal of the State. It had snow-capped mountains in it; and tunnels, and shafts, and pickaxes, and quartz-mills, and pack-trains, and mule-teams. These things were good; what there were of them. And it has railroads in it, and telegraphs, and stars, and suspension-bridges,

Seal for Territory of Nevada, designed by Orion Clemens, Mark Twain's brother.

and other romantic fictions foreign to sand and sage-brush. But the richest of it was the motto. It took them thirty days to decide whether it should be "Volens et Potens" (which they said meant "Able and Willing"), or "The Union Must and Shall be Preserved." Either would have been presumptuous enough, and surpassingly absurd just at present. Because we are not able and willing, thus far, to do a great deal more than locate wild-cat mining-claims and reluctantly sell them to confiding strangers at a ruinous sacrifice—of conscience. And if it were left to us to preserve the Union, in case the balance of the country failed in the attempt, I seriously believe we couldn't do it. Possibly, we might make it mighty warm for the Confederacy if it came prowling around here, but ultimately we would have to forsake our high trust, and quit preserving the Union. I am confident of it. And I have thought the matter over a good deal, off and on, as we say in Paris. We have an animal here whose surname is the "jackass rabbit" It is three feet long, has legs like a counting-house stool, ears of monstrous length, and no tail to speak of. It is swifter than a greyhound, and as meek and harmless as an infant. I might mention, also, that it is as handsome as most infants: however, it would be foreign to the subject, and I do not know that a remark of that kind would be popular in all circles. Let it pass, then—I will say nothing about it, though it would be a great comfort to me to do it, if people would consider the source and overlook it. Well, somebody proposed as a substitute for that pictorial Great Seal, a figure of a jackass-rabbit reposing in the shade of his native sage-brush, with the motto "Volens enough, but not so d—-d Potens."

—"Doings in Nevada," *New York Sunday Mercury* newspaper, February 7, 1864

∽⌒

Twain wrote many articles for the Territorial Enterprise *in Virginia City, Nevada.*

Territorial Enterprise, May 18, 1862

HOW TO PROSPECT A MINE!

By watching the operations of miners in Washoe we are enabled to lay down the following rules: First, find a lead; no matter what it looks like, or how much bed-rock is mixed with it, so you have something that seems to be running somewhere. If you can't find something that has length, breadth and direction, drive a peg and stick up your notice on the first spot of ground you can see that looks red or yaller—them's indications, and there's nothing like indications in this county. In locating your claim put in as many stripes of men as you can get—

"variety is the spice of life," as you will soon find. A mixture of Dutch, French, Spanish, Irish, Scotch, American, English and Norwegian makes a very lively company. No matter how rich the prospect you may be able to get on the surface of your lead, go off about 2,000 feet and start a tunnel towards it—nothing like getting deep enough the first thing—nothing like a tunnel, especially a long one. 2,000 or 3,000 feet is about the distance most companies "kalkerlate" to run, but a company anxious to do the big thing might go further off from the lead.

Having got your claim located, and having decided upon a sufficiently long tunnel, organize. Nothing like organizing, as you will find, with a very little experience. You can't have too much of it. Get up by-laws; they are very useful, as all members of mining companies are greatly addicted to respecting them. No such thing as getting them too long; their great length will make them more binding. You want a number of officers; the more officers you have, the more plans will be found for prosecuting the work, and you can't have too many plans. Having a President makes you look weighty; it takes well with men from the Bay. All the men you see that are from the Bay believe in having Presidents. You may never have any use for a Treasurer, but it looks well, and men from the Bay will expect it; therefore, it is best to have one. Be sure to have a provision in your by-laws allowing each member to work out his assessments; then the work can go on, whether the company is rich or not, and it will give your foreman something to do, to see that each member does his share of the work. Let the members work two days each, by turns.

Have meetings every two or three days—nothing like meetings, you get to know each other so well, and the more you know of each other the better you will be apt to agree. Every time you make 5 feet in your tunnel is not too often to have meetings, you will soon become very fond of these "feasts of reason." Having members representing a variety of nations gives you a splendid opportunity for gaining some insight into their languages; you are sure to hear them talk at ll the meetings. You cannot have too many meetings.

Territorial Enterprise, October 30 or 31, 1866

The following is an *Enterprise* Staff report on upcoming Twain lecture.

Tomorrow night our citizens will be afforded an opportunity to gratify their curiosity and offer a fitting testimonial to their fellow-townsman, Mark Twain, who will do up the Sandwich Islands at the Opera House on that occasion.

The enthusiasm with which his lecture was everywhere greeted is still ringing throughout California, and now that his foot is in his native heath, we expect to see the very mountains shake with a tempest of applause.

Our state can justly claim Mark Twain as its own peculiar production. It was while a resident here and associated with the *Enterprise* that he assumed the name of Mark Twain and developed that rich and inexhaustible vein of humor which has made the title famous. True he has since warmed his fancy in tropical climes and expanded his thought by ocean pilgrimage and heated his

eloquence in volcanic fires; but all these rest upon the solid foundation which was originally laid in our native alkali and sagebrush.

From present appearances he will receive an ovation seldom if ever equalled in our city and it is pleasing to know that such an event will be equally gratifying to the audience and speaker.

Twain at about the time the *Enterprise* article was published.

This is an excerpt from a Twain lecture on his then new book Roughing It, *given December 14, 1871.*

The (Lansing Michigan) State Republican,

LADIES AND GENTLEMEN...

Now when I first started out on this missionary expedition, I had a lecture which I liked very well, but by-and-by I got tired of telling that same old stuff over and over again, and then I got up another lecture, and after that another one, and I am tired of that: so I just thought tonight I would try something fresh, if you are willing. I don't suppose you care what a lecturer talks about if he only tells the truth—at intervals. Now I have got a book in press (it will be out pretty soon), over 600 octavo pages, and illustrated after the fashion of the *Innocents Abroad*. Terms—however I am not around canvassing for the work. I should like to talk a little of that book to you tonight. It is very fresh in my mind, as it is not more than three months since I wrote it. Say 30 or 40 pages— or if you prefer it the whole 600.

Ten or twelve years ago, I crossed the continent from Missouri to California, in the old overland stagecoach, a good while before the Pacific Railway was built. Over 1,900 miles. It was a long ride, day and night, through sagebrush, over sand and alkali plains, wolves and Indians, starvation and smallpox— everything to make the journey interesting. Had a splendid time, a most enjoyable pleasure trip, in that old stagecoach. We were bound for Nevada, which was then a bran' new Territory nearly or about as large as the state of Ohio. It was a desolate, barren, sterile, mountainous, unpeopled country, sagebrush and deserts of alkali. You could scarcely cast your eye in any direction but your gaze would be met by one significant object, and that was the projecting horns of a dried, shrunken carcass of an ox, preaching eloquent sermons of the hardships suffered by those emigrants, where a soil refused to clothe its nakedness, except now and then a little rill (or, as you might call it, a river) goes winding through the plain. Such is the Carson River, which clothes the valley with refreshing and fragrant hayfields. However, hay is a scant crop, and with all the importations from California the price of that article has never come under $300 per ton. In the winter the price reaches $800, and once went up to $1,200 per ton, and then the cattle were turned out to die, and it is hardly putting the figure too strong to say that the valleys were paved with the remains of these cattle.

It is a land where the winters are long and rigorous, where the summers are hot and scorching, and where not a single drop of rain ever falls during eleven tedious months; where it never thunders, and never lightens; where no river finds its way to the sea or empties its waters into the great lakes that have no perceptible outlet, and whose surplus waters are spirited away through mysterious channels down into the ground. A territory broad and ample, but which has not yet had a population numbering 30,000, yet a country that produced $20,000,000 of silver bullion in the year 1863, and produces $12,000,000 to $16,000,000 every year, yet the population has fallen away until now it does not number more than 15,000 or 18,000. Yet that little handful of people vote just as strongly as they do anywhere, are just as well represented in the Senate of the United States as Michigan, or the great state of New York with her 3,000,000 or 4,000,000 of people. That is equality in representation.

I spoke of the sagebrush. That is a particular feature of the country out there. It's an interesting sort of shrub. You see no other sort of vegetable, and clear from Pike's Peak to California's edge the sagebushes stand from three to six feet apart, one vast greenish-gray sea of sage brush. It was the emigrant's fast friend, his only resource for fuel. In its appearance it resembles a venerable live oak with its rough bark and knotty trunk, everything twisted and dwarfed, covered with its thick foliage. I think the sagebrush are beautiful—one at a time is, anyway. Of course, when you see them as far as the eye can reach, seven days and a half in the week, it is different. I am not trying to get up an excitement over sagebrush, but there are many reasons why it should have some mention from an appreciative friend.

I grant you that as a vegetable for table use sagebrush is a failure. Its leaves taste like our ordinary sage; you can make sage tea of it; but anybody in this audience who has ever been a boy or a girl, or both, in a country where doctors were scarce and measles and grandmothers plenty, don't hanker after sage tea. And yet after all there was a manifest providence in the creation of the sagebrush, for it is food for the mules and donkeys, and therefore many emigrant trains are enabled to pull through with their loads where ox teams would lie down and die of starvation. That a mule will eat sagebrush don't prove much, because I know a mule will eat anything. He don't give the toss up of a copper between oysters, lead pipe, brick dust, or even patent office reports. He takes whatever he can get most of.

In our journey we kept climbing and climbing for I don't know how many days and nights. At last we reached the highest eminence—the extreme summit of the great range of the Rocky Mountains, and entered the celebrated South Pass.

Now the South Pass is more suggestive of a straight road than a suspension bridge hung in the clouds though in one place it suggests the latter. One could look below him on the diminishing crags and canyons lying down, down, down, away to the vague plain below, with a crooked thread in it which was the road, and tufts of feathers in it which were trees—the whole country spread out like a picture, sleeping in the sunlight, and darkness stealing over it, blotting out feature after feature under the frown of a gathering storm—not a film or shadow to mar the spectator's gaze. I could watch that storm break forth down there; could see the lightnings flash, the sheeted rain drifting along the canyon's side, and hear the thunder crash upon crash reverberating among a thousand rocky cliffs. This is a familiar experience to traveling people. It was a miracle of sublimity to a boy like me, who could hardly say that he had ever been away from home a single day in his life before.

We visited Salt Lake City in our journey. Carson City, the capital of Nevada, had a wild harem-scarem population of editors, thieves, lawyers, in fact all kinds of blacklegs. Its desperadoes, gamblers, and silver miners went armed to the teeth, every one of them dressed in the roughest kind of costumes, which looked strange and romantic to me and I was fascinated. . . .

The original Ormsby House in downtown Carson City, Nevada in 1863. Twain references the Ormsby in his letter to Robert Fulton.

In this letter to Robert Fulton, Twain is turning down an invitation to a pioneer's reunion that was taking place in 1905. The author was seventy years old at the time and reminisced about his time in Nevada.

In the Mountains, New Hampshire
May 24th, 1905.

Dear Mr. Fulton:

I remember, as if it were yesterday, that when I disembarked from the overland stage in front of the Ormsby in Carson City, in August, 1861, I was not expecting to be asked to come again. I was tired, discouraged, white with alkali dust and did not know anybody; and if you had said then, "Cheer up, desolate stranger, don't be down-hearted—pass on and come again in 1905," you cannot think how grateful I would have closed the contract. Although I was not expecting to be invited I was watching out for it, and was hurt and disappointed when you started to ask me and changed it to "How soon are you going away?" for I was an orphan at that time, and had been one so many years that I was getting sensitive about it.

But you have made it all right now, and the wound is closed. And so I thank you sincerely for the invitation; and with you, all Reno, and if I were a few years younger I would accept it, and promptly. I would go, I would let someone else do the oration, but as for me, I would talk—just talk. I would renew my youth; and talk—and talk—and talk—and have the time of my life! I would march the unforgotten and unforgettable antiques by, and name their names, and give them reverent hail and farewell as they passed: Goodwin, McCarthy, Gillis, Curry, Baldwin, Winters, Howard, Nye, Stewart, Neely Johnson, Hall, Clayton, Jones, North, Root—any my brother, upon whom be peace!—and then the desperadoes, who made life a joy and the "slaughter house" a precious possession: Sam Brown, Farmer Pete, Bill Mayfield, Six Fingered Jack, Jack Williams and the rest of the crimson discipleship—so on, so on. Believe me, I would start a resurrection it would do you more good to look at than the next one will, if you go on the way you are doing now.

Those were the days!—those old ones. They will come no more. Youth will come no more. They were full to the brim with the wine of life. There have been no others like them. It chokes me up to think of them. Would you like me to come out there and cry? It would not become my white head.

Good-bye. I drink to you all. Have a good time and take an old man's blessing.

Mark Twain

On Sea Voyages

The Quaker City Steamer

In the fullness of time the ship was ready to receive her passengers. I was introduced to the young gentleman who was to be my roommate, and found him to be intelligent, cheerful of spirit, unselfish, full of generous impulses, patient, considerate, and wonderfully good-natured. Not any passenger that sailed in the *Quaker City* will withhold his endorsement of what I have just said. We selected a stateroom forward of the wheel, on the starboard side, "below decks." It had two berths in it, a dismal dead-light, a sink with a washbowl in it, and a long, sumptuously cushioned locker, which was to do service as a sofa—partly—and partly as a hiding place for our things. Notwithstanding all this furniture, there was still room to turn around in, but not to swing a cat in, at least with entire security to the cat. However, the room was large, for a ship's stateroom, and was in every way satisfactory.

The vessel was appointed to sail on a certain Saturday early in June.

A little after noon on that distinguished Saturday I reached the ship and went on board. All was bustle and confusion. [I have seen that remark before somewhere.] The pier was crowded with carriages and men; passengers were arriving and hurrying on board; the vessel's decks were encumbered with trunks and valises; groups of excursionists, arrayed in unattractive traveling costumes, were moping about in a drizzling rain and looking as droopy and woebegone as so many molting chickens. The gallant flag was up, but it was under the spell, too, and hung limp and disheartened by the mast. Altogether, it was the bluest, bluest spectacle! It was a pleasure excursion—there was no gainsaying that, because the program said so—it was so nominated in the bond—but it surely hadn't the general aspect of one.

Finally, above the banging, and rumbling, and shouting, and hissing of steam rang the order to "cast off!"—a sudden rush to the gangways—a scampering ashore of visitors-a revolution of the wheels, and we were off—the pic-nic was begun! Two very mild cheers went up from the dripping crowd on the pier; we answered them gently from the slippery decks; the flag made an effort to wave, and failed; the "battery of guns" spake not—the ammunition was out.

An original illustration of the *Quaker City Steamer* from *Innocents Abroad*.

We steamed down to the foot of the harbor and came to anchor. It was still raining. And not only raining, but storming. "Outside" we could see, ourselves, that there was a tremendous sea on. We must lie still, in the calm harbor, till the storm should abate. Our passengers hailed from fifteen states; only a few of them had ever been to sea before; manifestly it would not do to pit them against a full-blown tempest until they had got their sea-legs on. Toward evening the two steam tugs that had accompanied us with a rollicking champagne-party of young New Yorkers on board who wished to bid farewell to one of our number in due and ancient form departed, and we were alone on the deep. On deep five fathoms, and anchored fast to the bottom. And out in the solemn rain, at that. This was pleasuring with a vengeance.

It was an appropriate relief when the gong sounded for prayer meeting. The first Saturday night of any other pleasure excursion might have been devoted to whist and dancing; but I submit it to the unprejudiced mind if it would have been in good taste for us to engage in such frivolities, considering what we had gone through and the frame of mind we were in. We would have shone at a wake, but not at anything more festive.

However, there is always a cheering influence about the sea; and in my berth that night, rocked by the measured swell of the waves and lulled by the murmur of the distant surf, I soon passed tranquilly out of all consciousness of the dreary experiences of the day and damaging premonitions of the future.

—Innocents Abroad

SS Minneapolis

Mark Twain's trip across the Atlantic would seem to have been a pleasant one. The *Minneapolis* is a fine, big ship, and there was plenty of company. Prof. Archibald Henderson, Bernard Shaw's biographer, was aboard; [Professor Henderson has since then published a volume on Mark Twain— an interesting commentary on his writings—mainly from the sociological point of view.] also President Patton, of the Princeton Theological Seminary; a well-known cartoonist, Richards, and some very attractive young people— school-girls in particular, such as all through his life had appealed to Mark Twain. Indeed, in his later life they made a stronger appeal than ever. The years had robbed him of his own little flock, and always he was trying to replace them. Once he said:

"During those years after my wife's death I was washing about on a forlorn sea of banquets and speech-making in high and holy causes, and these things furnished me intellectual cheer, and entertainment; but they got at my heart for an evening only, then left it dry and dusty. I had reached the grandfather stage of life without grandchildren, so I began to adopt some."

He adopted several on that journey to England and on the return voyage, and he kept on adopting others during the rest of his life. These companionships became one of the happiest aspects of his final days, as we shall see by and by.

There were entertainments on the ship, one of them given for the benefit of the Seamen's Orphanage. One of his adopted granddaughters—"Charley" he called her—played a violin solo and Clemens made a speech. Later his autographs were sold at auction. Dr. Patton was auctioneer, and one autographed postal card brought twenty-five dollars, which is perhaps the record price for a single Mark Twain signature. He wore his white suit on this occasion, and in the course

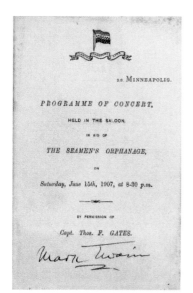

Signed ship menu of the SS *Minneapolis* from Twain's 1907 voyage to London to receive the honor of a Doctor of Literature degree from Oxford University in London.

of his speech referred to it. He told first of the many defects in his behavior, and how members of his household had always tried to keep him straight. The children, he said, had fallen into the habit of calling it "dusting papa off." Then he went on:

"When my daughter came to see me off last Saturday at the boat she slipped a note in my hand and said, 'Read it when you get aboard the ship.' I didn't think of it again until day before yesterday, and it was a 'dusting off.' And if I carry out all the instructions that I got there I shall be more celebrated in England for my behavior than for anything else. I got instructions how to act on every occasion. She underscored 'Now, don't you wear white clothes on ship or on shore until you get back,' and I intended to obey. I have been used to obeying my family all my life, but I wore the white clothes to-night because the trunk that has the dark clothes in it is in the cellar. I am not apologizing for the white clothes; I am only apologizing to my daughter for not obeying her."

He received a great welcome when the ship arrived at Tilbury. A throng of rapid-fire reporters and photographers immediately surrounded him, and when he left the ship the stevedores gave him a round of cheers. It was the beginning of that almost unheard-of demonstration of affection and honor which never for a moment ceased, but augmented from day to day during the four weeks of his English sojourn.

—*Mark Twain Biography* by Albert Bigelow Paine

BATH.

On Great Britain

Mark Twain was, later in life, made a Knight of Bath, as shown the clever cartoon on the previous page entitled "The Connecticut Yankee in King Edward's Court." He was very proud of this achievement and for his honorary degree from Oxford. However, it was a younger, brasher Twain that wrote this piece about the British. His tune obviously changed later in life.

Wherever they can stick a name so that it shall glorify anything pertaining to England, there they stick it. You never hear of an Englishman speak of the Hawaiian Islands—no, he calls them the Sandwich Islands; Cook discovered them second-hand, by following a Spanish chart three hundred years old, which is still in the British Museum, and named them for some one-horse Earl of Sandwich, that nobody had heard of before, and hasn't since—a man that probably never achieved any work that was really gorgeous during his earthly mission, excepting his invention for confining a slice of ham between two slices of bread in such a manner as to enable even the least gifted of our race to eat bread and meat at the same time, without being bewildered by too elaborate a conjunction of ideas. I suppose, if the real truth were known, some foreigner invented the Sandwich, but England gave it a name, in her usual cheerful fashion. They never even speak of the whale that swallowed Jonah merely as a whale, but as the Prince of Wales. They think it suggests that he was an English whale. If he was that, that is sufficient. That covers up any probable flaws in his character. It is nothing to them that he went about gobbling up the prophets wherever he found them; it is nothing that he interfered with their business—nothing that he put them to infinite delay, discomfort and annoyance; it is nothing that he disgorged prophets in such a condition, as to personal appearance, that they might well feel a delicacy about preaching in a strange city. No—being an English whale was sufficient to make this infamous conduct excusable; and being English, they are willing to let the "great fish" pass for a whale, notwithstanding a whale's throat is not large enough to let a man do down.

—Letter to San Francisco Alta California, February 11, 1868

Cartoon depicting Twain being made a Knight of Bath from the *Journal*, Minneapolis.

Our kindred blood and our common language, our kindred religion and political liberty, make us feel nearer to England than to other nations, and render us more desirous of standing well there than with foreign nationalities that are foreign to us in all particulars.

— The New Pilgrim's Progress

Here is Twain's speech from a Fourth of July celebration in London, 1899.

Mr. Chairman and ladies and gentlemen: I thank you for the compliment which has just been tendered me, and to show my appreciation of it I will not afflict you with many words. It is pleasant to celebrate in this peaceful way, upon this old mother soil, the anniversary of an experiment which was born of war with this same land so long ago, and wrought out to a successful issue by the devotion of our ancestors. It has taken nearly a hundred years to bring the English and Americans into kindly and mutually appreciative relations, but I believe it has been accomplished at last. It was a great step when the two last misunderstandings were settled by arbitration instead of cannon. It is another great step when England adopts our sewing-machines without claiming the invention—as usual. It was another when they imported one of our sleeping-cars the other day. And it warmed my heart more than I can tell, yesterday, when I witnessed the spectacle of an Englishman ordering an American sherry cobbler of his own free will and accord—and not only that but with a great brain and a level head reminding the barkeeper not to forget the strawberries. With a common origin, a common language, a common literature, a common religion and—common drinks, what is longer needful to the cementing of the two nations together in a permanent bond of brotherhood?

This is an age of progress, and ours is a progressive land. A great and glorious land, too—a land which has developed a Washington, a Franklin, a William M. Tweed, a Longfellow, a Motley, a Jay Gould, a Samuel C. Pomeroy, a recent Congress which has never had its equal (in some respects), and a United States Army which conquered sixty Indians in eight months by tiring them out—which is much better than uncivilized slaughter, God knows. We have a criminal jury system which is superior to any in the world; and its efficiency is

Mark Twain in his Oxford robes after receiving his honorary degree in 1907.

only marred by the difficulty of finding twelve men every day who don't know anything and can't read. And I may observe that we have an insanity plea that would have saved Cain. I think I can say, and say with pride, that we have some legislatures that bring higher prices than any in the world.

I refer with effusion to our railway system, which consents to let us live, though it might do the opposite, being our owners. It only destroyed three thousand and seventy lives last year by collisions, and twenty-seven thousand two hundred and sixty by running over heedless and unnecessary people at crossings. The companies seriously regretted the killing of these thirty thousand people, and went so far as to pay for some of them—voluntarily, of course, for the meanest of us would not claim that we possess a court treacherous enough to enforce a law against a railway company. But, thank Heaven, the railway companies are generally disposed to do the right and kindly thing without compulsion. I know of an instance which greatly touched me at the time. After an accident the company sent home the remains of a dear distant old relative of mine in a basket, with the remark, "Please state what figure you hold him at—and return the basket." Now there couldn't be anything friendlier than that.

But I must not stand here and brag all night. However, you won't mind a body bragging a little about his country on the fourth of July. It is a fair and legitimate time to fly the eagle. I will say only one more word of brag—and a hopeful one. It is this. We have a form of government which gives each man a fair chance and no favor. With us no individual is born with a right to look down upon his neighbor and hold him in contempt. Let such of us as are not dukes find our consolation in that. And we may find hope for the future in the fact that as unhappy as is the condition of our political morality to-day, England has risen up out of a far fouler since the days when Charles I. ennobled courtesans and all political place was a matter of bargain and sale. There is hope for us yet.

—*Sketches New and Old*

On France

Buffalo Express

TO THE READER.

The accompanying map explains itself.

The idea of this map is not original with me, but is borrowed from the "Tribune" and the other great metropolitan journals.

I claim no other merit for this production (if I may so call it) than that it is accurate. The main blemish of the city-paper maps of which it is an imitation, is, that in them more attention seems paid to artistic picturesqueness than geographical reliability.

Inasmuch as this is the first time I ever tried to draft and engrave a map, or attempt anything in the line of art at all, the commendations the work has received and the admiration it has excited among the people, have been very grateful to my feelings. And it is touching to reflect that by far the most enthusiastic of these praises have come from people who know nothing at all about art.

By an unimportant oversight I have engraved the map so that it reads wrong end first, except to left-handed people. I forgot that in order to make it right in print it should be drawn and engraved upside down. However, let the student who desires to contemplate the map stand on his head or hold it before her looking-glass. That will bring it right.

The reader will comprehend at a glance that that piece of river with the "High Bridge" over it got left out to one side by reason of a slip of the graving-tool, which rendered it necessary to change the entire course of the river Rhine or else spoil the map. After having spent two days in digging and gouging at the map, I would have changed the course of the Atlantic ocean before I would have lost so much work.

I never had so much trouble with anything in my life as I did with this map. I had heaps of little fortifications scattered all around Paris, at first, but every now and then my instruments would slip and fetch away whole miles of batteries and leave the vicinity as clean as if the Prussians had been there.

The reader will find it well to frame this map for future reference, so that it may aid in extending popular intelligence and dispelling the wide-spread ignorance of the day.

MARK TWAIN.

OFFICIAL COMMENDATIONS.

It is the only map of the kind I ever saw.
U. S. GRANT.

It places the situation in an entirely new light.
BISMARCK.

I cannot look upon it without shedding tears.
BRIGHAM YOUNG.

It is very nice, large print.
NAPOLEON.

~⁓

My wife was for years afflicted with freckles, and though everything was done
for her relief that could be done, all was in vain. But, sir, since her first glance
at your map, they have entirely left her. She has nothing but convulsions now.
J. SMITH.

~⁓

If I had had this map I could have got out of Metz without any trouble.
BAZAINE.

~⁓

I have seen a great many maps in my time,
but none that this one reminds me of.
TROCHU.

~⁓

It is but fair to say that in some respects it is a truly remarkable map.
W. T. SHERMAN.

~⁓

I said to my son Frederick William, "If you could only make a map like that,
I would be perfectly willing to see you die—even anxious.
WILLIAM III

The Can-Can

The dance had begun, and we adjourned to the temple. Within it was a
drinking saloon, and all around it was a broad circular platform for the
dancers. I backed up against the wall of the temple, and waited. Twenty sets
formed, the music struck up, and then—I placed my hands before my face
for very shame. But I looked through my fingers. They were dancing the
renowned "Can-can." A handsome girl in the set before me tripped forward
lightly to meet the opposite gentleman, tripped back again, grasped her dresses
vigorously on both sides with her hands, raised them pretty high, danced an

extraordinary jig that had more activity and exposure about it than any jig I ever saw before, and then, drawing her clothes still higher, she advanced gaily to the center and launched a vicious kick full at her vis-a-vis that must infallibly have removed his nose if he had been seven feet high. It was a mercy he was only six.

That is the can-can. The idea of it is to dance as wildly, as noisily, as furiously as you can; expose yourself as much as possible if you are a woman; and kick as high as you can, no matter which sex you belong to. There is no word of exaggeration in this. Any of the staid, respectable, aged people who were there that night can testify to the truth of that statement. There were a good many such people present. I suppose French morality is not of that straight-laced description which is shocked at trifles.

I moved aside and took a general view of the can-can. Shouts, laughter, furious music, a bewildering chaos of darting and intermingling forms, stormy jerking and snatching of gay dresses, bobbing beads, flying arms, lightning flashes of white-stockinged calves and dainty slippers in the air, and then a grand final rush, riot, a terrific hubbub, and a wild stampede! Heavens!

—*Innocents Abroad*

Original illustration from *Innocents Abroad*.

On Russia

On Czars

Taking the kind expression that is in the Emperor's face and the gentleness that is in his young daughter's into consideration, I wondered if it would not tax the Czar's firmness to the utmost to condemn a supplicating wretch to misery in the wastes of Siberia if she pleaded for him. . . . It seemed strange— stranger than I can tell—to think that the central figure in the cluster of men and women, chatting here under the trees like the most ordinary individual in the land, was a man who could open his lips and ships would fly through the waves, locomotives would speed over the plains, couriers would hurry from village to village, a hundred telegraphs would flash the word to the four corners of an Empire that stretches its vast proportions over a seventh part of the habitable globe, and a countless multitude of men would spring to do his bidding. I had a sort of vague desire to examine his hands and see if they were of flesh and blood, like other men's. Here was a man who could do this wonderful thing, and yet if I chose I could knock him down. The case was plain, but it seemed preposterous, nevertheless—as preposterous as trying to knock down a mountain or wipe out a continent. If this man sprained his ankle, a million miles of telegraph would carry the news over mountains— valleys—uninhabited deserts—under the trackless sea—and ten thousand newspapers would prate of it; if he were grievously ill, all the nations would know it before the sun rose again; if he dropped lifeless where he stood, his fall might shake the thrones of half a world! If I could have stolen his coat, I would have done it. When I meet a man like that, I want something to remember him by.

—*Innocents Abroad*

∽

After the Czar's morning bath it is his habit to meditate an hour before dressing himself.—*London Times Correspondence*

[Viewing himself in the pier-glass.] Naked, what am I? A lank, skinny, spider-legged libel on the image of God! Look at the waxwork head—the face, with the expression of a melon—the projecting ears—the knotted elbows—the dished breast—the knife-edged shins—and then the feet, all beads and joints and bone-sprays, an imitation X-ray photograph! There is nothing imperial about this, nothing imposing, impressive, nothing to invoke awe and reverence. Is it this that a hundred and forty million Russians kiss the dust before and worship? Manifestly not! No one could worship this spectacle, which is Me. Then who is it, what is it, that they worship ? Privately, none knows better than I: it is my clothes. Without my clothes I should be as destitute of authority as any other naked person. Nobody could tell me from a parson, a barber, a dude. Then who is the real Emperor of Russia ? My clothes. There is no other.

As Teufelsdröckh suggested, what would man be—what would any man be— without his clothes? As soon as one stops and thinks over that proposition, one realizes that without his clothes a man would be nothing at all; that the clothes do not merely make the man, the clothes are the man; that without them he is a cipher, a vacancy, a nobody, a nothing.

Titles—another artificiality—are a part of his clothing. They and the dry-goods conceal the wearer's inferiority and make him seem great and a wonder, when at bottom there is nothing remarkable about him. They can move a nation to fall on its knees and sincerely worship an Emperor who, without the clothes and the title, would drop to the rank of the cobbler and be swallowed up and lost sight of in the massed multitude of the inconsequentials; an Emperor who, naked in a naked world, would get no notice, excite no remark, and be heedlessly shouldered and jostled like any other uncertified stranger, and perhaps offered a kopek to carry somebody's gripsack; yet an Emperor who, by the sheer might of those artificialities—clothes and a title—can get himself worshipped as a deity by his people, and at his pleasure and unrebuked can exile them, hunt them, harry them, destroy them, just as he would with so many rats if the accident of birth had furnished him a calling better suited to his capacities than empering. It is a stupendous force—that which resides in the all-concealing cloak of clothes and title; they fill the onlooker with awe; they make him tremble ; yet he knows that every hereditary regal dignity commemorates a usurpation, a power illegitimately acquired, an authority conveyed and conferred by persons who did not own it. For monarchs have been chosen and elected by aristocracies only: a Nation has never elected one.

There is no power without clothes. It is the power that governs the human race. Strip its chiefs to the skin, and no State could be governed; naked officials could exercise no authority; they would look (and be) like everybody else— commonplace, inconsequential. A policeman in plain clothes is one man; in his uniform he is ten. Clothes and title axe the most potent thing, the most formidable influence, in the earth. They move the human race to willing and spontaneous respect for the judge, the general, the admiral, the bishop, the ambassador, the frivolous earl, the idiot duke, the sultan, the king, the emperor. No great title is efficient without clothes to support it. In naked tribes of savages the kings wear some kind of rag or decoration which they make sacred to themselves and allow no one else to wear. The king of the great Fan tribe wears a bit of leopard-skin on his shoulder—it is sacred to royalty; the rest of him is perfectly naked, Without his bit of leopard-skin to awe and impress the people, he would not be able to keep his job.

—Mark Twain, from The Czar's Soliloquy,
North American Review, March, 1905

On Austria

I. THE GOVERNMENT IN THE FRYING-PAN.

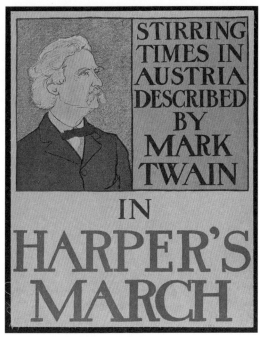

STIRRING TIMES IN AUSTRIA DESCRIBED BY MARK TWAIN

IN

HARPER'S MARCH

Cover of *Harper's Magazine*, 1898.

Here in Vienna in these closing days of 1897 one's blood gets no chance to stagnate. The atmosphere is brimful of political electricity. All conversation is political; every man is a battery, with brushes overworn, and gives out blue sparks when you set him going on the common topic. Everybody has an opinion, and lets you have it frank and hot, and out of this multitude of counsel you get merely confusion and despair. For no one really understands this political situation, or can tell you what is going to be the outcome of it.

Things have happened here recently which would set any country but Austria on fire from end to end, and upset the Government to a certainty; but no one feels confident that such results will follow here. Here, apparently, one must wait and see what will happen, then he will know, and not before; guessing is idle; guessing cannot help the matter. This is what the wise tell you; they all say it; they say it every day, and it is the sole detail upon which they all agree.

There is some approach to agreement upon another point: that there will be no revolution. Men say: "Look at our history, revolutions have not been in our line; and look at our political map, its construction is unfavourable to an organised uprising, and without unity what could a revolt accomplish? It is disunion which has held our empire together for centuries, and what it has done in the past it may continue to do now and in the future."

The most intelligible sketch I have encountered of this unintelligible arrangement of things was contributed to the *Traveler's Record* by Mr. Forrest Morgan, of Hartford, three years ago. He says:

> The Austro-Hungarian Monarchy is the patchwork-quilt, the Midway Plaisance, the national chain-gang of Europe; a state that is not a nation, but a collection of nations, some with national memories and aspirations and others without, some occupying distinct provinces almost purely their own, and others mixed with alien races, but each with a different language, and each mostly holding the others foreigners as much as if the link of a common government did not exist. Only one of its races even now comprises so much as one-fourth of the whole, and not another so much as one-sixth; and each has remained for ages as unchanged in isolation, however mingled together in locality, as globules of oil in water. There is nothing else in the modern world that is nearly like it, though there have been plenty in past ages; it seems unreal and impossible even though we know it is true; it violates all our feeling as to what a country should be in order to have a right to exist; and it seems as though it was too ramshackle to go on holding together any length of time. Yet it has survived, much in its present shape, two centuries of storms that have swept perfectly unified countries from existence and others that have brought it to the verge of ruin, has survived formidable European coalitions to dismember it, and has steadily gained force after each; forever changing in its exact make-up, losing in the West but gaining in the East, the changes leave the structure as firm as ever, like the dropping off and adding on of logs in a raft, its mechanical union of pieces showing all the vitality of genuine national life.

That seems to confirm and justify the prevalent Austrian faith that in this confusion of unrelated and irreconcilable elements, this condition of incurable disunion, there is strength—for the Government. Nearly every day some one explains to me that a revolution would not succeed here. "It couldn't, you know. Broadly speaking, all the nations in the empire hate the Government—but they all hate each other too, and with devoted and enthusiastic bitterness; no two of them can combine; the nation that rises must rise alone; then the others would joyfully join the Government against her, and she would have just a fly's chance against a combination of spiders. This Government is entirely independent. It can go its own road, and do as it pleases; it has nothing to fear. In countries like England and America, where there is one tongue and the public interests are common, the Government must take account of public opinion; but in Austria-Hungary there are nineteen public opinions—one for each state. No—two or three for each state, since there are two or three nationalities in each. A Government cannot satisfy all these public opinions; it can only go through the motions of trying. This Government does that. It goes through the motions, and they do not succeed; but that does not worry the Government much."

The next man will give you some further information. "The Government has a policy—a wise one—and sticks to it. This policy is—*tranquillity*: keep this hive of excitable nations as quiet as possible; encourage them to amuse themselves with things less inflammatory that politics. To this end it furnishes them an abundance of Catholic priests to teach them to be docile and obedient, and to be diligent in acquiring ignorance about things here below, and knowledge about the kingdom of heaven, to whose historic delights they are going to add the charm of their society by-and-by; and further—to this same end—it cools off the newspapers every morning at five o'clock, whenever warm events are happening." There is a censor of the press, and apparently he is always on duty and hard at work. A copy of each morning paper is brought to him at five o'clock. His official wagons wait at the doors of the newspaper offices and scud to him with the first copies that come from the press. His company of assistants read every line in these papers, and mark everything which seems to have a dangerous look; then he passes final judgment upon these markings. Two things conspire to give to the results a capricious and unbalanced look: his assistants have diversified notions as to what is dangerous and what isn't; he can't get time to examine their criticisms in much detail; and so sometimes the very same matter which is suppressed in one paper fails to be damned in another one, and gets published in full feather and unmodified. Then the paper in which it was suppressed blandly copies the forbidden matter into its evening edition—provokingly giving credit and detailing all the circumstances in courteous and inoffensive language—and of course the censor cannot say a word.

Sometimes the censor sucks all the blood out of a newspaper and leaves it colorless and inane; sometimes he leaves it undisturbed, and lets it talk out its opinions with a frankness and vigour hardly to be surpassed, I think, in the journals of any country. Apparently the censor sometimes revises his verdicts upon second thought, for several times lately he has suppressed journals after their issue and partial distribution. The distributed copies are then sent for by the censor and destroyed. I have two of these, but at the time they were sent for I could not remember what I had done with them.

If the censor did his work before the morning edition was printed, he would be less of an inconvenience than he is; but, of course, the papers cannot wait many minutes after five o'clock to get his verdict; they might as well go out of business as do that; so they print and take their chances. Then, if they get caught by a suppression, they must strike out the condemned matter and print the edition over again. That delays the issue several hours, and is expensive besides. The Government gets the suppressed edition for nothing. If it bought it, that would be joyful, and would give great satisfaction. Also, the edition would be larger. Some of the papers do not replace the condemned paragraphs with other matter; they merely snatch they out and leave blanks behind—mourning blanks, marked "*Confiscated.*"

The Government discourages the dissemination of newspaper information in other ways. For instance, it does not allow newspapers to be sold on the streets: therefore the newsboy is unknown in Vienna. And there is a stamp duty of nearly a cent upon each copy of a newspaper's issue. Every American paper that reaches me has a stamp upon it, which has been pasted there in the post-office or downstairs in the hotel office; but no matter who put it there, I have to pay for it, and that is the main thing. Sometimes friends send me so many papers that it takes all I can earn that week to keep this Government going....

—"Stirring Times in Austria" *Harper's Magazine,* 1898

Berlin

Chicago Daily Tribune, April 3, 1892

THE CHICAGO OF EUROPE

I feel lost in Berlin. It has no resemblance to the city I had supposed it was. There was once a Berlin which I would have known, from descriptions in books—the Berlin of the last century and the beginning of the present one: a dingy city in a marsh, with rough streets, muddy and lantern-lighted, dividing straight rows of ugly houses all alike, compacted into blocks as square and plain and uniform and monotonous and serious as so many dry-goods boxes. But that Berlin has disappeared. It seems to have disappeared totally, and left no sign. The bulk of the Berlin of today has about it no suggestion of a former period. The site it stands on has traditions and a history, but the city itself has no traditions and no history. It is a new city; the newest I have ever seen. Chicago would seem venerable beside it; for there are many old-looking districts in Chicago, but not many in Berlin. The main mass of the city looks as if it had been built last week, the rest of it has a just perceptibly graver tone, and looks as if it might be six or even eight months old.

The next feature that strikes one is the spaciousness, the roominess of the city. There is no other city, in any country, whose streets are so generally wide. Berlin is not merely a city of wide streets, it is the city of wide streets. As a wide-street city it has never had its equal, in any age of the world. "Unter den Linden" is three streets in one; the Potsdamerstrasse is bordered on both sides by sidewalks which are themselves wider than some of the historic thoroughfares of the old European capitals; there seem to be no lanes or alleys; there are no short cuts; here and there, where several important streets empty into a common center, that center's circumference is of a magnitude calculated to bring that word spaciousness into your mind again. The park in the middle of the city is so huge that it calls up that expression once more.

The next feature that strikes one is the straightness of the streets. The short ones haven't so much as a waver in them; the long ones stretch out to prodigious distances and then tilt a little to the right or left, then stretch out on another immense reach as straight as a ray of light. A result of this arrangement is that at night Berlin is an inspiring sight to see. Gas and the

Berlin in the 1890s.

electric light are employed with a wasteful liberality, and so, wherever one goes, he has always double ranks of brilliant lights stretching far down into the night on every hand, with here and there a wide and splendid constellation of them spread out over an intervening "platz," and between the interminable double procession of street lamps one has the swarming and darting cab lamps, a lively and pretty addition to the fine spectacle, for they counterfeit the rush and confusion and sparkle of an invasion of fireflies.

There is one other noticeable feature—the absolutely level surface of the site of Berlin. Berlin, to recapitulate, is newer to the eye than is any other city, and also blonder of complexion and tidier; no other city has such an air of roominess, freedom from crowding; no other city has so many straight streets; and with Chicago it contests the chromo for flatness of surface and for phenomenal swiftness of growth. Berlin is the European Chicago. The two cities have about the same population—say a million and a half. I cannot speak in exact terms, because I only know what Chicago's population was week before last; but at that time it was about a million and a half. Fifteen years ago Berlin and Chicago were large cities, of course, but neither of them was the giant it now is.

But now the parallels fail. Only parts of Chicago are stately and beautiful, whereas all of Berlin is stately and substantial, and it is not merely in parts but uniformly beautiful. There are buildings in Chicago that are architecturally finer than any in Berlin, I think, but what I have just said above is still true. These two flat cities would lead the world for phenomenal good health if London were out of the way. As it is, London leads by a point or two. Berlin's death rate is only nineteen in the thousand. Fourteen years ago the rate was a third higher.

Berlin is a surprise in a great many ways—in a multitude of ways, to speak strongly and be exact. It seems to be the most governed city in the world, but one must admit that it also seems to be the best governed. Method and system are observable on every hand—in great things, in little things, in all details, of whatsoever size. And it is not method and system on paper, and there an end— it is method and system in practice. It has a rule for everything, and puts the rule in force; puts it in force against the poor and powerful alike, without favor or prejudice. It deals with great matters and minute particulars with equal faithfulness, and with a plodding and painstaking diligence and persistency which compel admiration—and sometimes regret. There are several taxes, and they are collected quarterly. Collected is the word; they are not merely levied, they are collected—every time. This makes light taxes. It is in cities and countries where a considerable part of the community shirk payment that taxes have to be lifted to a burdensome rate. Here the police keep coming, calmly and patiently, until you pay your tax. They charge you 5 or 10 cents per visit after the first call. By experiment you will find that they will presently collect that money.

In one respect the 1,500,000 of Berlin's population are like a family: the head of this large family knows the names of its several members, and where the said members are located, and when and where they were born, and what they do for a living, and what their religious brand is. Whoever comes to Berlin must furnish these particulars to the police immediately; moreover, if he knows how long he is going to stay, he must say so. If he takes a house he will be taxed on the rent and taxed also on his income. He will not be asked what his income is, and so he may save some lies for home consumption. The police will estimate his income from the house rent he pays, and tax him on that basis.

Duties on imported articles are collected with inflexible fidelity, be the sum large or little; but the methods are gentle, prompt, and full of the spirit of accommodation. The postman attends to the whole matter for you, in cases where the article comes by mail, and you have no trouble and suffer no inconvenience. The other day a friend of mine was informed that there was a package in the post-office for him, containing a lady's silk belt with gold clasp, and a gold chain to hang a bunch of keys on. In his first agitation he was going to try to bribe the postman to chalk it through, but acted upon his sober second thought and allowed the matter to take its proper and regular course. In a little while the postman brought the package and made these several collections: duty on the silk belt, 7 1/2 cents; duty on the gold chain, 10 cents; charge for fetching the package, 5 cents. These devastating imposts are exacted for the protection of German home industries.

The calm, quiet, courteous, cussed persistence of the police is the most admirable thing I have encountered on this side. They undertook to persuade me to send and get a passport for a Swiss maid whom we had brought with us, and at the end of six weeks of patient, tranquil, angelic daily effort they succeeded. I was not intending to give them trouble, but I was lazy and I thought they would get tired. Meanwhile they probably thought I would be the one. It turned out just so.

One is not allowed to build unstable, unsafe, or unsightly houses in Berlin; the result is this comely and conspicuously stately city, with its security from conflagrations and breakdowns. It is built of architectural Gibraltars. The building commissioners inspect while the building is going up. It has been found that this is better than to wait till it falls down. These people are full of whims.

One is not allowed to cram poor folk into cramped and dirty tenement houses. Each individual must have just so many cubic feet of room-space, and sanitary inspections are systematic and frequent.

Everything is orderly. The fire brigade march in rank, curiously uniformed, and so grave is their demeanor that they look like a Salvation Army under conviction of sin. People tell me that when a fire alarm is sounded, the firemen assemble calmly, answer to their names when the roll is called, then proceed to the fire. There they are ranked up, military fashion, and told off in detachments by the chief, who parcels out to the detachments the several parts of the work which they are to undertake in putting out that fire. This is all done with low-voiced propriety, and strangers think these people are working a funeral. As a rule, the fire is confined to a single floor in these great masses of bricks and masonry, and consequently there is little or no interest attaching to a fire here for the rest of the occupants of the house.

There is abundance of newspapers in Berlin, and there was also a newsboy, but he died. At intervals of half a mile on the thoroughfares there are booths, and it is at these that you buy your papers. There are plenty of theaters, but they do not advertise in a loud way. There are no big posters of any kind, and the display of vast type and of pictures of actors and performance framed on a big scale and done in rainbow colors is a thing unknown. If the big show bills existed there would be no place to exhibit them; for there are no poster fences, and one would not be allowed to disfigure dead walls with them. Unsightly things are forbidden here; Berlin is a rest to the eye.

—Mark Twain

Switzerland

The Lion of Lucerne was designed by Bertel Thorvaldsen and created by Lukas Ahorn in about 1820. It commemorates the Swiss Guards who were massacred in 1792 during the French Revolution. Mark Twain praised the sculpture in A Tramp Abroad.

The commerce of Lucerne consists mainly in gimcrackery of the souvenir sort; the shops are packed with Alpine crystals, photographs of scenery, and wooden and ivory carvings. I will not conceal the fact that miniature figures of the Lion of Lucerne are to be had in them. Millions of them. But they are libels upon him, every one of them. There is a subtle something about the majestic pathos of the original which the copyist cannot get. Even the sun fails to get it; both the photographer and the carver give you a dying lion, and that is all. The shape is right, the attitude is right, the proportions are right, but that indescribable something which makes the Lion of Lucerne the most mournful and moving piece of stone in the world, is wanting.

The Lion of Lucerne

The Lion lies in his lair in the perpendicular face of a low cliff—for he is carved from the living rock of the cliff. His size is colossal, his attitude is noble. His head is bowed, the broken spear is sticking in his shoulder, his protecting paw rests upon the lilies of France. Vines hang down the cliff and wave in the wind, and a clear stream trickles from above and empties into a pond at the base, and in the smooth surface of the pond the lion is mirrored, among the water-lilies.

Around about are green trees and grass. The place is a sheltered, reposeful woodland nook, remote from noise and stir and confusion—and all this is fitting, for lions do die in such places, and not on granite pedestals in public squares fenced with fancy iron railings. The Lion of Lucerne would be impressive anywhere, but nowhere so impressive as where he is.

—*A Tramp Abroad*

On the Sandwich Islands

After writing about the Sandwich Islands for the Alta California *newspaper, Twain returned to San Francisco. It had been his first time outside of America. He had spent almost five months there. Upon his return, Twain decided to give a humorous lecture on his travels.*

The native language is soft and liquid and flexible and in every way efficient and satisfactory—till you get mad; then there you are; there isn't anything in it to swear with.

—*Mark Twain's Speeches*

～૭

Nearby is an interesting ruin—the meager remains of an ancient temple—a place where human sacrifices were offered up in those old bygone days . . . long, long before the missionaries braved a thousand privations to come and make [the natives] permanently miserable by telling them how beautiful and how blissful a place heaven is, and how nearly impossible it is to get there; and showed the poor native how dreary a place perdition is and what unnecessarily liberal facilities there are going for it; showed him how, in his ignorance, he had gone and fooled away all his kinfolk to no purpose; showed him what rapture it is to work all day long for fifty cents to buy food for next day with, as compared with fishing for a pastime and lolling in the shade through eternal summer, and eating of the bounty that nobody labored to provide but Nature. How sad it is to think of the multitudes who have gone to their graves in this beautiful island and never knew there was a hell.

—Roughing It

This became Twain's favorite lecture. He performed it almost 100 times, first in San Francisco on October 2, 1866. It was his debut as a professional platform entertainer. He gave it for the last time on December 8, 1873, to a delighted audience in London, England.

The lecture usually began something like this: "The Sandwich Islands will be the subject of my lecture—when I get to it—and I shall endeavor to tell the truth as nearly as a newspaper man can. If I embellish it with a little nonsense, that makes no difference; it won't mar the truth; it is only as the barnacle ornaments the oyster by sticking to it. That figure is original with me! I was born back from tidewater and don't know as the barnacle does stick to the oyster. . . ."

On Bermuda

Twain in Bermuda.

Bermuda is the right country for a jaded man to "loaf" in. There are no harassments; the deep peace and quiet of the country sink into one's body and bones and give his conscience a rest and chloroform the legion of invisible small devils that are always trying to whitewash his hair.

—"Some Rambling Notes of an Idle Excursion", *The Atlantic*

There are no newspapers, no telegrams, no mobiles, no trolleys, no trams, no tramps, no railways, no theatres, no noise, no lectures, no riots, no murders, no fires, no burglaries, no politics, no offences of any kind, no follies but church, & I don't go there.

—Letter to Elizabeth Wallace, March 10, 1910

Bermuda is not large, and is like the earlier Garden of Eden, in that everybody in it knows everybody else, just as it was in the serpent's headquarters in Adam's time.

—*Autobiography*

On the Orient

Kelley's Weekly, *a publication that was similar to* Harper's Weekly, *published this story in 1867. It was probably the first printing of any part of* Innocents Abroad.

"A Yankee in the Orient. Mark Twain Takes a Turkish Bath."

For years and years I have dreamed of the wonders of the Turkish bath; for years and years I have promised myself that I would yet enjoy one. Many and many a time, in fancy, I have lain in the marble bath, and breathed the slumbrous fragrance of Eastern spices that filled the air; then passed through a weird and complicated system of pulling and hauling, and drenching and scrubbing, by a gang of naked savages who loomed vast and vaguely through the steaming mists, like demons; then rested for a while on a divan fit for a king; then passed through another complex ordeal, and one more fearful than the first; and, finally, swathed in soft fabrics, been conveyed to a princely saloon and laid on a bed of eider down, where eunuchs, gorgeous of costume, fanned me while I drowsed and dreamed, or contentedly gazed at the rich hangings of the apartment, the soft carpets, the sumptuous furniture, the pictures, and drank delicious coffee, smoked the soothing narghili, and dropped, at the last, into tranquil repose, lulled by sensuous odors from unseen censers, by the gentle influence of the narghili's Persian tobacco, and by the music of fountains that counterfeited the pattering of summer rain.

Cover of *Kelley's Weekly* from November 30, 1867.

That was the picture, just as I got it from incendiary books of travel. It was a poor, miserable imposture. The reality is no more like it than the Five Points are like the Garden of Eden. They received me in a great court, paved with marble slabs; around it were broad galleries, one above another, carpeted with seedy matting, railed with unpainted balustrades, and furnished with huge rickety chairs, cushioned with rusty old mattresses, indented with impressions left by the forms of nine successive generations of men who had reposed upon them. The place was vast, naked, dreary; its court a barn, its galleries stalls for human horses. The cadaverous, half nude varlets that served in the establishment had nothing of poetry in their appearance, nothing of romance, nothing of Oriental splendor. They shed no entrancing odors—just the contrary. Their hungry eyes and their lank forms continually suggested one glaring, unsentimental fact—they wanted what they term in California "a square meal."

I went into one of the racks and undressed. An unclean starveling wrapped a gaudy table-cloth about his loins, and hung a white rag over my shoulders. If I had had a tub then, it would have come natural to me to take in washing. I was then conducted down stairs into the wet, slippery court, and the first things that attracted my attention were my heels. My fall excited no comment. They expected it, no doubt. It belonged in the list of softening, sensuous influences peculiar to this home of Eastern luxury. It was softening enough, certainly, but its application was not happy. They now gave me a pair of wooden clogs—benches in miniature, with leather straps over them to confine my feet (which they would have done, only I do not wear No. 13s.) These things dangled uncomfortably by the straps when I lifted up my feet, and came down in awkward and unexpected places when I put them on the floor again, and sometimes turned sideways and wrenched my ankles out of joint. However, it was all Oriental luxury, and I did what I could to enjoy it.

They put me in another part of the barn and laid me on a stuffy sort of pallet, which was not made of cloth of gold, or Persian shawls, but was merely the unpretending sort of thing I have seen in the negro quarters of Arkansas. There was nothing whatever in this dim marble prison but five more of these biers. It was a very solemn place. I expected that the spiced odors of Araby were going to steal over my senses now, but they did not. A copper-colored skeleton, with a rag around him, brought me a glass decanter of water, with a lighted tobacco pipe in the top of it, and a pliant stem a yard long, with a brass mouth-piece to it.

It was the famous "narghili" of the East—the thing the Grand Turk smokes in the pictures. This began to look like luxury. I took one blast at it, and it was sufficient;

the smoke went in a great volume down into my stomach, my lungs, even into the uttermost parts of my frame. I exploded one mighty cough, and it was as if Vesuvius had let go. For the next five minutes I smoked at every pore, like a frame house that is on fire on the inside. Not any more narghili for me. The smoke had a vile taste, and the taste of a thousand infidel tongues that remained on that brass mouthpiece was viler still. I was getting discouraged. Whenever, hereafter, I see the cross-legged Grand Turk smoking his narghili, in pretended bliss, on the outside of a paper of Connecticut tobacco, I shall know him for the shameless humbug he is.

This prison was filled with hot air. When I had got warmed up sufficiently to prepare me for a still warmer temperature, they took me where it was—into a marble room, wet, slippery and steamy, and laid me out on a raised platform in the centre. It was very warm. Presently my man sat me down by a tank of hot water, drenched me well, gloved his hand with a coarse mitten, and began to polish me all over with it. I began to smell disagreeably. The more he polished the worse I smelt. It was alarming. I said to him:

"I perceive that I am pretty far gone. It is plain that I ought to be buried without any unnecessary delay. Perhaps you had better go after my friends at once, because the weather is warm, and I can not 'keep' long."

He went on scrubbing, and paid no attention. I soon saw that he was reducing my size. He bore hard on his mitten, and from under it rolled little cylinders, like maccaroni. It could not be dirt, for it was too white. He pared me down in this way for a long time. Finally I said:

"It is a tedious process. It will take hours to trim me to the size you want me; I will wait; go and borrow a jack-plane."

He paid no attention at all.

After a while he brought a basin, some soap, and something that seemed to be the tail of a horse. He made up a prodigious quantity of soap-suds, deluged me with them from head to foot, without warning me to shut my eyes, and then swabbed me viciously with the horse-tail. Then he left me there, a snowy statue of lather, and went away. When I got tired of waiting I went and hunted him up. He was propped against the wall, in another room, asleep. I woke him. He was not disconcerted. He took me back and flooded me with hot water, then turbaned my head, swathed me with dry table-cloths, and conducted me to a latticed chicken-coop in one of the galleries, and pointed to one of those Arkansas beds.

—*Innocents Abroad*

On Siam

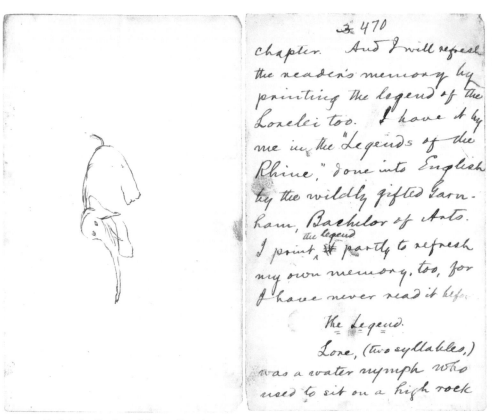

3. 470

chapter. And I will refresh
the reader's memory by
printing the legend of the
Lorelei too. I have it by
me in the "Legends of the
Rhine," done into English
by the wildly gifted Garnham, Bachelor of Arts.
I print the legend ⌗ partly to refresh
my own memory, too, for
I have never read it before.

The Legend.
Lore, (two syllables,)
was a water nymph who
used to sit on a high rock

Twain's doodles from *A Tramp Abroad*.

While Twain wrote he sometimes flipped over his sheets and indulged in a little mental free play. The manuscript of A Tramp Abroad *contains two sketches of elephants then a sketch of a gentleman being dragged from the customs house by an elephant's trunk. The image leaves much of the action off page.*

For A Tramp Abroad, *Twain wrote a sketch entitled "A Stolen White Elephant," that was not included in the final version. However, it was published separately in 1882 by James R. Osgood. The story began:*

"The following curious history was related to me by a chance railway acquaintance. He was a gentleman more than seventy years of age, and his thoroughly good and gentle face and earnest and sincere manner imprinted the unmistakable stamp of truth upon every statement which fell from his lips. He said:

You know in what reverence the royal white elephant of Siam is held by the people of that country. You know it is sacred to kings, only kings may possess it, and that it is, indeed, in a measure even superior to kings, since it receives not merely honor but worship. Very well; five years ago, when the troubles concerning the frontier line arose between Great Britain and Siam, it was presently manifest that Siam had been in the wrong. Therefore every reparation was quickly made, and the British representative stated that he was satisfied and the past should be forgotten. This greatly relieved the King of Siam, and partly as a token of gratitude, but partly also, perhaps, to wipe out

₤ 47 ½

there with his son the Count Hermann, a youth of twenty. Hermann had heard a great deal about the beautiful Lore, & had finally fallen in love with her without having yet seen her. So he used to wander to the neighborhood of the Lei, evenings, with his zither and "Express his tou Longing in low Sing-ing," as Garnham says. On one of these occasions, "Suddenly there hovered

any little remaining vestige of unpleasantness which England might feel toward him, he wished to send the Queen a present—the sole sure way of propitiating an enemy, according to Oriental ideas. This present ought not only to be a royal one, but transcendently royal. Wherefore, what offering could be so meet as that of a white elephant?

Homecoming

The *New York Times*, October 13, 1900

MARK TWAIN'S HOMECOMING.

Payment of His Debts, Though Not Legally Liable for Them All—A Five Years' Absence—No Plans Yet to Do Him Honor.

Ere this the Minnehaha may have poked her nose into her New York dock, and the doyen of American letters, Mark Twain, been landed, together with his baggage, with which, according to a letter he recently wrote to Secretary Gage, the steamer "would be loaded."

It is a little over five years since Samuel L. Clemens left his native land, inspired by a lofty motive, to which the history of literature, cannot show a parallel. Six years ago the publishing firm of Charles L. Webster & Co., of which Mr. Clemens was the financial backer, failed, owing a little over $200,000. At the time it was known that the author was heavily involved, and that he would practically have to "begin life over again," as the saying goes, but what was not even then suspected was that Mr. Clemens has assumed responsibility for all the firm's debts. This was made known later in a statement issued to the American public just before he sailed westward from Vancouver, in August, 1895:

> It has been reported that I sacrificed, for the benefit of the creditors, the property of the publishing firm whose financial backer I was, and that I am now lecturing for my own benefit.
>
> This is an error. I intend the lectures, as well as the property, for the creditors. The law recognizes no mortgage on a man's brain, and a merchant who has given up all he has may take advantage of the rules of insolvency and start free again for himself. But I am not a business man; and honor is a harder

master than the law. It cannot compromise for less than a hundred cents on the dollar, and its debts never outlaw. I had a two-thirds interest in the publishing firm, whose capital I furnished. If the firm had prospered, I should have expected to collect two-thirds of the profit. As it is, I expect to pay all the debts. My partner has no resources, and I do not look for assistance from him. By far the largest single creditor of this firm is my wife, whose contributions in cash, from her private means, have nearly equaled the claims of all the others combined. She has taken nothing. On the contrary, she has helped and intends to help me to satisfy the obligations due to the rest. It is my intention to ask them to accept that as a legal discharge, and trust to my honor to pay the other 50 per cent. as fast as I can earn it. From my reception thus far on my lecturing tour, I am confident that, if I live I can pay off the last debt within four years, after which, at the age of sixty-four, I can make a fresh and unincumbered start in life. I am going to Australia, India and South Africa, and next year hope to make a tour of the great cities of the United States. I meant, when I began, to give my creditors all the benefit of this, but I begin to feel that I am gaining something from it, too, and that my dividends, if not available for banking purposes, may be even more satisfactory than theirs.

And now the bravest author in all literature has returned, not only with debts paid, not only with the sublime consciousness that he has requited a self-imposed moral obligation but with the contentment, and it may be the pride, that such are the present unincumbered royalties from his books that if he were never to put pen to paper again, or never again stand upon the lecture platform, he could pass the rest of his life far removed from the strain of affairs and the martyrdom of financial distress. In commenting upon

MARK TWAIN'S HOME-COMING.

Payment of His Debts, Though Not Legally Liable for Them All—A Five Years' Absence—No Plans Yet to Do Him Honor.

Ere this the Minnehaha may have poked her nose into her New York dock, and the doyen of American letters, Mark Twain, been landed, together with his baggage, with which, according to a letter he recently wrote to Secretary Gage, the steamer "would be loaded."

It is a little over five years since Samuel L. Clemens left his native land, inspired by a lofty motive, to which the history of literature cannot show a parallel. Six years ago the publishing firm of Charles L. Webster & Co., of which Mr. Clemens was the financial backer, failed, owing a little over $200,000. At the time it was known that the author was heavily involved, and that he would practically have to "begin life over again," as the saying goes, but what was not even then suspected was that Mr. Clemens had assumed responsibility for all the firm's debts. This was made known later in a statement issued to the American public just before he sailed westward from Vancouver, in August, 1895:

It has been reported that I sacrificed for the benefit of the creditors the property of the publishing firm whose financial backer I was, and that I am now lecturing for my own benefit.

This is an error. I intend the lectures as well as the property for the creditors. The law recognizes no mortgage on a man's brain, and a merchant who has given up all he has may take advantage of the laws of insolvency and start free again for himself. But I am not a business man, and honor is a harder master than the law. It cannot compromise for less than 100 cents on the dollar, and its debts never outlaw. I had a two-thirds interest in the publishing firm, whose capital I furnished. If the firm had prospered I should have expected to collect two-thirds of the profits. As it is, I expect to pay all the debts. My partner has no resources, and I do not look for assistance from him. By far the largest single creditor of this firm is my wife, whose contributions in cash from her private means have nearly equaled the claims of all the others combined. She has taken nothing. On the contrary, she has helped, and intends to help me to satisfy the obligations due to the rest. It is my intention to ask my creditors to accept that as a legal discharge, and trust to my honor to pay the other 50 per cent. as I can earn it. From my reception thus far on my lecturing tour I am confident that if I live I can pay off the last debt within four years, after which, at the age of sixty-four, I can make a fresh and unincumbered start in life. I am going to Australia, India, and South Africa, and next year I hope to make a tour of the great cities of the United States. I meant, when I began, to give my creditors all the benefit of this, but I am beginning to feel that I am gaining something from it, too, and that my dividends, if not available for banking purposes, may be even more satisfactory than theirs.

And now the bravest author in all literature has returned, not only with debts paid, not only with the sublime consciousness that he has requited a self-imposed moral obligation, but with the contentment, and it may be the pride, that such are the present unincumbered royalties from his books that if he were never to put pen to paper again, or never again stand upon the lecture platform, he could pass the rest of his life far removed from the strain of affairs and the martyrdom of financial distress. In commenting upon this fine example of the very chivalry of probity, The London News has dwelt lovingly upon the closing wards of what may go down to history as "Mark Twain's Vancouver Manifesto," and said:

The last touch is very fine, both as literature and as feeling. He has gained something, and that is the esteem of all men of honor throughout the world. This act is the best of all critical commentaries on the high moral teaching of his books. He needs all the encouragement of sympathy. He has paid his debts, but he has still to make another fortune, and he is sixty-three!

Mark Twain did not return to lecture in the United States, as he had expected. His itinerary in the Far East, however, was practically carried out as he had at first planned, a permanent record of which may be considered to exist in "Following the Equator." But Old Europe was loath to part with one whom, from afar, it had regarded purely as a humorist, but who on near approach proved to be a finished man of letters, one in whom humor had gradually become a means, and not an end. About three years ago Mr. Clemens took up his abode in London, and thence would run over to the Continent whenever his interests, or, let us say, those of his creditors, demanded his presence there. In this way he spent nearly a year in Italy, with a Winter divided between Paris, Berlin, and Vienna. Everywhere a most cordial welcome was extended to him, not only by men of his profession, journalists and men of letters, but by royalties as well. Some day he may write out for us his impressions of the German Kaiser, or his conversations with the late King Humbert and with the Emperor Francis Joseph. In Vienna he lingered long. There no literary or artistic function was complete without him. On one occasion, on being entertained by the Vienna Press Club, to the surprise of its members he spoke in German, discoursing with sparkling philosophy upon the terrors of German syn-

this fine example of the very chivalry of probity, The *London News* has dwelt lovingly upon the closing words of what may go down to history as "Mark Twain's Vancouver Manifesto," and said:

> The last touch is very fine, both as literature and as feeling. He has gained something, and that is the esteem of all men of honor throughout the world. This act is the best of all critical commentaries on the high moral teaching of his books. He needs all the encouragement of sympathy. He has paid his debts, but he has still to make another fortune, and he is sixty-three!

Mark Twain did not return to lecture in the United States, as he had expected. His itinerary in the Far East, however, was practically carried out as he had at first planned, a permanent record of which may be considered to exist in "Following the Equator." But Old Europe was loath to part with one whom, from afar, it had regarded purely as a humorist, but who on near approach proved to be a finished man of letters, one in whom humor had gradually become a means, and not an end. About three years ago Mr. Clemens took up the abode in London, and thence would run over to the Continent whenever his interests, or, let us say, those of his creditors, demanded his presence there. In this way he spent nearly a year in Italy, and a Winter divided between Paris, Berlin, and Vienna. Everywhere a most cordial welcome was extended to him, not only by men of his profession, journalists and men of letters, but by royalties as well. Some day he may write out for us his impressions of the German Kaiser, or his conversations with the late King Humbert and with the Emperor Francis Joseph. In Vienna he lingered long. There no literary or artistic function was complete without him. On one occasion, on being entertained by the Vienna Press Club, to the surprise of its members he spoke in German, discoursing with sparkling philosophy upon the terrors of German syntax. This speech, so rich in humor, yet withal so logical and analytical as to receive serious consideration from German savants, was reprinted in the original or in translation throughout the world.

It was the same in London, where he appeared before the Parliamentary Committee on Copyright, and in one humorous discourse, interspersed with queries and answers, accomplished more practical results for British letters than had been achieved by the lengthy and learned arguments presented by his English brethren of the pen. Besides the lectures that occupied a considerable part of his European sojourn, articles and sketches have from time to time appeared in American and English magazines, showing that his pen has not been idle. Some of these have just appeared in book form under the title of "The Man That Corrupted Hadleyburg." So great has been the demand for him over there, and so indispensable has been his presence, that a record of his London sojourn alone would prove a most fascinating volume. Possibly the last words that he addressed to a British public before sailing were those uttered on the occasion of opening a reading room at Kensal Rise, London. The ceremony took place on the Saturday proceeding his departure for America. Here is an account of the event, reproduced from the report in the London papers:

> Mark Twain formally declared the room open, and said he thought it a superbly good idea that the Legislature should not compel a community to provide itself with intellectual food, but give it the privilege of providing it for itself, if is so desired. If it was willing to have it, it would put its hand in its pocket and bring out—the penny rate. He thought it a proof of the moral, financial, and mental condition of the community if it would tax itself for its mental food. A reading room was the proper introduction to a library, reading up through the newspapers and magazines to other literature. He did not know what they would do without the newspapers, and instanced his experience in obtaining news in the Sandwich Islands and San Francisco. He referred to the rapid manner in which the news of the Galveston disaster was made known to the world, which reminded him of an episode that occurred fifteen years ago when at church at Hartford. The clergyman decided to make a collection for the survivors, if any, of a similar disaster, but did not include him in the leading citizens who took plates round. He complained to the Governor of the want of financial trust in him, and he replied, "I would trust you myself—if you had a bell punch," one of those articles used to protect bus and tram companies against the conductors. In reply to a vote of thanks, he said he liked to listen to compliments. He indorsed all Cr. Crone, the mover, said about the union of England and America. Mr. Irwin Cox, the seconder, had alluded to his nom de plume, which he was rather fond of. A little girl wrote him from New Zealand the previous day, stating that her father said his proper name was not "Mark Twain," but Clemens. She knew better, because Clemens was the man who sold the patent medicine. She like the name of Mark—why Mark Antony was in the Bible. He replied to her that he was glad to get that expression from her, and as Mark Antony had got into the Bible, "I am not without hopes myself."

Mark Twain returns to America bearing with him the evidence of many distinctions and honors. Most of the leading associations and societies of merit on the Continent have taken him unto themselves. But how lightly he wears these decorations was once betrayed by him to a friend who had congratulated him on receiving the ribbon of the Legion of Honor. "Few escape it," he remarked simply.

It is doubtful if any of his Continental friends and admirers knew anything about the great task he was working out among them. To have told them would have been like revealing a domestic secret to a public that had no business to know it. It was, therefore, simply because of his mental attributes that they found pleasure in honoring him. There is more for Americans to honor in him than this, for he took us into his confidence at the very beginning. He told us about the task he had undertaken to perform. There was not an American heart which did not bid him godspeed when he set out upon his mission five years ago.

Now that he has overcome all obstacles and has triumphantly accomplished the work he believed he ought to do, some peculiar recognition of this fact should come to him from Americans - something that should appeal to Samuel L. Clemens, the man, rather than to Mark Twain, the literateur. Just what form this recognition should take is doubtful, for the case, as we have said, has no exact precedent. No attempt should be made to rival even in significance the decorations that have been bestowed upon him by the Old World. They are things apart. A dinner, with a memorial of welcome, would perhaps, be the most satisfactory and appropriate form of recognition.

An extended inquiry among writers and publishers of this city has failed to reveal the presence of any plans for this purpose. Everybody, however, recognizes the appropriateness of such a demonstration, and expresses the hope that one might be made. So much good will and friendliness should not be allowed to spend itself in isolated expression. It should be molded into some common and distinctive form. The question is, Who will do the molding? The material is ready. No time should be wasted. Why not the Authors Club?

—Mark Twain

BIBLIOGRAPHY

Paine, Albert Bigelow. *Mark Twain: A Biography*, Harper & Brothers Publishers, 1912

Paine, Albert Bigelow. *Mark Twain's Letters*, Harper & Brothers Publishers, 1917

Paine, Albert Bigelow. *The Boy's Life of Mark Twain*, Harper & Brothers Publishers, 1916

Twain, Mark. *The American Claimant,* Charles L. Webster, 1892.

Twain, Mark. *A Connecticut Yankee in King Arthur's Court.* Charles L. Webster and Co., 1889

Twain, Mark. *A Double Barreled Detective Story*, Harper & Brothers Publishers, 1902

Twain, Mark. *Fables of Man*, University of California Press, 1972

Twain, Mark. *Innocents Abroad* (also known as *The New Pilgrims' Progress*), American Publishing Company, 1869

Twain, Mark. *Life on the Mississippi,* James R. Osgood & Co., 1883

Twain, Mark. *Pudd'nhead Wilson.* Charles L. Webster and Co., 1889

Twain, Mark. *Roughing It*, American Publishing Company, 1872

Twain, Mark. *Sketches New and Old*, American Publishing Company, 1875

Twain, Mark. *A Tramp Abroad*, American Publishing Company, 1880

Twain, Mark. *Fenimore Cooper's Literary Offenses*, North American Review 161 (July *1895*)

Twain, Mark. *Following the Equator*, American Publishing Company, 1897

Twain, Mark. *Letters from the Earth*, Harper & Row, 1962

Twain, Mark. *Personal Recollections of Joan of Arc*, Harper & Brothers Publishers, 1896

Twain, Mark. *Mark Twain's Autobiography*, Harper & Brothers Publishers, 1923

PHOTO CREDITS

Beinecke Rare Book and Manuscript Library, 43, 63, 78, 134

"The Boyhood Home of Mark Twain" by Rev. Henry M. Wharton. *Century Magazine*, September 1902, 37

The *Buffalo Express*, 1869, 200

Chemung County Historical Society, Elmira, NY, 203

Clifton Waller Barrett Library of American Literature, Special Collections, University of Virginia, Charlottesville, VA., 56, 68-69, 159, 161, 171, 175

Courtesy of the Mark Twain Project, The Bancroft Library, University of California, Berkeley, 106, 116, 153, 176, 181, 207, 208, 209, 210, 214, 253, 254, 255, 256, 262

Courtesy of Dartmouth College Library, 316-317

Courtesy of Dave Thomson, 104, 185 (top)

Courtesy of Kevin Mac Donnell, 13, 166, 168, 169, 170, 173

Courtesy of Willi Heidelbach, 14

Division of Rare and Manuscript Collections, Cornell University Library, 28-29, 74, 155, 167

Harpers Weekly, published by Harper & Brothers from 1857-1916, 16, 59, 117, 150, 230-242, 299

Houghton Library, Harvard University, bMS Am 1429 (1153), 34

Library of Congress 2, 15 (top) 20, 22 (top), 32, 51, 64, 65, 79, 82, 94, 98, 99, 102, 199, 121, 123, 143, 145, 174, 192, 217, 243, 249, 268, 289, 297, 304-305, 309

The *Missouri Democrat*, 197

Morristown National Historical Park Museum & Library, 141

New York Public Library, 272

Nevada Historical Society, 276

The *New York Times*, 183, 318

Paine, Albert Bigelow. *Mark Twain: A Biography*, Harper & Brothers Publishers, 1912: 9, 11, 15 (bottom), 17, 19, 21, 22 (bottom), 24, 25, 40, 48, 87, 125, 164, 258, 277, 291

Paine, Albert Bigelow. *Mark Twain's Letters*, Harper & Brothers Publishers, 1917, 45, 270

Photograph by GH Jones, dated 1850, 89

Photograph by Napoleon Sarony, 1895, 7

Photographer, unknown. 1903, 245

The Pierpont Morgan Library/Art Resource, 46, 52, 72, 172, 220-221

Rowan Public Library, 285

Shapell Manuscript Foundation, 227

The *Saturday Press*, 31

Scientific American, March 9, 1901, 41

Twain, Mark. *The Adventures of Huckleberry Finn*, Charles L. Webster And Company, 1884, 36, 226, 39

Twain, Mark. *The Adventures of Tom Sawyer*, American Publishing Company, 1876, 36, 226

Twain, Mark. *Innocents Abroad* (also known as *The New Pilgrims' Progress*), American Publishing Company, 1869, 283

Twain, Mark. *Life on the Mississippi,* James R. Osgood & Co., 1883: 3, 180,

Twain, Mark. *Roughing It*, American Publishing Company, 1872, 55, 273

Wiener Bilder, 17. Oktober 1897, S. 3, 110

The Western Nevada Historic Photo Collection, 280

INDEX

Actors' Fund of America, 165-166; promotional letter, **166**

Adjectives, Twain on, 58

Admiration, Twain on, 105

Adventures of Huckleberry Finn, The, 38-39, 249; autographed copy, 165, **166**; Finn's home, *38*; First edition cover, 39; signed copy, **43**; Twain on, 38-39; unused introduction, **93**

Adventures of Tom Sawyer, The, 21, **36, 226**, 249, 250; Becky Thatcher character, 249-251; manuscript page, **21**; Twain on, 36-37

Adverbs, Twain on, 58

Advice to Youth speech, 89-92

Advice, Twain on, 105

Affection, Twain on, 195

Ah, Sin!, 65, 66-67; script, **68-69**

Aldrich, Thomas Bailey, 33-35; Twain letter to, 33, **34**, 35

American Abroad speech, 268

American Claimant, The, 49

American Publisher, 134

American Publishing Company, 33, 152-153, 158

Amusing Game of Innocence Abroad, **168**, 169

Animal testing, Twain on, 260-261

Animals, Twain on, 252-265

Anniversaries, Twain on, 207

Anti-slavery, 199-201

Atlantic Monthly, The, 13, 56, 57, 58, 66, 243, 312

Austen, Jane, Twain on, 70

Austria, Twain on, 299-302

Autobiography, 31, 37, 38-39, 49, 50, 58, 97, 122, 139, 155, 160, 193, 201, 226, 257, 312; preface, **116**

Automobiles, Twain in 1906 Oldsmobile, **124**; Twain on, 124

Babies, Twain on, 211-213

Bats, Twain on, 257

Bazaine, 293

Beard, Frank Carter, 134

Belasco, David, 24

Bell, Alexander Graham, 121

Berlin, Twain on, 303, **304, 305**, 306-308

Bermuda, **311**; Twain on, 311-312

Bible, Twain on, 138-139

Billiards, Twain on, 122-123

Birthdays, Twain on, 125-130

Bismarck, 292

Bixby, Horace, 8, **9, 182-183**,186

Blankenship, Tom, 38

Bliss Jr., Elisha, 33, 155; Twain letter to, **152**, 153

Boardman, Jenny, 97

Book selling, Twain on, 153-160

Boston *Daily Globe*, 120

Bowen, Will, 266

Bowker, Richard R., 81

Bowser, D.W., 58

Boy's Life of Mark Twain, The, 8

Boys, Twain on, 226-227

Bravery, Twain on, 105

Brooklyn Academy of Music, Twain lecture, 162-165; caricature, **164**

Brown, Colonel William L, 64; Twain on, 64

Buffalo Express, 16-17, 199, **200**, 201, 291

Cable, George Washington, 117, 160; book tour with Twain, 160, **161**

Cairo, Illinois, 9

Can-Can (dance), 293, 295

Card games, Twain on, **167, 168**, 169

Carson City, Nevada, Ormsby House, 280, 281

Cats, Twain on, 253, **254, 255, 256**

Celebrated Jumping Frog of Calaveras County, The, 28-29, 30-31; letter regarding, **28-29**, 30-31

Celebrations, Twain on, 125-133

Censorship, Twain on, 42-43

Charles L. Webster & Co., 318

Chicago compared to Berlin, 303, 306-308

Chicago Daily Tribune, 303

Children, books for, 227-228; history dates memory aids, 228-229, **230, 231**, 232, **233, 234, 235, 236, 237, 238, 239, 240, 241, 242**

Children, Twain on, 211-242

Christianity, Twain on, 139

Cigars, Twain image on boxes, **169**, 170

Clapp, Henry, 31

Clemens, Clara, **216, 217**, 218-221, **222**, 255-256; letters from Twain, **220, 221**

Clemens, Jane Lampton, Twain letter to, 209, **210**, 211, **270**, 271

Clemens, Jean, 221, **222, 223**, 224-225; death, 223-225

ACKNOWLEDGEMENTS

Any author of such an effort owes a great debt of gratitude to those who went before him. Several writers' works have proved invaluable, including Albert Bigelow Paine, Ron Powers, Justin Kaplan, Fred Kaplan, Charles Neider, William Dean Howells, Michael Shelden, Milton Meltzer, and of course Twain's children Sara Clemens and Susy Clemens, and, the many other historians who wrote about Twain throughout the years.

As ever, I owe a countless number of historians, experts, and librarians who were it not for them, this book would never have happened. I am indebted to Kevin Mac Donnell, Gretchen B. Witt, Frank C. Grace, Michael Lange, Sharon at the Mark Twain Project, Stephen Railton at University of Virginia and the Special Collections Department of University of Virginia Library, Dave Thomson for allowing us access to his very special collection, the folks at the Beinecke Library, Yale University, Special Collections Library, at the University of Arizona, The Morgan Library, Oakland Museum of California, The Chemung County Historical Society, Brent Colley, University of Oregon, Spinks Shreeves Gallery, Shapell Manuscript Foundation, Cornell University, George Eastman House, and of course the Gutenberg Project, the Library of Congress, and the New York Times. As always, special thanks to Patti Philipon the Beatrice Fox Auerbach Chief Curator of the Mark Twain House.

I would, of course, like to thank J.P. Leventhal of Black Dog & Leventhal Publishers, who helped make this book a reality. Were it not for his excitement, enthusiasm, and faith in me, I would not have had this opportunity. I also owe a huge debt of gratitude to Lisa Tenaglia, Katherine Furman, Liz Driesbach, Pamela Schechter, Ted Goodman, and everyone else who helped mold a rather large, unwieldy collection into a readable finished volume.

I would like to thank my sons, Dylan and Dawson, whom I have taken too much time away from in order to pursue not only this work, but also my other professional aspirations. I have tried to attend as many of their basketball, baseball and track meets as possible, but there is no replacement for a chat or a dinner out, many of which were robbed by my other pursuits. I vow to them to spend more time hanging out and less time working.